LIESTHAT KILL

THE SUPERNATURAL BATTLE FOR TRUTH

ROB RANDALL

Author of *The Invisible War*

Foreword by Dr. Jim Logan, Author and Counselor

PUBLISHERS
READING YOU LOUD AND CLEAR

www.21stcenturypress.com

LIES THAT KILL
The Supernatural Battle for Truth

First Edition: 2011

PUBLISHERS
READING YOU LOUD AND CLEAR

www.21stcenturypress.com

LIES THAT KILL

DEDICATION

To my precious Lord Jesus who is my life, my hope, and my ultimate joy. Without the sacrifice of Christ for my sins, what is offered in this book would be worthless. I am eternally grateful for the wonderful and holy privilege to work with Christ to bring His Kingdom on the earth as it is in Heaven. He is faithful. He is good. He is almighty. He is the truth that exposes the LIES THAT KILL.

My Dear Precious Lord Jesus Christ,

Thank You for Your willingness to speak through me Your eternal truth that sets the captives free. I am so grateful for Your love demonstrated on the Cross of Calvary. I ask You to put this book and all who read it in the circle of Your blood; for healing, cleansing and protection. I ask You Lord Jesus to shut the mouths of the liars, so only Your wonderful voice will be heard as You speak. I ask You, Lord Jesus to come and do what we cannot do for ourselves. Please:

Search me, O God, and know my heart: try me, and know my thoughts: And see if there be any wicked way in me, and lead me in the way everlasting (Psalms 139:23-24 KJV).

LIES THAT KILL

WITH A GRATEFUL HEART

To my wife and precious gift from my Lord Jesus, Pattie:
You are far more than I had ever hoped and prayed for in a wife. The light of our Lord Jesus has always shinned the brightest through you. Your love and faithfulness has encouraged my walk, lifted my song, and captured my heart for these 36 blessed years.

To my wonderful and gifted children—Tina and Jason, Bob and Amy, Mike and Lindsay:
What a joy to my heart to see each of you following, trusting, and serving our Lord Jesus. I'm so grateful to our Lord for His wonderful work in each of your lives.

To my precious grandchildren—Callum, Elise, Will, Matthew and all those to come:
As you grow, may you come to know how much Christ loves you with each passing day. You are a wonderful blessing from our Heavenly Father.

To Norm and Beverly Coad:
May Heaven's bounty be your reward for your tireless love and countless prayers offered to our Heavenly Father for the Randall Family.

To all my precious friends that have allowed me to pray with them:
Thank you for allowing me to witness the supernatural healing power of Christ manifested through His loving and faithful presence.

To my Precious Sisters in the Lord: Sherry Ball, Beverly Coad, Debbie Newhouse, Amy Randall, Pattie Randall, and Helen Rekerdres:
With a grateful heart, I give thanks to our precious Lord for you and your many sacrificial hours of work in preparing the manuscript of this book.

CONTENTS

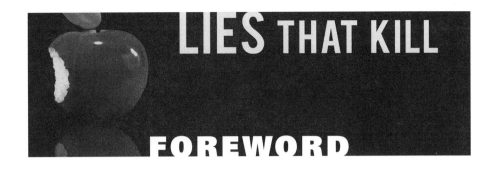

FOREWORD

Many Christians feel that their walk with God has come to a standstill. There seems to be a wall they can't get around or over. If this describes you, LIES THAT KILL is for you. This marvelous book is a guide to identifying these walls and how they can be removed. In Scripture these walls are called strongholds. The foundation of every stronghold is a false belief system. Jesus said it is the truth that sets you free, but lies will bind you and keep you from the freedom that is rightfully yours as a child of God. Christians who are going nowhere in their walk with God have these strongholds. They struggle with the Word of God, and many have a distorted view of Him which leads to a poor prayer life. They doubt that they can really trust God or His Word.

I wish I had written this marvelous book! I trust you will have the same experience I did—I couldn't put the book down! I want every person I counsel or disciple to have a copy. May you discover, as I have, that it is one of the best books to have in your library. LIES THAT KILL is a life-transforming book.

Dr. Jim Logan, Author and Counselor
Biblical Restoration Ministries, Sioux City, IA

LIES THAT KILL

PREFACE

In *LIES THAT KILL*, Dr. Rob Randall presents ten different perspectives that underline one basic truth—lies kill; truth sets us free. This book is extremely important because it exposes some common lies that are generally believed to be true, and it proclaims the biblical truth in juxtaposition to each of those lies. The basic lies of this age and all the philosophies attached to them are leading many to hell and destruction.

Dr. Randall, a multi-gifted man of God, convicts us as only the evangelist can. He effectively combines Scripture, historical references, charts, and personal testimonies to reveal areas of deception that are pervasive in our lives today. Our need is so great because the outcome of believing deception and lies is so profoundly destructive. The light that Randall sheds on our time and culture and our perishing life appears to us as light in darkness. The light of truth is starkly contrasted to the darkness of our present time and decadence. The choices given us are clearly stated.

This book will divide. Dr. Randall and *LIES THAT KILL* are to God the aroma of Christ among those who are being saved and those who are perishing—to the perishing, the smell of death; to those being saved, the fragrance of life (paraphrase of *2 Corinthians 2:15-16* NIV).

Dr. Norman Lee Coad, D.Min., LPC, LMFT, LCDC, Counselor
Coadword Christian Counseling Services, Burleson, TX

You are in possession of an America's "must read." My friend, Dr. Rob Randall, has concisely and wonderfully communicated the ten most often used lies of the Enemy in *LIES THAT KILL*. You may not initially think that the lies discussed in this work are truly falsehoods; you may not think the topics are that grave in nature. Allow me to testify, they are. As a minister for almost 20 years, I have personally witnessed one too many people being "killed" by their believing one or more of the Devil's lies discussed in these pages. Please read and study this book attentively so you will not become the next statistic.

Dr. Jeff Meyers, Ph.D., Pastor
First Baptist Church, Conyers, GA

It would be impossible for me to count the times I have been confronted with one of the "lies that kill" presented here by Dr. Rob Randall. Having served as a Senior Pastor for over 35 years, these questions and arguments have come from moms, dads, teenagers, prodigal sons, religious zealots, wounded families and doubting Thomases. In fact, I would bet that most of us have been confronted with one of these lies— maybe even in our own thinking. Before I trusted Christ as my Savior, I lived a hard life, but I was "religious;" and truthfully, I believed a few of these lies myself.

In this book, *LIES THAT KILL*, Dr. Rob Randall does a wonderful job laying out the truth. Many in our day are deceived and base their lives on these lies. It is crucial that we take a hard look at these lies and measure them against the Truth that we believe—the Truth found in the Word of God. As contemporary believers in Jesus Christ, we must arm ourselves to combat these "lies that kill." As you read the pages of this book, please be open to receive what the Lord has for you. Share this with a doubting Thomas in your life. Arm yourself for the fight.

Olen Griffing, Founding Pastor
Shady Grove Church, Grand Prairie, TX

LIES THAT KILL

INTRODUCTION

THE SUPERNATURAL BATTLE FOR TRUTH

Welcome to *LIES THAT KILL*. I bless you in Jesus' Name. All of us seek to know in what we can believe and put our trust. We want to be certain that our trust is secure and will not be betrayed. Before we begin our study together, I want to establish from the start, that this book is not market driven. It has not been written from a purely scholastic point of view so as to be accepted in academia. It is not a book of philosophy, psychology, or even merely religion. This book is not even written from a so-called "Christian Worldview," because there are many who claim to be Christian who have departed from biblical truth. *LIES THAT KILL* is unapologetically written from a Biblical Worldview. It is this author's premise that there is a truth established in Heaven that neither the changes of time nor the whims of man can alter.

When Jesus stood before the Roman Governor, Pontius Pilate, He was asked the most important question, any man could ask: *What is truth (John 18:38)?* Implied in this eternal question is the desire to understand reality. Pilate didn't understand it at the time, but He was looking into the eyes of truth. The search for truth is a sacred pursuit. I hold firmly to the conviction that, if anyone will sincerely and honestly search for truth, he will ultimately be led to Jesus. What you and I do with Him always determines our destiny.

The question often comes to me: "Why is it so important to believe and live in the truth?" The thinking goes like this: "Wouldn't it be best if I kept my stuff to myself? Then no one would be disappointed or get angry at me." Jesus tells us in *John 8:32—You shall know the truth, and the truth shall make you free*. What is at stake is our freedom in Christ. You may ask, "What do you mean by freedom?" In *Gal. 5:1* we find these words:

> *It was for freedom that Christ set us free; therefore keep standing firm and do not be subject again to a yoke of slavery (Gal 5:1).*

Of the several words used in the New Testament for freedom, the two I want to focus on for this study are ἐλευθερία—eleutheria and πολίτης —politace. Eleutheria carries with it the full meaning of liberty. Liberty is the freedom to become all God has created us to be in Him (*Col. 1:22*). The other word, politace is a word from which we get our word politic. This word relates to our position as a citizen of the Kingdom of God into which the Lord Jesus transfers us from the Kingdom of Darkness, when we are born of the Spirit of God into the Family of God (*Col. 1:13*). We may then conclude from these New Testament words a clear working definition of freedom. Freedom is the liberty for each of us to become what God has in His heart for us to become. Freedom is a gift of God made possible through the death and resurrection of Christ. It is freely offered to anyone who will receive it. Freedom in Christ is not merely an end in and of itself. It is also the means to an end. Freedom in Christ is as much a process as it is a position.

The process of spiritual freedom is for the ultimate purpose of becoming like Christ. The goal of our freedom in Christ is as the Apostle Paul wrote:

> *...in order to present you before God holy and blameless and beyond reproach (Col 1:22).*

Or as James the half-brother of our Lord Jesus wrote:

...that you may be perfect (τέλειον—mature) and complete, lacking in nothing (James 1:4).

Liberty and freedom are sacred words. The struggle for liberty and freedom has stained the soil of every nation with the sacrificial blood of its brave and courageous people. I submit to you that there is a greater battle that is raging for the liberty and freedom of our souls. This supernatural battle is between the truth of God and the spiritual powers of darkness who are ceaselessly perpetuating their murderous lies. According to Jesus in *John 8:32*, it is the *truth* that has the power to set us free. Truth is the liberating agent that keeps us becoming all God has in His heart for us to become. Without this freedom of God, we are left with a life of spiritual bondage that ultimately leads to death. The enemy of our souls, Satan, has had thousands of years to perfect his murderous craft. In *John 8:44* we discover the basic tactic of Satan that comes from his nature. This is so important. We must carefully pay attention to what the Holy Spirit is saying to us through Jesus:

"You are of your father the devil, and you want to do the desires of your father. He was a murderer from the beginning, and does not stand in the truth because there is no truth in him. Whenever he speaks a lie, he speaks from his own nature, for he is a liar and the father of lies."

It is not surprising that our Lord begins with TRUTH in explaining the armor that He has provided for each believer in his spiritual battle. Gird your loins with TRUTH. Notice, it is the Devil who is the father of lies. He is the arch-deceiver. All that he has done and will ever do is based upon man's willingness to believe his lies. The only remedy for a lie is the truth. In the worldview of our Western mindset, the concept of truth is often determined by nothing more than individual philosophy and/or opinion. We live in a postmodern Western mindset where the prevailing philosophy in American education is relativism. That is, there is no absolute truth. Truth is defined and practiced as that which you determine in your relative world to be true. That's why we have the problem of parents killing their children through selfish barbarism called abortion. That's why so many marriages end in divorce, leaving our children alone and easy prey for the Enemy. That's why our churches are full of self-seeking, self-centered, self-acclaimed lords ruling over their own kingdoms. So many today believe they can create their own realities, their own truth. They build their lives on the assumptions of their self-imposed truths instead of the foundation of the Word of God. Let the deception end! There is a truth that can never change. What God has said is forever settled—it has been established forever in Heaven *(Psalm 119:89)*.

To be victorious in the spiritual battle we must:

1. FACE the TRUTH! The truth may be very painful, but only lies will kill you. My father used to say, "Son, live your life as an open book. So, if anyone were to see any part of your life, you wouldn't be ashamed."

2. TELL the TRUTH! Confess your sins *(I John 1:9)*. Keep your sins hidden, and the Enemy will stay at work in your life. My parents were of a generation that didn't talk. They never admitted their problems. It somehow showed a lack of manners to discuss those things that were disturbing. In no small way, my parent's unwillingness to face the truth was the catalyst for the destruction of their marriage. Dear Friend, however challenging to the flesh it may be, tell the TRUTH! Remember, they overcame the Devil, by the word of their testimony *(Rev. 12:11)*. They told the truth. Satan can't handle the truth. All he does is through lies. Tell the truth!

3. BELIEVE the TRUTH! There is no freedom in Christ where there is unbelief.

> *But let him ask in faith without any doubting, for the one who doubts is like the surf of the sea driven and tossed by the wind. For let not that man expect that he will receive anything from the Lord, being a double minded man unstable in all his ways (James 1:6-7).*

4. TRUST the TRUTH! *You shall know the TRUTH and the TRUTH shall make you free (John 8:32).* The only thing we have to fear in the spiritual battles is our ignorance. We must trust the TRUTH of God if we are to be free.

5. LIVE the TRUTH! Whatever God says, do it. So discipline your life to live in the truth of the Word of God. *Thy word have I hidden in my heart, that I might not sin against Thee (Psalm 119:11).* Freedom in Christ comes through the TRUTH of God.

As you read these pages, would you be courageous enough to take a journey with me. This journey, at times, may be frightening and disturbing. It may lead us to places, where before now; we have not been willing to go. Although we may have to face Fear and look him square into his eyes, this journey into truth has the power to bring us into the places of freedom that Christ has bought for us at Calvary. Come with me as we take a close look at LIES THAT KILL—The Supernatural Battle for Truth. May we be willing to follow the Holy Spirit as He leads us into all truth, just as Christ promised *(John 16:13).* May He lead us to those places where we have bought into the deceptive lies of the Enemy. May Christ Himself give us the courage to confess where we have been deceived and were willing participants in and with Satan's lies. Then, and only then, will we come to know the truth of God, that can set us FREE *(John 8:32)*!

In any study of the supernatural truths of God, it is important that terms are clearly defined. Words such as demon, blasphemy, cult, curses, etc., carry different meanings to different people. When you encounter such words in this book, please refer to the Glossary provided on page 269 in the back of the book. This list will give a clear understanding how these words are used in this study.

LIES THAT KILL should be studied with an open Bible and an open heart. For it is the Word of God through which the truth of God is revealed in these most important eternal matters presented in these pages. *LIES THAT KILL* is offered to you with the prayer that our Lord Jesus will use these truths to bring its readers into spiritual cleansing and freedom to the glory of God.

THE BIBLE CAN'T BE THE WORD OF GOD. MEN WROTE IT.

When it all comes down to it, this is the one lie that has the power to derail everything our Lord has provided for us. I begin this book with this lie for it may very well be the seed bed for all others perpetrated by the Enemy. It is, without question, the cornerstone of all satanic deceptions. If Satan can get us to question at any level the authenticity and reliability of God's Word, he will have found a foothold for his murderous craft. When we fall for this lie, all others are bound to follow. From the very beginning of recorded time in the Garden of Eden, we find Satan using this lie when he challenged Eve's faith in God's Word:

> *Now the serpent was more crafty than any beast of the field which the LORD God had made. And he said to the woman, "Indeed, has God said, 'You shall not eat from any tree of the garden (Gen 3:1)?'"*

Notice how Satan is checking her out to see if she really believes what God has said. Now, of course, you know the rest of the story. We live in a fallen and cursed world today because of the sin that entered into it through our first parents' disregard for God's Word.

As one looks at the question of the infallibility and subsequent authority of Scripture in church history, just a casual student finds that the authority of Scripture was never brought into question. George Duncan Barry in his book, *The Inspiration and Authority of Holy Scripture, A Study in the Literature of the first Five Centuries*, surveys the early church fathers' view on Scripture and concludes, "The fact that, for fifteen centuries, no attempt was made to formulate a definition of the doctrine of inspiration of the Bible, testifies to the universal belief of the Church that the Scriptures were the handiwork of the Holy Spirit..."[1]

In the 1800's questions about the authority of Scripture began to arise. Since then, every major denomination has entangled itself in a vigorous battle over the Bible and its authority over our lives. Even Charles Haddon Spurgeon (1834-1872), considered the greatest preacher of the 19th century, did not escape the fray. He described the seriousness of the matter thus: "Believers in Christ's atonement are now in declared union with these who make light of it; believers in holy Scripture are in confederacy with those who deny plenary inspiration; those who hold evangelical doctrine are in open alliance with those who call the Fall a fable, who deny the personality of the Holy Spirit, who call justification by faith immoral, and hold there is another probation after death; to be very plain, we are unable to call these things Christian Unions (A clear reference to the Baptist Union of England), they begin to look like confederacies in evil."[2]

This is precisely why this author has been compelled to write this book on the Enemy's lies. When the church is brought to the place of doubt and entertains the thought that the Word of God is full of errors, it is then left with a life that has no compass; a dead religion without the possibility of faith. Without faith, there is no way of cooperating with the power of God in and through His body—the church. Simply put, the Kingdom of God does not come, and the will of God is not done on the earth as it is in Heaven *(Matt. 6:10)*.

As a young preacher, I attended what was then the largest Baptist

University in the world. As a student I had my faith in God's Word challenged most every day. The barrage of attacks was not intended to strengthen my faith as a young preacher. They seemed to be aimed at destroying what faith I had. It was as if my professors believed reasoning had no room for faith. It seemed as though many of my professors believed that the Bible may have been inspired in certain spots, and somehow, by their educational prowess, they were inspired to pick out those spots. They held to a more classical, liberal position concerning the Scriptures. That position, simply stated, holds to the belief that "the Bible is a human witness to divine revelation."[3] It is not divine revelation in its substance or essence. The late W.A. Criswell, my Pastor, mentor, and friend, succinctly defines a theological liberal: one "who turns aside from the Word of God and substitutes for it his own speculations. He is a theological liberal who judges the Holy Scriptures by his own subjective experience and not his experience by the Scriptures."[4] The truth is, the Bible welcomes intelligent and honest reason:

> *"Come now, and let us reason together," Says the LORD (Isaiah 1:18).*

In fact, the Bible promises that if we ask for wisdom, God will abundantly give it:

> *But if any of you lacks wisdom, let him ask of God, who gives to all men generously and without reproach, and it will be given to him (James 1:5).*

My Friend, the Bible speaks of two kinds of wisdom available to all. One wisdom comes from God above. The other comes from the powers of darkness:

> *But if you have bitter jealousy and selfish ambition in your heart, do not be arrogant and so lie against the truth. This wisdom is not that which comes down from above, but is earthly, natural, demonic. For where jealousy and selfish ambition exist, there is disorder and every evil thing. But the wisdom from above is first pure, then peaceable, gentle, reasonable, full of mercy and good*

fruits, unwavering, without hypocrisy (James 3:14-17).

Would you join me right now in asking our Lord to give us His wisdom as we study these amazing truths concerning the Scriptures?

THE BIBLE IS THE WORD OF GOD IN ITS ORIGINATION

In the beginning was the Word, and the Word was with God, and the Word was God (John 1:1).

And the Word became flesh, and dwelt among us, and we beheld His glory, glory as of the only begotten from the Father, full of grace and truth (John 1:14).

These passages link the Word of God to the Person of Christ. That is, the Living Word of God and the written Word of God cannot and therefore must not be separated. Jesus did not have his beginnings as a baby in Bethlehem. Jesus has always been. Before time and creation, the Scripture refers to Him as a part of the Godhead:

Then God said, "Let <u>Us</u> make man in <u>Our</u> image, according to <u>Our</u> likeness; and let them rule over the fish of the sea and over the birds of the sky and over the cattle and over all the earth, and over every creeping thing that creeps on the earth" (Gen. 1:26).

He was present at creation. Why is this so important? To try to separate the written Word from the Living Word leads us to a place of powerlessness in the spiritual battles of life. The written Word is the perfect revelation of God to man. Yes, men wrote the Bible, but God is the one who has linked Himself to it to reveal and manifest His holy presence. Without God there is no Bible.

THE BIBLE IS THE WORD OF GOD IN ITS INSPIRATION

"Surely the Bible can't be God's truth. After all it was written by men." How often has this old worn-out argument been heard, whether stated or implied? Why, it sounds so "logical." After all, we attempt to impose what we know concerning our frail inconsistencies and spiritual compromises upon the writers of Scripture. While it is clear from the teaching of Scripture that men wrote the Bible, it is God who supernaturally gave them the words to speak. He used their personalities, gifting, and experiences. It was the Holy Spirit of God who gave them His words to speak and to write.

My dear friend and long time counselor, Dr. Bill Nix wrote a timeless textbook with Dr. Norm Geisler on the Bible, *A General Introduction to the Bible*. The authors brilliantly lay the groundwork for the understanding of biblical inspiration. Two prominent New Testament passages set the stage for the discussion of inspiration:

1.   All Scripture is inspired by God and profitable for teaching, for reproof, for correction, for training in righteousness (2 Tim 3:16).

The word used here for *inspired* is *theopneustos*. This is the only occurrence of the word *theopneustos* (God-breathed) in the New Testament:

2.   No prophecy was ever made by an act of human will, but men moved by the Holy Spirit spoke from God (2 Peter 1:21).

So in literal biblical terminology, inspiration is the process by which Spirit-moved writers recorded God-breathed writings. Hence, when inspiration is viewed as a total process, it includes both the writer and the writings; but, when it is seen as a product (as in *2 Tim. 3:16*), it relates only to the writings—*graphe*. This picture is well summarized in *Hebrews 1:1*: "God spoke of old to our fathers by the prophets," to which *2 Timothy 3:16* would add the thought "…in their writings." The whole process of inspiration begins with the matter of divine revelation. The prime mover in inspiration is God:

> *No prophecy ever came by the impulse of man, but men moved*
> *by the Holy Spirit spoke from God (2 Peter 1:21).*

In other words, God moved and the prophet mouthed these truths; God revealed and man recorded His Word. The Bible is God's Word in the sense that it originates with Him and is authorized by Him, even though it is articulated by men. God moved the prophets in such a way as to breathe out (literally, *spirate*) their writings. In other words, God spoke to the prophets and is speaking through their writings.[5] The Word of God is the revelation of God. In it we have the manifestation of the presence and power of almighty God. The Scriptures claim for themselves to be theopneustos. This word comes from two words; theo which means God and pneustos which means breath. It literally means all Scripture comes to us from the very breath of God:

> *All Scripture is inspired (theopneustos) by God and profitable for teaching, for reproof, for correction, for training in righteousness; that the man of God may be adequate, equipped for every good work (2 Timothy 3:16-17).*

That's right. God did it. It's God's Word. Satan hates it because the Bible always exposes his murderous strategies of lies. If it were a mere book of man's exploits and imaginations, the Devil wouldn't even be impressed. But because the Bible is the Word of God, all of Hell and its evil inhabitants tremble at its truth.

THE BIBLE IS THE WORD OF GOD IN ITS COMPILATION

The Bible is not one book; It is sixty-six books. There are thirty-nine in the Old Testament and twenty-seven in the New Testament. It was written during a period of 1600 years, extending from 1492 BC to AD 100. The sixty-six books were written by about forty different authors: Kings such as David and Solomon, statesmen, such as Daniel and Nehemiah, priests such as Ezra, and by men learned in the wisdom of Egypt such as Moses. It comes to us through men learned in Jewish law like Paul, through a herdsman like Amos, and through a tax-gatherer named Matthew. Men who were fisherman like Peter, James, and John; unlearned and ignorant men, penned the words of the Bible. This word of the Bible comes to us through the careful attention of a trained physician by the name of Luke and such mighty seers as Isaiah, Ezekiel, and Zechariah. The Bible was written on two continents, in countries hundreds of miles apart. One man wrote one part of the Bible in Syria, another man another part in Arabia, and a third man wrote another portion in Italy and in Greece. They wrote in the desert of Sinai, in the wilderness of Judea, in the cave of Adullam, in the public prison of Rome, on the Isle of Patmos, in the palaces of Mount Zion and Shushan, by the rivers of Babylon, and on the banks of Chebar.[6] Can you imagine another book compiled like this? Let's say, sixty-six medical books written by forty different physicians and surgeons during a period of 1600 years.

The Bible is as much a miracle in its form as it is in its substance. There is a process of revelation in it. There is a clear line of doctrine that runs through it. The New Testament is built on the Old Testament, and the Old Testament cannot be understood without The New Testament. The Bible is a patchwork of carefully intertwined and overlapping doctrinal and eternal truth. One cannot comprehend Leviticus without Hebrews, nor can we grasp Daniel without the book of The Revelation. We cannot fully seize the intricacies and depth of meaning of the Passover or Isaiah 53 without an understanding of the Gospels of Matthew, Mark, Luke, and John. Yes, the Bible was written by men of different cultures, different ages, different educational backgrounds, and vastly different experiences. It is clear that the Bible gives all of mankind something far more than the writings of mere human personalities and perspectives.

THE BIBLE IS THE WORD OF GOD IN ITS PRESERVATION

No consideration of the Bible as the Word of God would be complete without looking carefully at how God has preserved the text from its early writers to us today. Whole books have been written on this subject. I will not attempt to repeat what has already been established by the many volumes of scholarly material offered to us through this last century on the issue of the preservation of Scripture. Let's look, however, at the most convincing evidence that our Bible has been preserved by God, and how its journey through the centuries to us has been guided by His omnipotent, supernatural hand.

It was the responsibility of the scribes to maintain the integrity of each word and phrase of the Bible. It was their life's work to copy and carefully protect the manuscripts of the Bible so as to hand over an unchanged text to each passing generation. Whole museums are full of these beautifully transcribed documents of immeasurable worth. Each page is a beautiful piece of art no less priceless than a Rembrandt or Picasso; no less awesome or breathtaking as a sculpture or painting by Michelangelo. Down through the centuries, the untold thousands of scribes painstakingly have left us page after page of carefully copied manuscripts of the Bible.

Between the autograph and the modern Bible extends an important link in the overall chain "from God to us" known as transmission. It provides a positive answer to the question: Do Bible scholars today possess an accurate copy of the autographs? Obviously, the authenticity and authority of the Bible cannot be established unless it be known that the present copies have integrity. For the New Testament, beginning with the second century ancient versions and manuscript fragments and continuing with abundant quotations of the Fathers and thousands of manuscript copies from that time to the modern versions of the Bible, there is virtually an unbroken line of testimony. Furthermore, there are not only countless manuscripts to support the integrity of the Bible (including the Old Testament since the discovery of the Dead Sea Scrolls), but a study of the procedures of preparation and preservation of the biblical manuscript copies reveals the fidelity of the transmission process itself. In fact, it may be concluded that no major document from antiquity comes into the modern world with such evidence of its integrity as does the Bible.[7]

One might argue, "How can we be certain of the lack of errors in the transmission of the Bible down through the centuries, since no one has discovered an original manuscript?" One of the great privileges and subsequent overwhelming joys of my life was visiting the British Museum with my late Evangelist Father, Dr. Bob Randall. (He, like his Father before him, preached the Bible as God's Word literally all over the world while calling people to repentance and faith in Christ as Savior and Lord. The Randall Family has been preaching the claims of the Word of God on people's lives for over 100 years, which includes six generations as far as we have discovered.) That day in London was one of those unique and special moments, when God validated His call upon my life. In the ancient document section of the museum, we inquired about the location of two manuscripts by the name of Codex Vaticanus and Codex Sinaiticus (Aleph). Codex Vaticanus is perhaps the most important witness to the text of the New Testament because of its early date (c. A.D. 325-50). Codex Sinaiticus (Aleph) is generally considered to be the most important witness to the text because of its antiquity (c. A.D. 340) accuracy, and lack of omissions.[8] Not only do we have these magnificent collections of the New Testament books that date within a little more than 200 years of the original writings, we also have Old Testament Bible texts that have been discovered from papyri in Aramaic cursive that predate these amazing collections to the fourth century B.C..

Yes, it is true we don't have an original manuscript of the Bible. However, through the science of Textual Criticism, an unbroken line of transmission of the biblical text from the original writings to our Bible is easily recognized. Why is this so important? It is important because we now have the ability to look at these ancient texts of the Bible that have brought to us our Bible. Gleason Archer observes that the two copies of Isaiah discovered in Qumran Cave #1 "proved to be word for word identical with our standard Hebrew Bible in more than 95% of the text. The 5% of variation consisted chiefly of obvious slips of the pen and the variations in spelling.[9]

As we look carefully at these Bible passages and compare them to these ancient manuscripts, it is with great joy and amazement that we discover we do have a Bible that is consistent with the most ancient text. Think of it, God has overseen the preservation of His Word to us in the Bible. It can only be concluded by any honest person that the Bible we hold in our hands is in fact trustworthy and reliable.

THE BIBLE IS THE WORD OF GOD IN ITS DECLARATION

The Bible itself claims to be the Word of God. The Old Testament writers claimed to be speaking for God. The expressions *The Lord said, The Lord spoke saying*, and *Thus saith the Lord* occurs 560 times in the first five books of the Old Testament known as the Pentateuch, 300 times in the historical and prophetical books, and 1200 times in the Prophets. In all, over 2000 times in the Old Testament, the writers claimed that the words that they were to speak and write were given to them by God. Jeremiah even said that God put the words in his mouth to speak:

> *Then the LORD stretched out His hand and touched my mouth, and the LORD said to me, "Behold, I have put My words in your mouth" (Jeremiah 1:9).*

In the New Testament, Jesus leaves no doubt as to His understanding concerning the nature of Scripture as the Word of God. Christ recognized that there was true Divine revelation there, that He was the goal of it all. He came to fulfill the law and the prophets. The Scriptures are the last word with Him.[10] Notice what Jesus said concerning what He believed about the Scriptures:

> *"Have you not read?" (Matt. 12:3,5, 19:4, 21:16, 42, 22:31, Mark 2:25, 12:10, 12:26, Luke 6:3, 10:26), But Jesus answered and said to them, "You are mistaken, not understanding the Scriptures, or the power of God" (Matt 22:29).*

The most convincing of all the proofs and arguments for the verbal inspiration of the Bible is the fact that the Lord Jesus Christ regarded it and treated it as such. Look at such passages as *Matthew 19:4-5; 22:29; 23:35, Mark 7:13, Luke 24:44; John 5:39, 10:35.* Jesus taught the infallibility of Scripture. He regarded it as divine authority and as the final court of appeal concerning all questions.[11] In the story of the temptation of Jesus, we read that three times He used the Word of God from the book of Deuteronomy. It is remarkable that the Lord Jesus refused to overwhelm Satan with the force of His superior wisdom.

He scorned to crush him with a display of His almighty power. His defense for each assault plainly and simply was, "It is written." We see Jesus in *Matthew 4* overcoming the tempter in the wilderness by three quotations from Deuteronomy without note or comment except the words, "It is written." [12]

We find these words in Hebrews as to what the Scriptures claim for themselves:

> *For the word of God is living and active and sharper than any two-edged sword, and piercing as far as the division of soul and spirit, of both joints and marrow, and able to judge the thoughts and intentions of the heart (Hebrews 4:12).*

No counselor, however trained or educated, can do this. No pastor or church can do this. Only the Word of God has the power to judge our thoughts and secret intentions. The Bible is as alive and active as it was when it first came forth from God's heart; when He first spoke it to man. It is timeless in its power, for it is timeless in its essence. God spoke it, and God still speaks in it and through it.

THE BIBLE IS THE WORD OF GOD IN ITS DURATION

In this life nothing stays the same. Every day change is inevitable. Time and change are like inseparable twins. However, when all changes around us, one thing never changes and that is the Word of God:

> *Heaven and earth will pass away, but My words shall not pass away (Matt 24:35).*

> *The grass withers, the flower fades, But the word of our God stands forever (Isaiah 40:8).*

The testimony of history confirms over and over again that the Bible is the Eternal and never-changing Word of God. As it declares for itself:

> *Forever, O LORD, Thy word is settled in heaven (Psalms 119:89).*

The Word of God is forever settled, it is forever established in the courts of Heaven. The testimony of the many fulfilled biblical prophecies, as well as those which are being fulfilled, give clear evidence that the Bible is the Word of God. The evidence from prophecy fulfilled is just such that its careful study results in a coffin for skepticism. One thousand prophetic statements mark the pages of the Old and New Testaments. It is estimated by careful scholars that over seven hundred of these have been fulfilled to the very letter. History is still running in the mold of prophecy. Notice the following list of biblical prophecies and how they relate to history.

These prophecies relate to cities: Babylon *(Isaiah 13:19-22)*, Nineveh *(Zephaniah 2:13)*, Tyre *(Ezekiel. 26:4)*, Israel and Judah *(Deut. 28:64-67)*. There are prophecies that relate to the nations, ancient and modern, *(Dan. 2:31-46)*; to the First and Second Coming of Christ, *(Gen. 3:15, Isaiah 9:7, Micah 5:2, Matt. 1, Acts 1:11, 1 Thess. 4:13-18)*; to the rise, progress and apostasies of the church. Then there are the prophecies that speak to wars and rumors of wars; of false prophets and false christs, of famine and earthquakes *(Matt. 24)*; to the coming Anti-Christ *(Rev. 13)*, to the coming Armageddon *(Rev. 9, 20: 7-9)*. The remaining prophecies are, at this moment, so clearly in evidence as to cast their shadows before them. All of this is a supernatural proof of a supernatural and forever enduring Bible.[13]

The Bible was one of the first major books ever translated, around 250 B.C., from Hebrew to Greek. It has been translated into more than 2,200 languages. In all translations, it has touched more than 90% of the world's population. The Bible has been rejected and criticized by kings, peasants, cults, other religions, fanatics, and scholars and yet it remains one of the most trusted and reliable books ever penned. In its translation activity, no other book in history compares with the Bible.[14]

It late Spring of 1996, I was invited by a couple of wonderful evangelist friends, Jim Ponder and Joe Atkinson, to partner with them for evangelistic meetings in the Ukraine. They had been going to the Ukraine for several years and wanted the Ukrainian experience for me. Allow me to put our time in the Ukraine in historical context. Kiev, the mother city of old mother Russia, is the capitol and center of Ukrainian history and life. It is a place well known for its murderous dictators like Joseph Stalin and Adolf Hitler. It is a horribly bloody place in human history. Ukrainian life has been extremely hard for nearly 100 years. Our visit to the Ukraine was just a few years after the dismantling of the Soviet Union. The newly found freedom of the people was best demonstrated in an open expression of religion, manifesting itself in these evangelistic gatherings that were being held all over the country. As a result of these meetings, evangelistic churches were springing up all across the Ukrainian landscape.

Through the day, we would travel out to the countryside into the towns and villages. We held evangelistic services primarily in the open marketplaces. Folks from all over the area would come and listen to the claims of Christ upon their lives. I was told that I was the first preacher of the Gospel of Christ ever seen or received in many of the villages where I had the blessed opportunity to preach. In front of the Hammer and Sickle, many hundreds of precious Ukrainians gave their hearts to Christ. In the evenings, the team would join together at Kiev's Opera House for an evangelistic crusade. There many on the team would sing, play our instruments and share what Christ had done for us. My late dear friend, and wonderfully gifted evangelist, Jim Ponder would stand and give God's message. As he proclaimed the Word of God, folks would fill the aisles coming forward to give their lives to Christ.

We soon learned that the meetings we were conducting were being broadcast live over Ukrainian television to millions of people across that great nation. These wonderful men of God with whom I partnered, had printed thousands of Ukrainian Bibles. At the end of each service, we would give out those Bibles to anyone who wanted one. Forever etched in my heart and mind is that scene. Before me a vast sea of people pressing in, hundreds of opened hands lifted upward with the hope of receiving their first Bible. You see, it had been a crime for over two generations for a person to have a Bible in the old communistic, secularist, and atheistic state of the Soviet Union. You would have thought we were giving out $1,000.00 bills. With sobbing and open tears of joy, many received their first Bible. My dear Friend, that's just a small example of the Bible's enduring role around the world in the lives and hearts of millions, even when those in power have tried to eradicate it from their land.

THE BIBLE IS THE WORD OF GOD IN ITS APPLICATION

If you have made the journey this far, and if you have studied with me the theological definitions of inspiration and scriptural authority, good for you. Let me say something here that must be stated firmly. As important as it is to believe good doctrine, if it is not applied to daily life, defeat is certain in the spiritual battle. This book is not merely a theological statement of faith for the purpose of bringing its readers into doctrinal compliance. If we stop with mere doctrinal beliefs, but do not apply the truth, then the Devil wins; lives will continue to be destroyed. If we are to believe the Word of God, then that belief must lead us to take up the Sword of the Spirit (which is the Word of God), and use it against the Enemy and his murderous schemes *(Eph. 6:17).*

For the word of God is living and active and sharper than any two-edged sword, and piercing as far as the division of soul and spirit, of both joints and marrow, and able to judge the thoughts and intentions of the heart (Hebrews 4:12).

The Word of God used by the Spirit of God has the power to change anything—any life, any home, any business, any sickness, any church, anything. How? Through its life…the Word of God is alive. It's alive! The Word of God can even change the atmosphere when used by the Spirit of God. Why do you think untold billions of dollars have been spent by all kinds of churches all over the world, in every culture, to build sanctuaries and places of worship? These houses of worship have been built with the primary center of their purpose and function to be the preaching of the Word of God. When the Word of God is applied by the Spirit of God, there is an encounter with the eternal Kingdom of God and its authority. God's supernatural and eternal life comes as we receive the Word of God:

But He answered and said, "It is written, 'Man shall not live on bread alone, but on every word that proceeds out of the mouth of God'" (Matt 4:4).

For there to be victory in spiritual warfare, one must come to believe that what God has said is truth. The Bible doesn't just contain the Word of God; it is the Word of God!

"Then I shall answer the one who taunts me, for I trust in your word. Do not snatch the word of truth from my mouth, for I have put my hope in your laws" (Psalm 119:42-43, NIV).

As has already been discussed in this chapter, it is not a coincidence that every major denomination has fought a fierce battle over the issue of the inspiration and authority of the Bible. If you take the authority of the Word of God out of the battle, if you take the "Sword of the Lord" out of the hands of the spiritual warrior, defeat is certain. We must see that *"the world through its wisdom did not come to know God" (1 Cor. 1:21).* TRUTH comes through God's revelation. This is how we know where to stand; it is written in the Word of God.

The Bible is the most important weapon for fighting the lying ones and their murderous schemes. I have always had a high view of Scripture. Anyone who knows the life and ministry of Rob Randall knows that I have never been confused as to the authority of God's Word. However, let me say that through my experiences in spiritual warfare, I have come to an even greater respect and reverence for the Word of God than I have ever known. The authority of Scripture may be debated in the classrooms of our universities and seminaries. The authority of Scripture may be disbelieved in the everyday programs of the church. But understand! Demons have a HIGH view of Scripture! They tremble in the presence of Thus saith the Lord. You see, it is in the Word that they are judged. It is in the Word of God that they are doomed and damned, and they know it. They are constantly looking for those who are confused about the Word of God to bring their evil agenda into the world. Truth exposes the work of the Enemy. Everything he does is in the darkness, covered in lies. Truth shines the light into the darkness and exposes his lies and deception.

Think of it! Through the Word of God, the work of God is done. The Sword of the Lord is able to separate that which is holy from that which is unholy. The Sword of the Lord is able to penetrate the heart of man and determine that which is of the flesh and that which is of the spirit. Wow, what power! No psychiatrist, however educated, is able to do that. Only God's Word is used by God to determine the truth, or its absence in our hearts. There is no substitute for the use of the Word of God against Satan. The great Scottish preacher, John Knox, said it well, "Christ might have repulsed Satan with a word or by commanding him to silence, as He to whom all power was given in heaven and earth; but it pleased his mercy to teach us how to use the sword of the Holy Ghost, which is the Word of God, in battle against our spiritual Enemy."[15] Even Jesus recognized the use of the Word of God as His sword against Satan in his amazing encounter with him in the wilderness *(Luke 4:1-3)*.

To be able to effectively use the Word of God in spiritual warfare, the believer must first know the Word of God. Dear brother and sister in Christ, get into the Word and stay in the Word! Come to know the Scriptures. Internalize the Word of God, not as a matter of legalistic ritual, but as a foundation on which to build your life. You must know your sword well before you attempt to use it in battle. The word Jesus used for the Word of God as He faced the tempter in *Luke 4:4* was *rhema*. This word refers to a *personal word* to you from God. For every lie the Enemy uses against the believer, God has an answer in His Word. This answer to every lie of Satan believed in your life is God's *rhema*. How do you know that the answer is from the Lord? He will speak to you through His written Word. The Enemy can't use the Word of God to bring God's will into your life. Only the Spirit of God will bring to you a personal word from the written Word that will be used of the Holy Spirit to bring about God's will.

Remember, the Devil is about destruction based on lies. Our Lord has given us His Word that it might bring forth life. The Devil and his evil angels are eternally fearful of the Word of God. All demons tremble in the presence of the well-dressed spiritual warrior wielding the Sword of the Spirit. All of Satan's lies are exposed and expelled with the Word of God. All the ground that the Devil's imps have gained in our lives they have stolen through their strategy of deceit and lies. The Word of God is without a doubt the most powerful weapon in the believer's arsenal against the powers of darkness. Remember, *And you shall know the truth, and the truth shall make you free (John 8:32)*. In Jesus' prayer for the church He makes the nature of the Word of God clear. *Sanctify them in the truth; Thy word is truth (John 17:17)*. Our foolish debates over the veracity and reliability of the Bible cannot change the fact that in Heaven and in Hell the debate is over. The Word of God is the truth of God used by the Spirit of God. It is the Sword of the Spirit. We must take it up and let the Spirit of God, who is within us, use it to destroy the works of the Enemy and uncover his murderous lies.

ENGAGING THE POWERS OF DARKNESS BY PRAYING THE WORD OF GOD

In the Scriptures, and through the Scriptures, we have the very presence of God. As has been stated, we must not separate the living Word of God from the written Word of God. Each is the living presentation of the presence and power of God. In a wonderful supernatural way, God is able to use our faith by using the Scriptures as a powerful weapon of warfare. The best example we have is the way Christ Jesus used the Scriptures in *Luke 4* to resist and rebuke the Enemy. The Word of God can be used as a prayer to confront the powers of darkness.

The following are examples of how to pray the Word of God in the battle for control over strongholds of the Enemy. The Scriptures listed here are just a sampling of how to use the Word of God in the process of spiritual cleansing. These particular scriptural passages have been found to be extremely powerful and effective in the cleansing process. As you pray the Scriptures over a person who is in battle with the powers of darkness, ask the Lord Jesus to cause the Word of God to become the sharp two-edged sword in the spirit world that He promises them to be: *2 Tim. 3:16-17*.

John 1:1, Eph. 6:17, Heb. 4:12, Jude, Col. 3, James 4, Psalm 35, Psalm 103.

Prayer

Dear Lord Jesus, I come to You as Your child; As a joint-heir with Christ Jesus, I thank You that You are able to do exceeding abundantly above all that I could ask, or even think. I thank You, Lord Jesus, that I am a victor, not a victim. I thank You that everything that I need to be free in Christ has been made available to me through the shed blood of Calvary. I thank You, Christ Jesus, that it was for freedom that You came to set me free *(Gal. 5:1)*. You came to destroy the works of the Devil. As I pray Your Word over this matter, I ask You to use Your Word as a sharp two-edged sword, separating righteousness from unrighteousness. Divide good from evil and the truth of God from the lies of the Enemy. I ask You, Lord Jesus, to make the evil ones hear and obey the Word of God. May what is done here today bring glory to Your Holy Name. May Your cleansing work cause all of the holy angels to rejoice and all the evil ones to be tormented—even to the very pit of Hell itself. As I pray these Scriptures back to You I ask, Lord Jesus, that You would use them to confront, rebuke, and dismantle the evil ones and their strongholds. As I pray the Word of God, use each word to set this captive one free for Your glory alone.

LIES THAT KILL

2

ANY GOD WILL DO—AS LONG AS I AM SINCERE.

It is important as we take a careful look at the LIES THAT KILL that we prioritize the ones in which so many others have their roots. It would be impossible to compile an exhaustive list of the terminal lies of the Enemy. Remember, Satan has had thousands of years to perfect his murderous, careful crafting of lies. In this chapter, I want to focus on a lie that is draped in political correctness. This lie may be socially acceptable; but, if someone accepts this fallacious notion that any god will do as long as we are sincere, it will lead them to death and destruction. I want us to investigate carefully what the Bible says concerning looking to other gods. We must look at the truth concerning the importance of worshiping only Jehovah God as revealed to us through His Son, Christ Jesus of Nazareth.

How many gods would you think there are around the world in different cultures? Gods that have specific names that have been worshiped and/or are being worshiped today? What would you guess? I did a search on the internet looking up the word god, or gods, and came up with several websites that list the major gods that have been worshipped, or are being worshipped by specific people groups around the world today. This is amazing to me. Man's need and ultimate desire to worship his creator has been replaced with the Enemy's vast number of counterfeits. Although I'm certain the following list is not exhaustive, it does give us a clear picture of how successful the Enemy has been to perpetrate his lies and man's eager willingness to believe them.

African gods—293
Australian gods—95
Aztec gods—175
Caribbean gods—86
Celtic gods—165
Chinese gods—470
Egyptian gods—358
Finnish gods—108
Greek gods—646
Inca gods—75
Japanese gods—160
Mayan gods—237
Mesopotamian gods—118
Middle Eastern gods—155
Native American gods—329
Norse Scandinavian gods—294
Oceanic (Pacific Islands) gods—261
Roman—Italy and Western Europe gods—241
Slavic and Baltic gods—195
South American gods—81
South East Asia—74

Imagine with me for a moment, if you will. According to this compiled list of gods there are 4,616 known gods with specific names that have been worshipped, or are being worshipped today. According to Van Der Toorn, Beckling and Van Der Hurst in their award-winning book, *Dictionary of Deities and Demons in the Bible*, a study of the Hebrew and Greek Bible, including the Apocrypha, yields some 635 listed gods.[1]

From a study of the compilation of serious anthropomorphic and religious scholars who have done their homework on the subject of religious systems, there are at least 5,251 gods that have been worshipped and/or are being worshipped today by people groups around the world. Think of it with me. There are over five thousand named gods that have taken the place of Jehovah God in the lives and hearts of people. If there were only one other god that was worshipped rather than Jehovah God, it would be one too many.

This failed argument, that the belief in a plurality of gods is stronger than belief in the one true and living Jehovah God as set forth in the Bible, has a shallow echo, as it travels down the corridors of time. Listen to some of these old, worn-out, and misguided arguments: "Just as long as folks are sincere, isn't that all that matters?" "Since there is only one God, does it really matter what you call Him?" "Isn't all that really matters is that we practice some kind of religion and follow the god of our choice to the best of our understanding?" "Isn't being religious the way we all become better people?" These sound pretty good until you look at the "fine print" of the offering of religion, without a relationship with Jehovah God through the sacrifice of Christ.

All that Satan has done, or will ever do, is based on our willingness to believe his lies. Jesus called the Devil "The Father of lies." Since we know the Devil is a murderer *"seeking someone to devour,"* then it must follow that his lies can kill. Believing Satan's lies can get you killed! The only answer for Satan's lies is the truth.

May I ask you today, "If what you believed about God was wrong, wouldn't you want to know it?" Boy, I sure would. No matter what we have been taught or how sincere a person may be, is it possible to be wrong in our beliefs? Of course it is. Sincerity does not carry with it the guarantee that all things will somehow turn out O.K. The only way we can know what we are believing in is truth is to ask ourselves, "Does what I am believing about God come from His revelation, or does it come from man's opinions or persuasions about God?"

It is crucial that we understand the Word of God given to us by Holy Spirit. It has come to us through the lives and pens of men, of course, but ultimately it was given to us by God; as we have thoroughly discussed in the previous chapter. Here is what is different about the Bible:

> *But know this first of all, that no prophecy of Scripture is a matter of one's own interpretation, for no prophecy was ever made by an act of human will, but men moved by the Holy Spirit spoke from God (2 Peter 1:20-21).*

AUTHENTIC BIBLICAL FAITH

Over 25 years ago, my father and I were conducting a series of meetings in a small town in the wheat fields of Western Kansas. One night during the revival meeting my Dad preached an especially powerful message on faith. While retiring for the evening to our motel room after the service Dad turned to me and asked, "Rob, what was wrong in the service tonight? Something was just not right." I replied, "Daddy, they didn't have a clue what you were preaching about." Tragically, many believers today do not understand true biblical faith.

Faith is not the process by which we just believe in something, however noble or religious. What, then, is faith? Is faith the unyielding desire to see or feel something from God? Is it a trigger when pulled, men can manipulate God to do their bidding? Is faith an exercise of mental weakness by which we ignore all matters of science and education? What is faith? Faith is not subjective. For faith to be true biblical faith, it must be objective. That is, faith does not begin with us. Faith is the response to what God has said. The writer of Hebrews put it this way:

> *Now faith is the assurance of things hoped for, the conviction of things not seen (Hebrews 11:1).*

Let's look carefully at the words <u>assurance</u> and <u>conviction</u>. In what are we to invest our assurance? In what must our conviction be placed? Faith is the assurance and conviction that God will do what He has said in His Word. In *Hebrews Chapter 11*, we find listed for us God's examples of men and women who were willing to obey what God had told them. In each example of biblical faith listed in the great "Hall of the Faithful," we see that God spoke first before these men and women could obey. Through the witness of their obedience to God, these great men and women became the "superstars of faith" that our Lord decided to use to teach us how to live by faith. Charles H. Spurgeon said it well: "Then you must see to it that your faith is that which rests only upon truth, for if there be any error or false notion in the fashioning of it, that shall be a joint in it which the spear can pierce. You must take care that your faith is agreeable to God's Word, that you depend upon true and real promises, upon the sure word of testimony and not upon the fictions and fancies and dreams of men."[2] Note carefully the three aspects of authentic biblical faith:

1. Revelation—For there to be authentic faith, we must respond to "Thus saith the Lord" God must speak first before faith can exist. Faith is simply this, believing what God has said is true.

> *By faith Noah, being warned by God about things not yet seen, in reverence prepared an ark for the salvation of his household (Heb. 11:7).*

Faith is the response to the revelation of God. Faith believes what God says.

2. Decision—Before faith can be born, a decision must be made in our hearts. That decision is whether or not to accept what God has said as true. The active will is necessary for faith to have its rightful place in the life of the believer.

> *By faith even Sarah herself received ability to conceive, even beyond the proper time of life, since **she considered Him faithful who had promised** (Heb. 11:11).*

3. Action—After God has spoken and after the decision is made to believe what God has said, the believer still has not entered into faith. Faith is the action based upon belief in what God has said. I like what one evangelist friend has said, "What we believe is what we do; everything else is just talk."

> *By faith Abraham, when he was called, obeyed by going out to a place which he was to receive for an inheritance; **and he went out**, not knowing where he was going (Heb. 11:8).*

Faith is not just a belief in a doctrine or teaching. NO, faith is responding to what God has said to the extent of ordering our lives on the basis of His revelation. Let us now look at the testimony of Scripture concerning the significance of Jehovah God being the only one true and living God.

THE TESTIMONY OF SCRIPTURE
If God says it, it would be wise and prudent for all men to believe it!

- God's Word says that all things were created by God, and for God:

> *For by Him all things were created, both in the heavens and on earth, visible and invisible, whether thrones or dominions or rulers or authorities—all things have been created by Him and for Him (Col. 1:16).*

- God's Word says that Jesus was God's only Son, born of a virgin and conceived by the Holy Spirit:

> *But when he had considered this, behold, an angel of the Lord appeared to him in a dream, saying, "Joseph, son of David, do not be afraid to take Mary as your wife; for that which has been conceived in her is of the Holy Spirit. And she will bear a Son; and you shall call His name Jesus, for it is He who will save His people from their sins." Now all this took place that what was spoken by the Lord through the prophet might be fulfilled, saying, "BEHOLD, THE VIRGIN SHALL BE WITH CHILD, AND SHALL BEAR A SON, AND THEY SHALL CALL HIS NAME IMMANUEL," which translated means, "GOD WITH US" (Matt. 1:20-23).*

- God's Word says that Jesus was sacrificed for our sins:

He made Him who knew no sin to be sin on our behalf, that we might become the righteousness of God in Him (2 Cor. 5:21).

- God's Word says that three days after Jesus died for our sins and was buried, He arose from the dead. Because God raised Him from the dead, the Heavenly Father has given Him a Name which is greater in authority and power than all other names:

And He is the radiance of His glory and the exact representation of His nature, and upholds all things by the word of His power. When He had made purification of sins, He sat down at the right hand of the Majesty on high; having become as much better than the angels, as He has inherited <u>a more excellent name</u> than they (Heb 1:3-4).

And being found in appearance as a man, He humbled Himself by becoming obedient to the point of death, even death on a cross. Therefore also God highly exalted Him, and bestowed on Him the name which is above every name, that at the name of Jesus EVERY KNEE SHOULD BOW, of those who are in heaven, and on earth, and under the earth, and that every tongue should confess that Jesus Christ is Lord, to the glory of God the Father (Phil 2:8-11).

- God's Word says that Jesus is coming again to rule and reign over this world from Jerusalem:

Then the moon will be abashed and the sun ashamed, For the LORD of hosts will reign on Mount Zion and in Jerusalem, and His glory will be before His elders (Isaiah 24:23).

And I saw heaven opened; and behold, a white horse, and He who sat upon it is called Faithful and True; and in righteousness He judges and wages war. And His eyes are a flame of fire, and upon His head are many diadems; and He has a name written upon Him which no one knows except Himself. And He is clothed with a robe dipped in blood; and His name is called The Word of God. And the armies which are in heaven, clothed in fine linen, white and clean, were following Him on white horses. And from His mouth comes a sharp sword, so that with it He may smite the nations; and He will rule them with a rod of iron; and He treads the wine press of the fierce wrath of God, the Almighty. And on His robe and on His thigh He has a name written, "KING OF KINGS, AND LORD OF LORDS" (Rev 19:11-16).

This wonderful Lord Jesus is coming again to rule and reign over the earth in righteousness and justice!

The Bible says that His Name is the only Name which men can call on to be saved:

And there is salvation in no one else; for there is no other name under heaven that has been given among men, by which we must be saved (Acts 4:12).

In Paul's letter to his son in the ministry, Timothy, we find these words:

For there is one God, and one mediator also between God and men, the man Christ Jesus (I Timothy 2:5).

THE TESTIMONY OF AMERICA'S RELIGIOUS HERITAGE

Folks may foolishly want to ignore America's religious heritage, but it is evident from the documents of history—many penned by our Founding Fathers—that the establishing of our own nation was an act of faith in its dedication to Jehovah God. Virtually everyone of the 55 writers and signers of the 1787 United States Constitution were members of Christian denominations: 29 were Anglicans, 16-18 were Calvinists, 2 were Methodists, 2 were Lutherans, 2 were Roman Catholic, 1 a lapsed Quaker/sometime Anglican, and one a practicing open Deist—Dr. Benjamin Franklin—who attended every kind of Christian worship, called for public prayer, and contributed to all denominations.[3]

In 1954 former Supreme Court Justice Earl Warren addressed the annual prayer breakfast of the International Council of Christian Leadership. Though never thought to be a fundamentalist Christian during his service as jurist, he clearly put himself in the company of those who are convinced of the Judeo-Christian worldview of the Founders when he said: "I believe no one can read the history of our country without realizing that the Good Book and the spirit of the Savior have from the beginning been our guiding geniuses...whether we look to the first Charter of Virginia...or to the Charter of New England...or the Charter of Massachusetts Bay...or to the Fundamental Orders of Connecticut... the same objective is present: a Christian land governed by Christian principles. I believe the entire Bill of Rights, came into being because of the knowledge our forefathers had of the Bible and their belief in it: freedom of belief, of expression, of assembly, of petition, the dignity of the individual, the sanctity of the home, equal justice under law, and the reservations of powers to the people...I like to believe we are living today in the spirit of the Christian religion."[4]

THE TESTIMONY OF MODERN EDUCATION IN AMERICA

Well documented is the history of modern education in America. Its beginning is forever a sober reminder that we should honor the one true and living Lord. Well documented is the history of the establishment of so many of the major educational institutions of higher learning in America to honor the one true and living Jehovah God. Of the 516 colleges and universities founded before the Civil War, only a few had no religious affiliation. Academics were often the product of an individual minister's zeal for learning, whereas the dominant motive in founding colleges was to provide an educated ministry. Prime examples are the divinity schools at Harvard (est. 1816), Yale (est. 1822), and Princeton (est. 1812) just to mention a few.[5] Did you know that Dartmouth College was established to reach the Dartmouth Indians for Christ? Did you know that the first university chartered in the Republic of Texas was my university—Baylor University? Baylor was founded out of its missionary founders passion that is represented by its President and subsequent namesake of the University, R.E.B. Baylor. He established the Texas Baptist Education Society for the primary purpose of helping support young men studying for the ministry from which Baylor University had its birth.[6]

THE TESTIMONY OF WESTERN CIVILIZATION

The history of the development and expansion of Western civilization was based on the mandate of the Bible to reach our world for Christ. England understood that to civilize was to Christianize the world. Through the timeless words of Winston Churchill, we can visit again a time of clarity of the Western World as the British were called into battle to maintain their very existence. His speech broadcast to a broken nation after the Blitz of Germany over Britain speaks to us today with laser precision as to their hearts' commitment to Jehovah God. "Arm yourselves, and be ye men of valor, and be in readiness for the conflict. For it is better for us to perish in battle than to look upon the outrage of our nation and our altar. As the Will of God is in Heaven, even so let it be."[7] In Churchill's message to the nation of England in the House of Commons given on June 18th, 1940, just hours before The Battle of Britain was initiated by Hitler's evil Nazi regime, we find a clear and precise reflection of Britain's understanding of her Christian destiny in world history. "...the battle of France is over, I expect that the Battle of Britain is about to begin. Upon this battle depends the survival of Christian civilization."[8]

THE TESTIMONY OF RELIGIOUS ARCHITECTURE

One need only to look at the hundreds of thousands of churches, synagogues, and mighty cathedrals built and dedicated to the worship of the one true and living God to see the evidence of God's love for His people as well as their love for Him. These sanctified structures of worship scattered throughout the world grace the landscape of every country and state, every town and village and in every culture and land where the freedom to worship God has been practiced. These great citadels of worship are not only the resounding testimony of man's devotion to Jehovah God, but the myriads of church steeples rising to the heavens also serve as sign posts to God's covenant He has made to His people through Christ Jesus.

THE TESTIMONY OF THE GREAT MUSICAL COMPOSERS

Even the greatest of composers of music the world has ever known wrote out of a deep and dedicated devotion to the one true and living Jehovah God. From George Frideric Handel to Franz Joseph Hayden, from Wolfgang Amadeus Mozart to Ludwig Van Beethoven, from Franz Shubert to Felix Mendelssohn, from Franz Lizst to Igor Stravinsky; over 300 years these great world redound gifts of musical genius composed their great masterpieces in concert to the glory of God. Johann Sebastian Bach as he sat composing, would frequently initial his blank manuscript pages with the marking "J.J." ("Jesu-Juva" —"Help me, Jesus"), or "I.N.S." ("In Nomine Jesu"—"In the Name of Jesus") At the manuscript end, Bach routinely initialed the letters "S.D.G." ("Soli Deo Gloria"—"To God alone, the glory").[9]

THE TESTIMONY OF THE DATING SYSTEM

All of human history cries out to every man that Jesus is the Christ, the Son of the one true and living God. The purpose of the western calendaring and dating system was ONLY to note the dividing point in the history of the world as it referenced Christ's birth. B.C. ('before Christ') and A.D. ('anno domini,' Latin for 'in the Year of our Lord').

THE CONSEQUENCES OF BREAKING THE FIRST COMMANDMENT

Now, some might want to ask: "Dr. Randall, you don't really believe that trusting in gods other than Jehovah God can get you killed, do you? I thought God was a loving God." God is a loving God. He is love. He loves everyone. He loves you and everyone who is in your family. He loves everyone who has lived, or who will ever live. He wants everyone to be saved from the consequences of their sin. That's why He sent His only Son Jesus Christ of Nazareth to die and pay the penalty for our sins. The Bible tells us in *2 Peter 3:9*, that it is God's will that *none perish*, but for *all* to come to repentance. Friend, God has set the rules. He has the right to do so. After all, He is God. There is a very good reason why the first commandment is:

You shall have no other gods before Me. You shall not make for yourself an idol, or any likeness of what is in heaven above or on the earth beneath or in the water under the earth. You shall not worship them or serve them; for I, the LORD your God, am a jealous God, visiting the iniquity of the fathers on the children, and on the third and the fourth generations of those who hate Me, but showing loving kindness to thousands, to those who love Me and keep My commandments (Deut. 5:7-10).

You shall not make for yourself an idol, or any likeness of what is in heaven above or on the earth beneath or in the water under the earth. You shall not worship them or serve them; for I, the LORD your God, am a jealous God, visiting the iniquity of the fathers on the children, on the third and the fourth generations of those who hate Me, but showing lovingkindness to thousands, to those who love Me and keep My commandments (Exodus 20:3-6).

In the book of *Judges*, we find these sobering words:

But you have abandoned Me and worshiped other gods. Therefore, I will not deliver you again (Judges 10:13).

The reason worshipping and trusting other gods is so dangerous, is because there is only one true and living God. All others are satanic counterfeits. All the other so-called gods are real. The Bible calls them real demons. Just don't take my word for it. Please study the Scriptures with me. We can't afford to get this wrong. In the following scripture, we find that there is only ONE LORD:

There is one body and one Spirit, just as also you were called in one hope of your calling; ONE Lord, one faith, one baptism, ONE God and Father of all who is over all and through all and in all (Eph 4:4-6).

All others who claim to be Lord are impostors. All other so-called lords or gods are liars. The Word of God calls them NO GODS and refers to them as demons *(Deut. 32:16-18, Psalm 106:37, 1 Cor. 10:20-21).*

They made Him jealous with strange gods; with abominations they provoked Him to anger. They sacrificed to demons who were not God, to gods whom they have not known, new gods who came lately, whom your fathers did not dread. You neglected the Rock who begot you, and forgot the God who gave you birth. (Deut 32:16-18).

In *Psalm 106:34* and following we find how God was enraged because His people did not obey Him. His judgment fell on them, because they refused to worship only Him:

They did not destroy the peoples, as the LORD commanded them, but they mingled with the nations, and learned their practices, and served their idols, which became a snare to them. They even sacrificed their sons and their daughters to the demons, and shed innocent blood, The blood of their sons and their daughters, whom they sacrificed to the idols of Canaan; and the land was polluted with the blood. Thus they became unclean in their practices, and played the harlot in their deeds. Therefore the anger of the LORD was kindled against His people, and He abhorred His inheritance. Then He gave them into the hand of the nations; and those who hated them ruled over them. Their enemies also oppressed them, and they were subdued under their power (Psalm 106:34).

In the New Testament, we find how God's people can be deceived into worshiping demons:

No, but I say that the things which the Gentiles sacrifice, they sacrifice to demons, and not to God; and I do not want you to become sharers in demons. You cannot drink the cup of the Lord and the cup of demons; you cannot partake of the table of the Lord and the table of demons. Or do we provoke the Lord to jealousy? We are not stronger than He, are we (1 Cor. 10:21-22)?

To invoke the name of any other god other than the one true and living Jehovah God for help or supernatural power is in fact the practice of witchcraft, which is forbidden by God. This evil practice carries with it the severe punishment of God:

But for the cowardly and unbelieving and abominable and murderers and immoral persons and <u>sorcerers</u> and <u>idolaters</u> and all <u>liars</u>, their part will be in the lake that burns with fire and brimstone, which is the second death (Rev 21:8).

In the Old Testament, we get a clear glimpse of what following after false gods will bring upon a foolish people:

"Yet you have forsaken Me and served other gods; therefore I will deliver you no more. Go and cry out to the gods which you have chosen; let them deliver you in the time of your distress." And the sons of Israel said to the LORD, 'We have sinned, do to us whatever seems good to Thee; only please deliver us this day.' So they put away the foreign gods from among them, and served the LORD; and He could bear the misery of Israel no longer (Judges 10:10-13).

Someone might ask, "Well, Dr. Randall, it is O.K. for you to believe that Jehovah is the only true and living God, but how can I know for certain that Jehovah God is the only true and living God?" Dear Friend, please hear my heart. It's time for you to put your faith and trust in Jehovah God through His Son, Jesus Christ of Nazareth. The reality of the one true living Jehovah God, revealed through Jesus Christ of Nazareth, can be verified.

GOD REVEALING HIMSELF

In *I Kings 18:20-40*, we find a showdown on Mount Carmel between

God's Prophet Elijah and 850 false prophets of the demons of Baal and Asherah:

> *So Ahab sent a message among all the sons of Israel, and brought the prophets together at Mount Carmel. And Elijah came near to all the people and said, "How long will you hesitate between two opinions? If the LORD is God, follow Him; but if Baal, follow him." But the people did not answer him a word. Then Elijah said to the people, "I alone am left a prophet of the LORD, but Baal's prophets are 450 men. Now let them give us two oxen; and let them choose one ox for themselves and cut it up, and place it on the wood, but put no fire under it; and I will prepare the other ox, and lay it on the wood, and I will not put a fire under it. Then you call on the name of your god, and I will call on the name of the LORD, and the God who answers by fire, He is God." And all the people answered and said, "That is a good idea."*

> *So Elijah said to the prophets of Baal, "Choose one ox for yourselves and prepare it first for you are many, and call on the name of your god, but put no fire under it." Then they took the ox which was given them and they prepared it and called on the name of Baal from morning until noon saying, "O Baal, answer us." But there was no voice and no one answered. And they leaped about the altar which they made. And it came about at noon, that Elijah mocked them and said, "Call out with a loud voice, for he is a god; either he is occupied or gone aside, or is on a journey, or perhaps he is asleep and needs to be awakened." So they cried with a loud voice and cut themselves according to their custom with swords and lances until the blood gushed out on them. And it came about when midday was past, that they raved until the time of the offering of the evening sacrifice; but there was no voice, no one answered, and no one paid attention.*

Then Elijah said to all the people, "Come near to me." So all the people came near to him. And he repaired the altar of the LORD which had been torn down. And Elijah took twelve stones according to the number of the tribes of the sons of Jacob, to whom the word of the LORD had come, saying, "Israel shall be your name." So with the stones he built an altar in the name of the LORD, and he made a trench around the altar, large enough to hold two measures of seed. Then he arranged the wood and cut the ox in pieces and laid it on the wood. And he said, "Fill four pitchers with water and pour it on the burnt offering and on the wood." And he said, "Do it a second time," and they did it a second time. And he said, "Do it a third time," and they did it a third time. And the water flowed around the altar, and he also filled the trench with water.

Elijah's Prayer

Then it came about at the time of the offering of the evening sacrifice, that Elijah the prophet came near and said, "O LORD, the God of Abraham, Isaac and Israel, today let it be known that Thou art God in Israel, and that I am Thy servant, and that I have done all these things at Thy word. Answer me, O LORD, answer me, that this people may know that Thou, O LORD, art God, and that Thou hast turned their heart back again." Then the fire of the LORD fell, and consumed the burnt offering and the wood and the stones and the dust, and licked up the water that was in the trench. And when all the people saw it, they fell on their faces; and they said, "The LORD, He is God; the LORD, He is God." Then Elijah said to them, "Seize the prophets of Baal; do not let one of them escape." So they seized them; and Elijah brought them down to the brook Kishon, and slew them there (I Kings 18:20-40).

Here are some truths we can glean from Elijah's confrontation with

Ahab and Jezebel's demonic false prophets:

• Just because we might be sincere in our religious fervor, we can find ourselves to be sincerely wrong. The prophets of Baal were so sincere and passionate in their misguided faith in Baal that they were willing to cut themselves and bleed for what they believed. Tragically, they had put their trust in a second-rate power.

• Never worry about the odds. God can handle it. Notice there were 850 prophets of Baal with demonic powers all backed up politically by the King and Queen. Poor old Elijah was seemingly all by himself. Looks can be deceiving…it didn't matter that he stood alone. You plus God always makes a majority, no matter what the circumstances.

• If we genuinely want God to manifest His presence so we can know who He is, we must first ask. In the Book of James we find these words:

You do not have because you do not ask. You ask and do not receive, because you ask with wrong motives, so that you may spend it on your pleasures (James 4:2-3).

• Not only do we need to ask, but we must ask with the right desires and the right motives. What is the proper motive for our asking God to reveal Himself? It is always the same no matter what our petitions or prayers. We must honestly desire that through His manifesting Himself, He would bring glory to His Name. Our hearts must first and foremost desire that all that is done, would be for His glory! This fateful day on Mt. Carmel wasn't Elijah's showdown. This was God's showdown with these demonic false prophets. Elijah was simply willing to cooperate with the purposes of Heaven for God's people that they would come to know and trust the one true and living Jehovah God.

When our eldest son, Bob, was a university student, he came home with a devastating confession. He revealed to his mother and me that he had fallen into a pit of addiction to a cheap and legal, but deadly, over-the-counter drug. I would love to tell you that one or two prayer meetings fixed the problem, but that's not at all what happened. This addiction led him on an eight-year journey into the Enemy's dark, secret and deadly places. I must admit there were times when his mother and I were doubtful that our son would return home alive. The Enemy had come to kill our son; and, in doing so, he came to destroy my family, ministry, and my life, as well. Night after night, prayer after endless prayer, we pleaded with the Lord to save our son's life from this evil destruction that had so entangled him. His root problem was much greater than his addiction, even though his addiction had become a dangerous problem. Our precious son's problem stemmed from his struggle with whether, or not, the Jesus he had heard about and had been taught about all his life, was real. Was God really who He says He is?

It's a much longer story, not mine to tell, for it is Bob's story. However, do you want to know what turned my son around? Do you want to know what led him back to living a life of faith in his Lord and Savior Jesus? It became apparent that the only thing that was going to change our son's life from his failed attempts at faith, to a true biblical faith, was an encounter with the living Lord Jesus Christ. I will never forget that night that changed our lives forever. I asked my wife, Pattie to go into prayer for us. I told her that I believed that the only thing that would stop this seemingly endless cycle of use, abuse, and torment was for God to reveal Himself to our Son.

So, I began to pray. I asked the Lord to be gracious. I pleaded for His mercy. I was fearfully aware we were sinners and that God is Holy. I was deeply concerned that coming into God's presence could have a deadly outcome; that His holiness and righteous indignation could consume us. I asked the Lord to remove every hindering spirit and their blocks that would keep us from the work of the Lord that night. I began to ask the Lord to come and show Himself to our son. My Friend, that is just what He did! That night, in our home, Jesus walked into the room. In a most dramatic way the Lord revealed Himself to our son, by literally taking his very breath away. He demonstrated to Bob that night that he alone held my son's life in His hands. As God gave breath back to him, our Lord Jesus told him that if he didn't turn back to God; if he didn't repent from his unbelief, he would not long be on this earth. After that amazing encounter, things were never the same. Deliverance and inner healing came much faster and much deeper with each passing day. That encounter with God changed everything. Today, Bob is serving the Lord and ministering in the power of God to those who are broken, tormented and wounded. Praise the almighty Name of our blessed Lord Jesus Christ. Eternity will not be long enough to praise our Great and Almighty God for what He has done for the Randalls.

Now to Him who is able to do exceeding abundantly beyond all that we ask or think, according to the power that works within us, to Him be the glory in the church and in Christ Jesus to all generations forever and ever. Amen (Eph. 3:20-21).

Ask the Lord to reveal Himself to you. Ask Him to show you who He is. Don't be afraid to ask the Lord to show you that He and He alone is God. If your heart is sincere and you are genuinely searching for the truth, God is so much more than willing and abundantly able to reveal Himself to you. Right now, I challenge you to ask the Lord to show Himself to you in His mighty love and power. Then you will come to understand how much God loves you. Then you will come to clearly understand the undying hatred the Enemy has for you and the deadly evil that is behind his lies that kill.

I CAN HANDLE MY OWN SIN.

SIN WON'T KILL ME.
I CAN MANAGE MY OWN SIN.

Well documented are the scandals of our time. Men and women pursuing a life of infidelity and deceit plunge recklessly headlong into a life of shame, humiliation and destruction. Blinded by the Enemy's lies, they have become the center of their own universe. Many foolishly come to the place where they believe the rules of God don't apply to them. Under the secret cover of a double life, a time bomb designed by the Evil One to take out as many as possible through these selfish acts is ticking. It is as though our society is drowning in a sea of refuse and filth of broken humanity. All around us are the bruised and battered remains of our broken homes, dead churches, and unnumbered wounded lives in the wake of these senseless self-centered exploits. As a result of the world of instant media we have been forced to witness the destruction of many of the fallen; from President Bill Clinton to Senator John Edwards, from Kobe Bryant to Tiger Woods, from Jimmy Swaggart to Ted Haggard, not to mention the untold number of Catholic priests who have fallen into the pit of twisted perversion that has led to a kind of spiritual dementia. The numbers in the "Hall of Shame" who have been deceived in believing they could manage their own sin staggers the mind. While serving churches as an itinerant evangelist for over 30 years, I found only a few churches had been spared the anguish and subsequent wounds of fallen leadership. All of this needless tragedy stems from this carefully crafted lie of the Enemy: "I can manage my own sin."

If this lie is not the most often used by the Enemy to foster his murderous schemes, it is certainly one of the most obvious. "I CAN HANDLE MY OWN SIN—Sin won't kill me. I can manage it on my own." It would be impossible for me to count the times I have witnessed the Enemy using this lie to keep folks in his demonic and deadly grip. The truth is, even the most ardent believer has a struggle with giving up control of his or her life completely to Christ. This is what I believe to be the great common denominator of the spiritual battles all men and women face. We desperately want to stay in control. We think we've got to be in charge of our lives. The greatest tragedy is our failure to embrace this truth: that in Christ there is no need for any more tragedies. As a result of our stubborn pursuit of maintaining self-control of our sin, lives needlessly remain broken, wounded, and headed for premature and unnecessary tragic destruction.

Let's begin our study of this most dangerous lie with a clear definition of what we are talking about when we use the word sin. What is sin? Is sin breaking someone's rules? Whose rules? Can we determine what is, and what is not, sin in our own lives according to our own situations, personal persuasions, and circumstances? The word for sin in the New Testament is ἁμαρτια—hamartia. It means to err, or to miss the mark. Think of it like an arrow missing its target. It has erred from its intended purpose. This New Testament word refers to not only missing the mark, but specifically to natural depravity; the corruption in nature not necessarily relating to specific sinful acts, but it refers to sinful nature, the sin principle in man.[1] Sin then is to fall short of the purpose for which we were created. God has created us for the heavenly purpose to glorify Him. We find this idea of glorifying God in the words He spoke when He first made man:

Then God said, "Let Us make man in Our image, according to Our likeness; and let them rule over the fish of the sea and over the birds of the sky and over the cattle and over all the earth, and over every creeping thing that creeps on the earth." And God created man in His own image, in the image of God He created him; male and female He created them (Gen. 1:26-27).

In this word *image*, we discover the purpose God created man. When you and I look in the mirror what do we see? Do we see ourselves? (Watch out, this is a trick question.) Of course not! If we saw ourselves in the mirror, there would be two of us. No, when we look into a mirror, we see the image of ourselves. It's not the real us, it's just an image. God made us in His image. We are not God—not in any way. However, we are, by design, to reflect His image in all we are, all we say, and all we do. Our lives were given to us by God so we might reflect His image—His glory, the fullness of who He is. When we cooperate with the lies of the Enemy and miss the mark, sin joins us to Satan's ongoing evil rebellion. This was Satan's great sin—rebellion for the purpose of stealing God's glory and position:

But you said in your heart, 'I will ascend to heaven; I will raise my throne above the stars of God, and I will sit on the mount of assembly, in the recesses of the north. I will ascend above the heights of the clouds; I will make myself like the Most High.' Nevertheless you will be thrust down to Sheol (Hell—the place of the dead), to the recesses of the pit (Isaiah 14:13-15).

When we sin, we have missed the mark God has set in His heart for us. His eternal and holy purposes are clearly spelled out in His Word. It is clear from Scripture that everyone has sinned. Everyone has missed the mark. Everyone has cooperated with the lies of the Enemy at one time or another:

...all have sinned and fall short of the glory of God (Romans 3:23),

That's right ...ALL—everyone: the butcher, the baker, the candlestick maker, rich man, poor man, beggar man, thief, doctor, lawyer, merchant chief, everyone. My good friend and wonderful encourager in the early days of my ministry, Dr. J.P. McBeth, wrote what I believe to be the best commentary on the book of Romans. In his wonderful work he clarifies man's sin condition: "For this refers especially to the Adamic sin (the propensity—programming toward sin) in every man. All sinned in Adam, and all sinned equally and there is no difference in men with reference to the Adamic sin."[2] You know what this says to me? No one, I mean not anyone, is better than anybody else. Preachers aren't better than used car salesmen. Priests aren't better than prostitutes. Everyone has sinned because everyone is born into a fallen and sinful world. That's why Jesus had to die for everyone *(John 3:16)*. Let's dig even deeper into the understanding of the definition of sin and look at another facet of this truth so we can better grasp how dangerous it is to try to manage our own sin. In the book of James we find these words:

Therefore, to one who knows the right thing to do, and does not do it, to him it is Sin (James 4:17).

The Holy Spirit tells us, through the pen of the Apostle Paul these most important words providing a clear definition of sin:

But he who doubts is condemned if he eats, because his eating is not from faith; and whatever is not from faith is Sin (Romans 14:23).

It is clear then, that according to the Scripture, sin can only be understood in the context of FAITH (or the lack of it). So to understand the definition of sin, we must first come to understand genuine biblical faith. In Chapter 2, pg. 44, I have covered the biblical truths concerning genuine faith. Let me concisely restate so as to better comprehend the definition of sin: Faith is not only believing what God has said, biblical faith also involves our doing (the act of obedience), based on what God has said. Then, according to this scriptural definition of faith, sin is the act of disobedience through unbelief to what God has said.

One of the reasons no one can manage their sin is because behind every temptation to sin there is an evil diabolical personality. These fallen angels of darkness are on assignment not only to tempt us, but also to lead us into sin so we will be destroyed. Anyone who tries to conquer the "evil ones," outside of the finished work of Christ, will always face certain defeat. Martin Luther stated it so well in his timeless hymn, *A Mighty Fortress Is our God*.

> *A mighty fortress is our God, a bulwark never failing;*
> *Our helper He, amid the flood of mortal ills prevailing:*
> *For still our ancient foe doth seek to work us woe;*
> *His craft and power are great, and armed with cruel hate,*
> *ON EARTH IS NOT HIS EQUAL.*[3]

There are no exceptions. In the face of these malevolent evil creatures, no one can hope to succeed in their own power against their murderous schemes. Evil is not merely a negative force that can be avoided by ignoring it. Evil is not merely a fabrication of a troubled mind. No, all evil comes from the mind and heart of the Evil One—Satan. The Devil and his minions must be confronted. These evil ones are on assignment to carry out his evil plan through the exploitation of man's sin. This confrontation can only be won through the work of Christ on Calvary. It is only through Christ's blood that the enemy of our souls is defeated.

SIN'S PERSONALITY

Notice in *Gen. 4:1-8* what the Scriptures tell us about the personality of sin. God personifies sin in this passage:

> *Then the Lord said to Cain, "Why are you angry? And why has your countenance fallen? If you do well, will not your countenance be lifted up? And if you do not do well, Sin is crouching at the door; and its desire is for you, but you must master it (Gen. 4:1-8)."*

> *The one who practices sin is of the devil; for the devil has sinned from the beginning (1 John 3:8)...*

By this the children of God and the children of the devil are obvious: anyone who does not practice righteousness is not of God (1 John 3:10)...

Sin is the highway the powers of darkness travel. Sin is the act of cavorting—cooperating with demons. Behind every temptation is a demon power waiting to take advantage of our unbelief and disobedience to God. These demon spirits are on assignment to steal, kill, and to destroy *(John 10:10)*. They have had thousands of years to perfect their murderous craft. In June of 2009, the world learned of the extramarital affair of the Governor of South Carolina, Mark Sanford. Willing to risk it all for a few fleshly hours of touching the taboo, and yes, dancing with demons, the Governor has lost all his credibility and integrity. The saddest loss may be the resulting spiritual damage that has been inflicted upon the lives of his sons. Even while facing the public humiliation of formal condemnation by the South Carolina Legislature, Governor Sanford could not manage his appetite for the darkness. His life seemed consumed with the search for an ill-conceived and demonically defined love counterfeit. His wife, Jenny, says it so well in an interview she had with *People Magazine*: "If there is any overriding message from that summer that I wanted our boys to remember, it was that you may choose your sin, but you cannot choose your consequences."[4] Why? Because the Enemy is in charge of exploiting our sin to the utmost of his evil intentions. Satan's plan cannot be defeated in our own power and strength. Not only are there demon personalities behind the temptation to sin, but there is an evil scheme and clear evil plan behind every act of sin. Another reason we cannot manage our sin is because of sin's supernatural eternal plan. Try as we dare, we cannot change it.

SIN'S PLAN

Sin's plan is to rule our lives. Sin always brings us into a life of spiritual bondage:

For we know that the Law is spiritual, but I am of flesh, sold into bondage to Sin (Romans 7:14).

Therefore do not let Sin reign in your mortal body that you should obey its lusts (Romans 6:12).

Jesus answered them, "Truly, truly, I say to you, everyone who commits Sin is the slave of Sin" (John 8:34).

Notice the words used here concerning the purpose and plan of sin: *reign*, *bondage*, and *slave*. These words demonstrate that sin has the power to carry us into a life of slavery. The Enemy doesn't care to which of his schemes we fall. He just wants us to be in bondage to him. He wants us to be in such bondage that God won't be able to get any glory from our lives. He wants to so enslave us that we cannot walk in the freedom of Christ. Not only can we not manage our sin, sin will always ultimately manage us. Sin's plan is not only to rule, but also to ruin our lives:

For the wages of Sin is death, but the free gift of God is eternal life in Christ Jesus our Lord (Romans 6:23).

But each one is tempted when he is carried away and enticed by his own lust. Then when lust has conceived, it gives birth to sin; and when sin is accomplished, it brings forth death (James 1:14-15).

In *Gen. 6:5-7*, we find the account of how God destroyed the earth because of sin. Think of it. Just one sin in the Garden of Eden has brought about all the sorrow and spiritual chaos we see in our world. So often, and to such tragic ends, we cooperate with sin...daily. One need only to study history to get a clear view of sin and the payment of destruction it brings with it. Wherever sin is practiced, death always follows. Sin has the power to enslave. Sin has the supernatural power to keep us in bondage. Listen to the tragic, but true, confession of the broken Tiger Woods. He is believed by many to be the greatest professional golfer of all time. In February 2010, Tiger faced the world in a press conference that was broadcast on every major network and revealed the trail of brokenness and subsequent sadness of his sin. His words say it all: "I knew my actions were wrong. I convinced myself that normal rules didn't apply. I never thought about whom I was hurting. Instead, I thought only about myself ... I thought I could get away with whatever I wanted to. I felt that I had worked hard my entire life and deserved to enjoy all the temptations around me. I felt I was entitled ... I was wrong."[5] As someone has correctly said, "The real problem with sin is a "Big I" problem. Notice how many references to the "Big I" in Tiger Woods' confession. Where did we ever get this idea that we can manage our sin? The truth is, no one can manage his or her own sin.

Man doesn't have the power to continue in sin without it bringing continual pain and sorrow. Sin always leads to destruction. It is sin that destroys our marriages. It is sin that destroys our children. It is sin that destroys our churches. It is sin that destroys our relationships. Sin always brings destruction in our lives. Please understand, that as certain as we put our hand on a hot stove we will be burned, if we sin without applying the sacrificial blood of Christ at Calvary through confession and repentance, it will kill us. It is an eternal law established in the heavens by God.

You might be thinking, "Dr. Randall, I haven't died yet. I'm still here. I've been living in sin for many years." Oh, Friend, please do not be deceived. If we would dare to be honest today, all of us would have to admit that much has been destroyed in our lives because of our cooperation with the Evil One through our sin. Look at all the divorce and the destruction of relationships. All of us know folks who are struggling with a disastrous variety of addictions. Everywhere we turn we see unnecessary sickness, diseases, and untimely deaths as a result of our sin. There is a danger, I know, that if all we have ever known is bondage to sin, then it will be difficult to accept that there is another way to live. But believe me when I say to you, there is another wonderful and blessed life promised to us in the Bible. It is a life of health, a life of love, and forgiveness. It is a life of freedom promised to us by Christ. Oh Friend, please understand sin won't just hurt you... SIN WILL KILL YOU! Another reason we aren't able to manage our sin is that God has already taken care of our sin at Calvary.

SIN'S ULTIMATE PAYMENT

Let's look at the Word of God together, and receive what God would say to us concerning His payment for our sin:

He made Him who knew no Sin to be Sin on our behalf, that we might become the righteousness of God in Him (2 Cor. 5:21).

There is therefore now no condemnation for those who are in Christ Jesus (Romans 8:1).

My little children, I am writing these things to you that you may not Sin. And if anyone Sins, we have an Advocate with the Father, Jesus Christ the righteous (I John 2:1).

Jesus took our sin to Calvary. It was there He paid the final sacrifice for all sin. He became sin. Yes, Jesus became our filthy junk. Jesus became the child molester and the sex addict. Jesus became the drug pusher. Jesus became the thief. Jesus became the drunk and the addict. Jesus became the liar and the murderer. On the Cross, the Heavenly Father allowed Jesus to not just take the place of sinners, but He literally became our sin. Jesus became sin, and in doing so, He paid the price for us to be free from what Paul called *the law of sin and death*. All He asks of us is to put our trust in Him. All He is asking of us is to receive His sacrifice on Calvary for the cleansing of our sin. If we continue to try to manage our sin, it means we are refusing to take it to Calvary. It is only at Calvary we can be washed clean of our sin and restored from its destruction in our lives.

There is only one plan for sin that God has approved and we can't change it. Trying to take Jesus' place for sin is an act of blasphemy. Jesus Christ died for our sin. He took our sin upon Himself. For us to try to carry our sin when He has already done it for us, is to try to take His place. It simply can't be done. There is only one Jesus *(1 Tim. 2:5)*. This one and only Savior made the one and final sacrifice for all sin *(Heb. 10:11-14)*. Our responsibility in this wonderful salvation is simply to receive the gift of Christ's sacrifice. This sacrificial work by which believers are sanctified is absolutely and wholly of God. It was done once for all when Christ died on the Cross; before we were in existence it was all done.[6] No more blood needs to be shed for our sin. Jesus has already paid the price of His blood for our sin. We must stop trying to carry our sin. We must give our guilt and all our sorrow to Him. Please stop believing that we can manage our own sin. It cannot be done without severe consequences. It is a load too heavy for anyone to carry alone.

Some might think. "Why, I think I will just keep my secret sins my little secret." What we must understand is that there are no secret sins. None! A significant part of the Enemy's strategy is to get us to believe that our sins that are hidden can't hurt us. Satan knows our secret sins can destroy us just as quick as any other of our sins. We will deal with the issue of our secrets in Chapter 4. Please stop listening to his lies. All the Devil wants is to keep us from life in Christ so he can kill us:

Thou hast placed our iniquities before Thee, Our secret Sins in the light of Thy presence (Psalm 90:8).

THREE SIN AREAS

To experience spiritual freedom, we must visit three sin areas in our lives to make certain the blood of Jesus has cleansed us from any place where the Enemy can take his murderous advantage. These sin areas are:

• **Sins we have committed**—Those times where we have disobeyed anything God has told us to do in His Word.

• **Sins that have been committed against us** -This is in the area of un-forgiveness and bitterness *(Matt. 6:14-15; Eph. 4:26-27)*. How to get clean from bitterness as well as learning to walk in forgiveness, is dealt with in great detail in Chapter 9, pg. 225.

• **Sins of our ancestors**—This is an area most of us might be aware of, however, we might not have studied the Scripture concerning the teaching of the sins of the fathers. To ignore the biblical teaching is to allow the Enemy of our souls a distinct advantage in the spiritual battles of life and death. We must visit these areas of ancestral sin. Our very destiny and the destiny of our families are in the balance.

Turn with me to the Scriptures. If our forefathers refused the cleansing of the Lord by not confessing their sin and by not turning to Christ by faith then those areas are open game for the Enemy to exploit for our destruction:

> *"You shall not worship them or serve them; for I, the LORD your God, am a jealous God, visiting the iniquity of the fathers on the children, on the third and the fourth generations of those who hate Me, but showing lovingkindness to thousands, to those who love Me and keep My commandments (Exodus 20:5)."*

> *The LORD is slow to anger and abundant in lovingkindness, forgiving iniquity and transgression; but He will by no means clear the guilty, visiting the iniquity of the fathers on the children to the third and the fourth generation (Numbers 14:18).*

> *Ah Lord GOD! Behold, Thou hast made the heavens and the earth by Thy great power and by Thine outstretched arm! Nothing is too difficult for Thee, who showest lovingkindness to thousands, but repayest the iniquity of fathers into the bosom of their children after them, O great and mighty God. The LORD of hosts is His name (Jeremiah 32:18);*

> *Our fathers sinned, and are no more; It is we who have borne their iniquities (Lamentations 5:7).*

It must be shouted from the housetops that God's will is blessing for His people! The blessing contract of God with His people is corporate. Abraham, Isaac, and Jacob are the ancestors of many nations; the covenant making of God, one-sided though it is, is designed to bring corporate blessing to many—if it is obeyed *(Gen. 17:4, 18:18, Psalm 112, Prov. 20:7)*. Now Satan, the great counterfeiter and exploiter, views this blessing as something to corrupt and then to exploit as corporate curses. The command, thou shalt have no other gods before

Me, has a penalty attached to it; violate it and be cursed, even to the third and fourth generation *(Exodus 20:5, Numbers 14:18)*. *Leviticus 26* and *Deuteronomy 28* are graphic in their description of the results of blessing for obedience and curses for disobedience. *Leviticus 26:39* says the descendants rot away because of their forefather's sin. *Isaiah 65:6-7* puts it in context of idolatry. *Jeremiah 32* is a forceful statement on the consequences of forsaking God and law breaking, in general. God promises blessing for obedience and the benefits thereof to a thousand generations *(Exodus 20, Deut. 5)*. He limits the curses to four generations, except for unkindness shown to Israel, and also to the illegitimate birth of children where it's indicated that the curse goes to ten generations *(Deut. 23:2-3)*.[7]

"Dr. Randall, are you saying that we are responsible for our fore-father's sin?" NO! Here me on this most important point. The Bible makes it clear in *Ezekiel 18:19* that everyone is responsible for their own sin. It's not a matter of responsibility unless, of course, we have at some time cooperated with the tempters and committed the sin. No, it's a matter of genetic predisposition. All of us have within our lives areas of weaknesses that were also present in our ancestors. Let me explain. Sins, like drunkenness, all kinds of addictions, abuse, raging anger, sexual immorality, and the like are often seen passing down through the generations of certain families. Demons know that, if these sins of our ancestors were not confessed in their lives, then there is a good chance that we too will not choose the way of spiritual cleansing through Christ through confession and repentance. The Bible calls these spirits famil-iar spirits. They are on generational assignments that can only be bro-ken through the application of the blood of Christ through the confes-sion of our sin. Demons claim that, if a parent was giving them ground through unconfessed sin in his or her life, they have the right to harass the offspring of that person. This does NOT make the child guilty of the sins of the parents; everyone is responsible for his or her own sins. The consequences of sin are still present and must be dealt with.[8]

How many of us know for certain that in the last four generations (120 years) of our family ancestry no one has made an evil promise or pact with the Devil? Such agreements may have been made for the sake of fame, money, healing, love and the like. How many know for certain that our great, great grandfather didn't call upon the "Wicked One" to give him what he wanted? Who knows what false gods have been sought and worshiped by those who have gone before us? From the eastern religions practiced in the 1960s, Indian worship of spirits and ancestors, to the secret oaths made in unholy rituals in secret lodge ceremonies; how many of us know with an absolute certainty it didn't happen? We don't, but the Devil does, and our Lord does. Our Lord was there when these blasphemous sins were committed against Him *(Lev. 17:7, Deut. 32:17, Psalm 106:37, 1 Cor. 10:20-21)*. He knows all about it. There are no secrets in Heaven *(Psalm 90:8)*. My dear Friend, the act of disobedience does not go away without bringing it to the Cross of Christ. Death doesn't cover, nor does it hide sin. Sin has eternal consequences, because sin is against God.

Some time ago I had a pastor challenge me on this subject of ancestral sin. He said, "Dr. Randall, all you're going to do is get people on a witch hunt." He said this teaching was only an Old Testament teaching, and now that we are in the New Testament times it no longer applied to believers. Please understand this is not just an Old Testament teaching. If it were only taught in the Old Testament, it would still be TRUE. Jesus did not come to destroy the law, but to fulfill it. Look with me how Jesus also taught the issue of ancestral sin in the New Testament:

> *Woe to you, scribes and Pharisees, hypocrites! For you build the tombs of the prophets and adorn the monuments of the righteous, and say, 'If we had been living in the days of our fathers, we would not have been partners with them in shedding the blood of the prophets.' Consequently you bear witness against yourselves, that you are sons of those who murdered the prophets. Fill up then the measure of the guilt of your fathers (Matt. 23:29-32).*

It's interesting to me how many want to receive the blessings of our forefathers, but when it comes to the curses they want to ignore the teaching of Scripture concerning the <u>sins of the fathers</u>. Please receive the truth today. You can't manage your sin. It will only destroy you. Some may want to argue, "I'm a Christian. I'm covered. I can do whatever I want because God's predestined plan for my life cannot be altered as the result of my sin and disobedience." Turn with me to *1 Cor. 11: 26-30*. Look at this chilling record of events concerning those in the church who took the Lord's Supper while carrying unconfessed sin:

> *For as often as you eat this bread and drink the cup, you proclaim the Lord's death until He comes. Therefore whoever eats the bread or drinks the cup of the Lord in an unworthy manner, shall be guilty of the body and the blood of the Lord. But let a man examine himself, and so let him eat of the bread and drink of the cup. For he who eats and drinks, eats and drinks judgment to himself, if he does not judge the body rightly. For this reason many among you are weak and sick, and a number sleep (1 Cor. 11: 26-30).*

We might ignore the truth of God, but we cannot escape its demands on our lives. The Word of God is forever settled; it is forever established in Heaven *(Psalm 119:89)*. Not only can we not manage our sin, trying to do so will only lead us into spiritual bondage. My Friend, the ultimate result of spiritual bondage is destruction. Be certain, *the soul who sins will die (Ezekiel 18:4)*. Here is the bottom line; hanging on to sin will destroy you. What is at stake is your very health and well-being. What is at stake is your family's health and well-being. What is at stake is the purpose and destiny for which God has created you. What is at stake is the glory of almighty God being manifested in and through your life.

Another reason you will not successfully manage your sin, is because you don't have the power to cleanse your heart. Only the Lord can cleanse your life and make it clean again. Sin can only be cleansed through the blood of Christ poured out for you at Calvary.

GOD'S PURIFICATION OF SIN
Is there any hope? OH YES! A thousand times, YES! There is a fountain

filled with blood drawn from Immanuel's veins. Sinners plunged beneath that flood, lose all their guilty stains.[9]

If we confess our sins, He is faithful and righteous to forgive us our sins and to cleanse us from all unrighteousness (1 John 1:9).

Would you begin your journey into cleansing? Would you confess your sin and be cleansed right now? I wish I could do it for you, but I can't. God loves you so much that he has paid the price of our sin through the Crucifixion of His Son Jesus on Calvary's Cross. Through believing in Him, all your sins can be forgiven and cleansed. You can be set free right now from the bondage of your sin. I don't care what you've done, or what has been done to you. Jesus' blood is enough for all sin and for all time. *It was for freedom that Christ came to set us free (Gal. 5:1).* Don't settle for anything less than the freedom bought for you by Christ when He died for you at Calvary. He purchased your freedom with His own blood.

The word used for *confession* in the New Testament is ὁμολογέο—*homologeo*. This word means to speak the same thing. It means to openly—many times publically—agree with what God is saying *(Luke 12:8)*. The practice of confessing sin is found throughout the Bible. We find the practice in the Old Testament *(Lev. 16:21, Psalm 32:5, Prov. 28:13, Daniel 9:20)*. We find it throughout the New Testament as an ongoing theme calling us to God. *I John 1:9* echoes the necessity of confessing our sin if we are to ever expect God's forgiveness and cleansing. Not only does the Bible promise the cleansing of our sin through confession, but this passage implies that we are obligated to confess our sins. By necessity, we ought to confess our sins. To confess sins is not merely to admit we are sinners, but to lay them before God and seek His forgiveness.[10]

Confession of sin is never easy. Our "old man," the flesh part of us, hates to admit it has ever been wrong. However, without the confession of our sin, the cleansing of our sin is just not possible. Let me make it very clear, the confession of our sin doesn't cleanse us from our sin.

Only the blood of Jesus shed on Calvary can cleanse sin. Why is this so important? Because confession is an act of humility and the act of humbling ourselves before God is essential to be able to come into the presence of Holy God and expect anything from Him *(James 4:6-10)*. Confession of our sin before God enables the blood of Christ to be applied and appropriated so His cleansing of our sin can take place.

> *But He gives a greater grace. Therefore it says, "GOD IS OPPOSED TO THE PROUD, BUT GIVES GRACE TO THE HUMBLE." Submit therefore to God. Resist the devil and he will flee from you. Draw near to God and He will draw near to you. Cleanse your hands, you sinners; and purify your hearts, you double-minded. Be miserable and mourn and weep; let your laughter be turned into mourning, and your joy to gloom. Humble yourselves in the presence of the Lord, and He will exalt you (James 4:6-10).*

Ask the Holy Spirit to lead you in a time of confession and cleansing. Go to a quiet place and pray the following passage of Scripture as your petition before our Lord. He knows your heart. You won't have to convince Him of your sincerity. This is not an exercise in judgment and condemnation. This is about cleansing. The Lord Jesus did not come to judge. It is sin that brings judgment. Jesus wants you to be free and clean far more than you could ever want. He came to set you free. Please hear me again when I say, "This is not about condemnation!" This is about you being set free from what most certainly will destroy you. Allow our Lord to show you where you have been in cooperation with the Enemy's lies. Confess them for what they are. It is sin to believe the Enemy's lies.

MAKING YOUR SIN LIST
Search me, O God, and know my heart;
Try me, and know my thoughts;
And see if there be any wicked way in me,
And lead me in the everlasting way
(Psalm 139:23-24).

The following list is not intended to be exhaustive. It is a guide. As the Lord reveals to you the sin that is in your heart, agree with Him that He's right and you have been wrong. Do not for any reason hang on to your sin, or argue with God about them. It will kill you! Continuing to ignore where you have cooperated with sin will allow the Enemy places in your life to steal, kill, and destroy. Ask the Lord to speak to you concerning these areas in your heart. Ask Him to silence all other voices but His as He speaks and as you listen. Believe what God's Word says:

> *If we confess our sins He is faithful and just to forgive us our sins And to cleanse us from all unrighteousness (I John 1:9).*

If you have already confessed any of these specific sins, forget about it. It's been taken care of by the blood of our Lord Jesus Christ. Don't go digging it back up. It's done:

> *There is therefore now no condemnation*
> *For those who are in Christ Jesus (Romans 8:1).*

SINS OF THE TONGUE
Have you made a vow and not kept it? *(Eccl. 5:1-5)*
Have you spoken against anyone (including yourself)? *(Matt. 5:44, Matt. 7:1-2)*
Have you spoken an oath in a secret lodge ceremony or anywhere else? *(Matt. 5:34, Exodus 23:32)*

SINS OF UNFORGIVENESS
Do you hold a grudge against anyone? *(Matt. 6:14-15, Matt. 7:1-2)*
Is there anyone you just can't forgive? *(Matt. 6:14-15)*
Do you resent yourself for any reason? *(Luke 10:27)*

SINS OF DISOBEDIENCE
Have you ever said no to the call of God? *(Jonah)*
Are you willing to go anywhere anytime the Lord speaks to you? *(Matt. 4:19-20)*
Have you been involved in the harming of a ministry or minister of the Gospel? *(Psalm 105:15)*

Have you dishonored your wife? *(I Peter 3:7)*

Have you said no to the Lord when He told you to give? *(Prov. 3:27-28)*

SINS OF REBELLION

Have you ever been involved in any form of witchcraft? *(Deut. 18:10-12, Rev. 21:8)*

Is there any area of rebellion in your life? *(I Samuel 15:23)*

Do you have trouble giving up control? *(Eph. 4:5)*

Are you unwilling to submit to your husband? *(Eph. 5:22-24)*

SINS OF ANGER

Have you let the sun go down on your anger? *(Eph. 4:26)*

Do you have trouble controlling your temper? *(Psalm 37:8)*

Do you feel you are better than others? *(Romans 3:10)*

Do you try to get your way by arguing? *(Gal. 5:20)*

Do you have a critical spirit? *(Matt. 7:1-2, Romans 14:4)*

SINS OF UNBELIEF

Does worry often control your thoughts? *(Phil. 4:6)*

Does fear control any area of your life? *(1 Tim. 1:7)*

Do you believe God will provide for you? *(Phil. 4:19)*

Do you fear your future? *(Rev. 1:17)*

Do you fear dying or death? *(Rev. 1:18)*

Is there any part of the Scriptures you just don't believe? *(2 Tim. 3:16, Matt. 4:4)*

Do you refuse to live by faith? *(Romans 14:23)*

SINS OF INGRATITUDE

Is worship time for you great joy or frustration? *(Psalm 111:1-4)*

Do you love the Lord with all your heart, all your soul, all your strength and all your mind? *(Luke 10:27)*

Do you resent God for anything He has or has not done? *(Psalm 143:6-12)*

SINS OF IMPURITY

Have you committed adultery or fornication? *(Matt. 5:27-28)*

Are you hiding any secret sin in your life? *(Psalm 90:8)*

Could you have stopped an abortion? *(Psalm 139:13-16)*

Does pornography have any part of your life? *(Gal. 5:19)*

Are your thoughts concerning women pure? *(Gal. 5:19)*

Are your thoughts concerning men pure? *(Gal. 5:19)*

SINS OF GREED

Do you possess anything that is not rightfully yours? *(Eph. 4:28, I Peter 4:15)*

Do you have unpaid debts? *(2 Kings 4:7, Romans 12:8)*

Have you robbed God by the withholding of His tithe? *(Malachi 3:8-10)*

Have you profited through misrepresentation of the value of goods? *(Prov. 21:6)*

Do you love money? *(1 Tim. 6:10)*

Do you want what others have? *(Gal. 5:20-21)*

Have you made money or taken advantage through the sorrows of others? *(2 Tim. 3:6-9)*

SINS OF PRIDE

Are you willing to allow the Lord to manifest His power through you? *(2 Tim. 3:5)*

Are you concerned about your reputation? *(Phil. 2:7)*

Do you have trouble humbling yourself? *(James 4:6)*

Do you have trouble receiving ministry from others? *(James 4:6)*

SINS OF IDOLATRY

Is there anyone or anything in your life more important to you than Christ? *(Gal. 5:20)*

Do you crave evil things? *(1 Cor. 10:5-6)*

Do you have a love for money? *(1 Tim. 6:10)*

Do you love the things of the world? *(James 4:4)*

SINS OF THE SPIRIT

Do you act like everything is all right when it isn't? *(Matt. 23:28)*

Are you too busy to pray? *(1 Tim. 2:1)*

Are you neglecting the study of God's Word? *(Matt. 4:4)*

Have you neglected the witnessing of your faith in Christ to others? *(Matt. 28:19-20)*

Have you been unwilling to love others? *(Mark 12:30, Matt. 22:36, I John 3:14)*

> *He who has my commandments and keeps them, he it is who loves Me; and he who loves Me shall be loved by my Father, and I will love him, and will disclose Myself to him (John 14:21).*

IF THEY KNEW THE REAL ME, THEY WOULDN'T LOVE ME.

IF PEOPLE KNEW WHAT I HAVE DONE, OR WHAT'S BEEN DONE TO ME, NO ONE WOULD EVER LOVE ME.

Believing the truth of God is necessary if we are to walk in the freedom Christ bought for us on Calvary. Jesus tells us in *John 8:32*: You shall know the truth, and the truth shall make you free. There is a truth that does not—cannot—change. What God has said is forever settled in Heaven. God's Word has been established in the Heavens as truth *(Psalm 119:89)*. As we continue our journey into the Enemy's Lies That Kill, let's take a careful look at one of the most dangerous and strategically crafted lies of Satan. This lie has the ability to open the flood gates of Hell into our lives. This lie carries with it the supernatural power to steal the eternal destiny of our lives: "IF THEY KNEW THE REAL ME, THEY WOULDN'T LOVE ME. If folks knew what I have done, or what's been done to me in secret, no one would ever love me."

Tragically, many folks today are living under the bondage of a false identity. This false identity may have been received from a father or mother, a brother or sister, a so-called friend or close acquaintance. Some get their false identity from a wounded and sick church or clergy. Sadly, many have come to believe that they are who their degrees, their ordination, man-made titles, or various other accomplishments say they are. The evil ones don't care who, or what, they use as their instruments of destruction. All they care about is that their message of false identity is believed. Through their never ceasing barrage of lies, the evil ones' purpose is to turn our hearts away from what God has in His heart for us. With just a casual look, we can see that this evil scheme has been successfully repeated to the sad destruction of many souls. I see people all the time confused as to why and who God made them to be. Please believe this truth..."You are not what your father says you are. You are not what your mother says you are. You are not what your brother or sister says you are. You are not what the church says you are. YOU ARE WHAT GOD SAYS YOU ARE!"

Maybe the following illustration will help. You and I can receive a false image of ourselves or we can receive our true identity from the heart of God. Our true identity is what God had in His heart for us to be when He formed us in our mother's womb:

YOUR FALSE IDENTITY vs. YOUR TRUE IDENTITY
(Illustration A)

YOUR FALSE IDENTITY The Lies of the Enemy Performance Based Roles Acceptance System	YOUR TRUE IDENTITY The Truth of God's Word Work of God Grace Acceptance System
Accident, Mistake	Planned Creation of God
Cursed	Blessed
Damaged Goods	Wonderful
Good Father, Mother, Son, Daughter	Joint-heir with Christ, Child of God
Good Husband, Wife	Bride and Body of Christ
Intelligent, Educator, Student	Gifted with the Mind of Christ
Preacher, Evangelist, Pastor, Deacon	Called of God
Rejected, Abandoned	Received, Accepted, Acceptable
Ugly	Beautiful – Inside and Out
Hated	Loved, Lovable
Provider	Provided for
Orphaned	Precious Son and Daughter of God
Talented	Gifted
Judged	Forgiven
Etc.	Etc.

Here's what we need to face: if we are who people say that we are, when we don't measure up to their expectations, we're toast. Self-hatred, self-rejection, and self-defeating attitudes will begin to control our lives; and, ultimately, the Enemy's lies will have worked to bring destruction and death. On the other hand, if we are who God says we are, if we are loved and accepted no matter what, then we are able to live a life filled with love, security, and with the hope that what God created us to be will be accomplished. God's Word says of man: *For as he thinks within himself, so he is (Prov. 23:7).* If we can't believe the truth, we can't live the truth. Believing the truth of God, rather than the lies of the Enemy, is the difference between a life of bondage and a life of freedom. Look with me at this most important warning in Scripture:

> *See to it that no one takes you captive through philosophy and empty deception, according to the tradition of men, according to the elementary principles of the world, rather than according to Christ (Col. 2:8).*

You and I have been given a clear choice. We can believe the lies of this world perpetrated by the *"god of this world" (2 Cor. 4:4)*—Satan, or we can believe the truth of God revealed to us in and through the life and work of Christ Jesus. This lie that 'no one would love me if they really knew what I have done or what's been done to me' is based on the assumption that righteousness is something that can be gained by our good deeds, or lost by our wrong deeds.

Although you have sinned, please understand YOU are not sin. I want to say it again. No matter what you have done, no matter what has been done to you, YOU are not sin! Notice what God said when He created the heavens and earth and all the animals. He said it was good. But when He added man and woman to His creation, He said it was very good:

> *And God saw all that He had made, and behold, it was very good (Genesis 1:31).*

Please look with me at a very important truth we find in the book of Ecclesiastes:

> *I know that everything God does will remain forever, there is nothing to add to it and there is nothing to take from it... (Ecclesiastes 3:14).*

The Bible declares that everything God does remains forever. Since God created you, you can neither add to, nor take anything from what He has created. Stated another way, nothing you have ever done, or could ever do, can take away from your eternal worth found in the heart of the One who created you. You may have grown up in a home where your worth was based upon your behavior, good or bad; or, worse still, you may have received the idea from certain members of your church that your eternal worth is based upon your behavior or performance. Please understand. **Your worth is based solely upon what God says you are worth in His eternal Word**:

> *For Thou didst form my inward parts; Thou didst weave me in my mother's womb. I will give thanks to Thee, for I am fearfully and wonderfully made; Wonderful are Thy works, And my soul knows it very well (Psalm 139:13-14).*

Do you see it? You are a wonderful creation of a Holy God. Do you believe it, or have you bought into this most dangerous and damaging lie of the Enemy? Jesus Christ did not come to condemn sinners! If your church condemns you, your church is not a 'Jesus kind of church.' JESUS DID NOT COME TO CONDEMN SINNERS! This wonderful truth needs to be shouted from the housetops until all come to understand.

JESUS CAME TO FORGIVE—NOT CONDEMN

> *For God did not send the Son into the world to judge the world, but that the world should be saved through Him (John 3:17).*

Jesus didn't come to make the righteous more righteous. There is no one who is righteous except Christ. Not one! Not even one person is righteous. All have missed the mark. All are sinners for all have sinned.

> *What then? Are we better than they? Not at all; for we have already charged that both Jews and Greeks are all under sin; as it is written, "There is none righteous not even one (Romans 3:9-10);..."*

Someone might say, "But, Dr. Randall, you don't know what I have done. It's really bad." Please, hear me! Jesus came and died for you and all your stuff. He came for sinners. Jesus did not come for the so-called righteous folks to reward their self-righteousness. Jesus came for you and me:

> *I have not come to call the righteous but sinners to repentance (Luke 5:32).*

Dear Friend, no one is better than anyone else. We are all a mess. All of us are messy people who have messed up lives and have made a mess of things in our lives. All families have secret bad stuff hidden in their "closets." All any of us have ever done, or could ever do, is fail. Please accept this truth and deal with it. All have sinned and fallen short of the glory of God:

> *For all of us have become like one who is unclean, and all our righteous deeds are like a filthy garment (Isaiah 64:6).*

> *As it is written, "There is none righteous not even one" (Romans 3:10);..."*

If what you have believed about God is a lie, wouldn't you want to know it? I don't care what you have heard or learned. If it is a lie, if it is not true, it must be denounced and confessed before our Lord Jesus so that you can walk in the freedom of Christ.

THE ROLE OF THE LAW

"But, Dr. Randall, since Jesus didn't come to abolish the law, what place does the law have in our lives?" In Chapter 6, the spiritual issues of the law and the dangers of living by the law are dealt with in detail; but for the sake of our study on this most important subject of our identity in Christ, let me say that the law was given to show all people that they are sinners. Because of our sin, we aren't capable of living up to God's perfect standards—His LAW. The Law of God, in a real sense, is like a mirror. In that mirror we are able to see that in and of ourselves we are totally inadequate, no matter how hard we try, to meet God's demands. Therefore, we can never attain His approval. The Apostle Paul refers to the law as our schoolmaster, our tutor:

Therefore the Law has become our tutor to lead us to Christ, that we may be justified by faith. But now that faith has come, we are no longer under a tutor. For you are all sons of God through faith in Christ Jesus. For all of you who were baptized into Christ have clothed yourselves with Christ *(Gal. 3:24-27)*. Jesus came to die for you and me. He died for our sins. The Bible puts it this way:

> *"He who knew no sin, became sin for us, that we might become the righteousness of God in Him" (2 Cor. 5:21).*

In dying for our sins, He fulfilled God's law. Therefore, putting our faith in Christ, puts us <u>in Christ</u>. He clothes us in His righteousness. Not by our works, but through the work of Christ we now can fulfill God's perfect law. Because Jesus did it for us!

GOD'S GIFT OF RIGHTEOUSNESS

Righteousness is a gift from a loving God. Our efforts, however good, cannot attain it. No one can be good enough to gain God's approval. It's simply not possible. His approval of us is only through the sacrifice of His Son on Calvary. It is at Calvary we begin to understand God's unconditional love as opposed to man's conditional kind of love. Man's love is based on the conditions which he sets, based on the false righteousness of our behavior or misbehavior. If we act right, then we will be loved and accepted. If we don't, then we are abandoned and rejected. Man's love is conditional, but God's love comes through the sacrifice of Christ. He became the payment for all our sin. God loves us so much that He offers us this free gift. If we will receive this gift by faith, believing Christ died for our sins and that He rose again, by no work of our own, we become accepted and clothed in Christ's righteousness. God's love offered to us through the sacrifice of Christ is unconditional! (I am dependent on Holy Spirit to communicate this wonderful eternal truth.)

It is here I want us to take a journey into the wonderful world of the eternal truth of God so we can come to understand who we really are in Christ. Our genuine worth is in our supernatural identity we have in Christ. The Enemy of our souls will do everything he can to keep us from understanding and believing the following truths.

THE BELIEVER'S INHERITANCE IN CHRIST

In our union with Christ, we become *joint-heirs* with Christ. Everything the Father has given His only Son, is legally ours, when we are placed in Christ through the receiving of His salvation. Since Jesus conquered sin, we too can be victorious over sin *(Hebrews 4:15, Romans 6:1-4)*. Since Jesus conquered Satan, we too can be victorious over the Devil and all his evil angels *(Luke 4, Col. 2:15, Rev. 12:11)*. Since Jesus conquered death, you and I will someday share in His victory over death *(Hebrews 2:14)*. Since Jesus was given a new body, you and I in Christ will also be given a new body. Since Jesus has a home in Heaven, in Christ, we also have a home in Heaven *(John 14:1-3)*. In our union with Christ we are more than conquerors through Him who loved us *(Romans 8:37)*. This is not just church chatter. This is the truth! Everything that Jesus has been given is rightfully ours in Christ. Look with me at the Book of *Ephesians Chapter 1* and 2. In *Chapter 1* beginning in *verse 19* to the end of the Chapter, the Holy Spirit reveals the truth that, when Christ was raised from the dead, God gave Him the ultimate power and authority over all things. Jesus Christ is Lord! He is Lord over all names, over all things *(vs. 21)*. God seated Him in the place of all authority—at His right hand *(vs. 20)*. Now don't miss this. This is huge! Notice carefully what God has done for us in Christ:

*But God, being rich in mercy, because of His great love with which
He loved us, even when we were dead in our transgressions,
made us alive together with Christ (by grace you have been
saved), and raised us up with Him, and seated us with Him in
the heavenly places, in Christ Jesus, in order that in the ages
to come He might show the surpassing riches of His grace in
kindness toward us in Christ Jesus (Eph. 2:4-7).*

Right now, if you are in Christ, you have been given a place to work
with Christ in His victory, at the right hand of God the Father. WOW!
How is this possible? Because everything the Father has given Jesus is
yours through your union with Christ. That's right! Everything! He has
given you the keys to the Kingdom of God *(Matt. 16:19)*. Why did He
do all this for you? So He might show His great love toward you. That's
how valuable you are to God. He loves you so much. He is willing to
share His life, His work, and His position of authority with you.

Too often we accept the Enemy's lies instead of God's truth. These
lies are well crafted evil time bombs that are programmed to bring destruction at the Evil One's strategic and sinister pleasure. All of his evil
lies are ultimately aimed to undermine our relationship with God. Many
times we mistakenly view our relationship with our Heavenly Father
through our disappointments with our early fathers. We must never allow our wounds to define who we are in Christ. If Satan can get us to
believe that God is not good, our inheritance as a child of God is not
secure, or for whatever reason we don't really belong in the Family of
God, his evil seeds of destruction will have been planted.

Today, we are hearing a wonderfully similar message from many
pulpits all around the world. Through sermons and in-depth Bible studies, we are being given the distinction between living like we are or-
phaned and living as accepted sons and daughters of God. This is a
powerful truth the Holy Spirit is evidently trying to remind the church
in these difficult days of intense warfare. The following illustration is
printed by permission from a dear Brother in Christ, Gary Stewart. It
helps us better understand the difference between living life with the
mindset of a son and living with the mindset of an orphan.

THE ORPHAN SPIRIT vs. THE SPIRIT OF SONSHIP
(Illustration B)

Concept:	Orphan Spirit	Mature Sons (Sonship)
Father's Love	Knowledge of	Experienced
Father's Blessing	Desires it	Walks in it
Father's Affirmation	Wants it	Has it
Father's Presence	Looks for Visitation	Walks in Habitation
Father's Provisions	Pleads for	Received; Know I have them
Sees God as	Almighty	Abba, Father
Felt Provisions	Slave, Child Delinquent	Son! Doing the Father's business
Living Life	Bound	Free (Free indeed!)
Walking in	Stress/Worry/Fear	Peace and Joy
Self Esteem	Low	High
Security	Insecure	Strong in the Father
Purpose in Life	Not sure	To do the Father's will/work
Serving God	Seeking Father's approval	Love motivated
Discipleship	Chore	Joy
Holy Spirit	Knows about	Depends on to lead
The Bible	Very good book	Book I live by—Bread of Life
Mind set	This Earth	Kingdom of God
Citizenship	Earthly	Heavenly
Church	My church/denomination	To advance Kingdom of God
Outreach	Numbers	Souls to disciple
Life Perspective	Present/Now/This moment	Eternal
Earthly Things	Grab hold of	Give away
Giving	Reluctant	Cheerful
Prayer	Want the Father to hear me	Knows the Father hears me
Prayer Focus	My wants	Father's wants
Faith	Doubt; Little Faith	Trust; Much faith
Righteous Living	Attempts; often fails	Does; Seldom fails
Troubles/Difficulties	Why? Why? Why?	Opportunities for growth!
Spiritual Expectation	Low	High
Focus	Me	Father/Son

We see this same difference manifested in the lives of the two sons mentioned in the parable of Jesus we know as the Story of the Prodigal Son in *Luke 15 vs. 11-32:*

THE DEMAND OF THE RECKLESS SON

And He said, "A certain man had two sons; and the younger of them said to his father, 'Father, give me the share of the estate that falls to me.' And he divided his wealth between them. "And not many days later, the younger son gathered everything together and went on a journey into a distant country, and there he squandered his estate with loose living."Now when he had spent everything, a severe famine occurred in that country, and he began to be in need. "And he went and attached himself to one of the citizens of that country, and he sent him into his fields to feed swine."And he was longing to fill his stomach with the pods that the swine were eating, and no one was giving anything to him.

THE PRODIGAL'S REVELATION

"But when he came to his senses, he said, 'How many of my father's hired men have more than enough bread, but I am dying here with hunger! I will get up and go to my father, and will say to him, "Father, I have sinned against heaven, and in your sight; "I am no longer worthy to be called your son; make me as one of your hired men."' "And he got up and came to his father."

THE BROTHER'S SELF-CENTEREDNESS

"Now his older son was in the field, and when he came and approached the house, he heard music and dancing."And he summoned one of the servants and began inquiring what these things might be. "And he said to him, 'Your brother has come, and your father has killed the fattened calf, because he has received him back safe and sound.' "But he became angry, and was not willing to go in; and his father came out and began entreating him."But he answered and said to his father, 'Look! For so many years I have been serving you, and I have never

neglected a command of yours; and yet you have never given me a kid, that I might be merry with my friends; but when this son of yours came, who has devoured your wealth with harlots, you killed the fattened calf for him.'

Here we have the biblical picture of what a son looks like when acting as an orphan. Here are some lessons that are exhibited by the older brother's response to his father's love:

• Anger carries him into a place of isolation. This is the great work of Satan. His goal is to destroy us. He can best accomplish his murderous task when we feel alone, abandoned, and discouraged. Anger left alone always leads to a place of destruction.

• He was more concerned about his pleasure than working for the pleasure of his father.

• Selfishness is the result of insecurity. Insecurity is the result of a lack of understanding of our position with the Father.

• His vision was impaired. All he could see was himself. He wasn't able to join the celebration of his lost brother coming home because his eyes were on himself.

• His self-centered spirit kept him from entering into the forgiving spirit of his father. What we don't have, we can't give away. Please understand that any accusation not dealt with toward the living or the dead is a finger of accusation directed in God's face. (See Chapter 9.)

THE FATHER'S UNFAILING LOVE

But while he was still a long way off, his father saw him, and felt compassion for him, and ran and embraced him, and kissed him. "And the son said to him, 'Father, I have sinned against heaven and in your sight; I am no longer worthy to be called your son.' "But the father said to his slaves, 'Quickly bring out the best robe and put it on him, and put a ring on his hand and sandals on his feet; and bring the fattened calf, kill it, and let us eat and be merry; for this son of mine was dead, and has come to life again; he was lost, and has been found.' And they began to be merry.

"And he said to him, 'My child, you have always been with me, and all that is mine is yours. 'But we had to be merry and rejoice, for this brother of yours was dead and has begun to live, and was lost and has been found (Luke 15:11-32).'"

"That's all fine and good, but what about me? I just don't believe God loves me." Beth Moore explains why so many folks today have a hard time in accepting God's love. She writes, "Why do we have so much trouble believing and accepting the love of God? You see, unbelief regarding the love of God is the ultimate slap in His face. The world came into being from the foundation of God's love. God nailed down His love for us on the cross. Can you imagine the grief of our unbelief after all He's done? You may say, 'But I just can't make myself feel like God loves me.' Belief is not a feeling. It's a choice. We may live many days when we don't feel loved or lovely; but in spite of our emotions, we can choose to take God at his Word."[1]

"But, Dr. Randall, what about those who have hurt me?" Please understand, no one is getting away with anything. God will take care of them. Trust Him to do the right thing. He always has and He always will do the right thing. He is a just God. Since Christ has forgiven us, we must forgive those who have hurt us. Please understand it is only through the love of God that is received by grace through faith that we are able to genuinely love and forgive ourselves as well as love and forgive others. Dear Friend, if those in your life are not walking in the forgiveness of God, then they are not capable of showing you genuine love. They can't help it. They can't give you what they don't have. Authentic love comes from God to you through the sacrifice of Christ. Please hear this with your heart. Only those who have been forgiven by Christ are able to forgive others *(Matt. 6:14-15)*. (See Chapter 9.)

My father used to say, "Our job as Christians is to present Christ in such a way that everyone would know how much He loves them." God does love you with an unfailing love. He loves you with a greater love than you could ever completely fully understand. It doesn't matter what you've done. It doesn't matter what's been done to you. God loves you! But you say, "I just can't believe it, because of what I have done." Dear Friend, please stop listening to the accusers and liars. Stop listening to the Devil and his demons. Here is the truth of God for you. Receive it right now. Let the truth of God's love toward you continually reverberate within your soul:

> *There is therefore now <u>NO CONDEMNATION</u> for those who are in Christ Jesus (Romans 8:1).*

Look to Calvary. It is at Calvary (and only at Calvary) you will find your true worth. You are worth the precious life and blood of God's only Son—the Lord Jesus Christ. Where should you be looking for your ultimate value? There is one place, and only one where you will find your genuine value. That place is at Calvary. It was at Calvary that God's greatest expression of His love was displayed for all to see. *Greater love has no one than this, that one lay down his life for his friends (John 15:13).* He loves you more than you could ever know. Would you allow Christ the privilege of baptizing you in the Father's love and forgiveness right now?

> *Behold what manner of love the Father has bestowed on us, that we should be called children of God (1 John 3:1)!*

The single most important concept for the child of God to know is this: ***The Father loves you, He really, really loves you!*** While I was a Baylor Student, we were visited on a regular basis by the gifted writer of worship songs, Kurt Kaiser. I remember the first time I heard this wonderful song. I can almost see Kurt right now sitting at the piano, as he began teaching us this new song of God's love. I know of no greater song that expresses the love of our Heavenly Father given to us through the death of Christ on Calvary:

O, how He loves you and me. O, how He loves you and me.
He Gave His Life what more could He give. O, how He loves
you. O, how he loves me. O, how He loves you and me.

Jesus to Calvary did go. His love for mankind to show.
What He did there brought hope from despair.
O, how He loves you. O, how He loves me.
O, how He loves you and me.[2]

Oh, how we need to respond to His love! Oh, how we need to truly love and worship Him for all He has done for us. I shall never forget when our first children were in elementary school. For the Christmas program all the children sang a brand new song. It was a song that even now captures my heart. Hearing the children's tender voices singing this sweet song was one of the greatest musical moments of my life. Can you imagine with me the sound coming from the hearts of those precious children as they sang?

I love You, Lord, and I lift my voice
To worship You. O my soul rejoice!
Take joy, my King, in what You hear
May it be a sweet, sweet sound in Your ear.[3]

Stop listening to the liars. All they want to do is to kill you. Their lies will kill your hope. Their lies will destroy your joy. Their lies will kill your relationships. Their lies will keep you from your destiny as a child of God. Their lies will ultimately kill your body. The lie that no one can love you because of what you have done or what has been done to you is just not true.

Pam Kanaly, Co-founder of Arise Ministries, speaks the truth concerning the identity we have in Christ in her wonderful book, *Will the Real Me Please Stand Up:* "For a number of years, God has given me an insatiable desire to see myself the way He sees me, not as others see me, or the ways I often see myself. As a result of quest for truth, He's pulled back the veil and allowed me to envision in part my illustrious new creation in Christ Jesus. I'm astonished at His delight in His children!"[4]

In Neil Anderson's materials on spiritual warfare, he is faithful to remind us of who we are in Christ. Would you receive the truth of who we are in Christ?

WHO I AM IN CHRIST: AFFIRMATIONS OF TRUTH

I am deeply loved by God the Father:

John 17:23 The Father loves me as much as He loves Jesus.

Ephesians 1:6 The Father accepts me in Christ, just as I am.

Ephesians 1:7-8 The Father has lavished His grace on me.

I Corinthians 6:20 The Father purchased me with the blood of His Son.

1 John 3:1 The Father has poured out His love on me.

Ephesians 2:10 I am my Father's workmanship; His "poem."

Zechariah 2:8 I am the apple of my Father's eye.

I am safe and secure in Christ:

John 15:5 I am connected to Jesus like a branch to a vine.

John 10:27 I am protected, held in Jesus' and the Father's hands.

2 Corinthians 5:21 I am the righteousness of God in Christ, therefore in Him I do measure up!

Romans 15:7 I am accepted in Christ to the glory of God.

Romans 6:3-4 I died with Christ to the rule of sin and have been raised up to live a new life.

Romans 7:4 I died to the law through the body of Christ.

Hebrews 13:5 I will never be deserted or forsaken by Christ.

I am indwelt by the Holy Spirit, Who is my strength:

I Corinthians.6:19 I am the temple of the Holy Spirit, Who was given to me by my Father.

Ephesians 1:13 I am sealed by the Spirit, Who was given to me as a pledge of my full inheritance in Christ.

Romans 8:14-15 I am led by the Spirit of adoption and am no longer a slave to fear; He enables me to cry out "Abba! Father!"

I Corinthians 12:13 I have been baptized by the Holy Spirit and placed into the body of Christ as a full member.

I Corinthians 12:4 I have been given spiritual gift(s) by the Holy Spirit.

Ephesians 5:18 I can be filled with Holy Spirit instead of leaning on substances to empower me.

Galatians 5:16-18 I can walk by the Spirit instead of giving into the lusts of my flesh.[5]

It has been well stated, "A person cannot rise above the revelation of God's understanding of himself." Have you had the Father experience? God is our Father, but He much more wants to be your Father. Can you say, "He is my Father?" Can you call Him "*Abba*"—my Father, my Daddy?

For all who are being led by the Spirit of God, these are sons of God. For you have not received a spirit of slavery leading to fear again, but you have received a spirit of adoption as sons by which we cry out, "Abba Father!" The Spirit Himself bears witness with our spirit that we are children of God, and if children, heirs also, heirs of God and fellow heirs with Christ, if indeed we suffer with Him in order that we may also be glorified with Him (Romans 8:14-17).

THE FATHER'S LOVE LETTER

Right now, will you open your heart and receive the love of the Heavenly Father. The following is a love letter written to YOU from the Heavenly Father:

My Child,

You may not know Me,
but I know everything about you.

Psalm 139:1

I know when you sit down and when you rise up.

Psalm 139:2

I am familiar with all your ways.

Psalm 139:3

Even the very hairs on your head are numbered.

Matthew 10:29-31

For you were made in My image.

Genesis 1:27

In me you live and move and have your being.

Acts 17:28

For you are My offspring.

Acts 17:28

I knew you even before you were conceived.

Jeremiah 1:4-5

I chose you when I planned creation.

Ephesians 1:11-12

You were not a mistake,
for all your days are written in My book.

Psalm 139:15-16

I determined the exact time of your birth
and where you would live.

Acts 17:26

You are fearfully and wonderfully made.

Psalm 139:14

I knit you together in your mother's womb.

Psalm 139:13

And brought you forth on the day you were born.

Psalm 71:6

I have been misrepresented
by those who don't know Me.

John 8:41-44

I am not distant and angry,
but am the complete expression of love.

1 John 4:16

And it is My desire to lavish My love on you.

1 John 3:1

Simply because you are My child
and I am your Father.

1 John 3:1

I offer you more than your earthly father ever could.

Matthew 7:11

For I am the perfect father.

Matthew 5:48

Every good gift that you receive comes from My hand.

James 1:17

For I am your provider and I meet all your needs.

Matthew 6:31-33

My plan for your future has always been filled with hope.

Jeremiah 29:11

Because I love you with an everlasting love.

Jeremiah 31:3

My thoughts toward you are countless
as the sand on the seashore.

Psalms 139:17-18

And I rejoice over you with singing.

Zephaniah 3:17

I will never stop doing good to you.

Jeremiah 32:40

For you are My treasured possession.

Exodus 19:5

I desire to establish you
with all My heart and all My soul.

Jeremiah 32:41

And I want to show you great and marvelous things.

Jeremiah 33:3

If you seek Me with all your heart,
you will find Me.

Deuteronomy 4:29

Delight in Me and I will give you
the desires of your heart.

Psalm 37:4

For it is I who gave you those desires.

Philippians 2:13

I am able to do more for you
than you could possibly imagine.

Ephesians 3:20

For I am your greatest encourager.

2 Thessalonians 2:16-17

I am also the Father who comforts you
in all your troubles.

2 Corinthians 1:3-4

When you are brokenhearted,
I am close to you.

Psalm 34:18

As a shepherd carries a lamb,
I have carried you close to My heart.

Isaiah 40:11

One day I will wipe away
every tear from your eyes.

Revelation 21:3-4

And I'll take away all the pain
you have suffered on this earth.

Revelation 21:3-4

I am your Father, and I love you
even as I love my son, Jesus.
John 17:23

For in Jesus, My love for you is revealed.
John 17:26

He is the exact representation of My being.
Hebrews 1:3

He came to demonstrate that I am for you,
not against you.
Romans 8:31

And to tell you that I am not counting your sins.
2 Corinthians 5:18-19

Jesus died so that you and I could be reconciled.
2 Corinthians 5:18-19

His death was the ultimate expression
of My love for you.
1 John 4:10

I gave up everything I loved
that I might gain your love.
Romans 8:31-32

If you receive the gift of My son Jesus,
you receive Me.
1 John 2:23

And nothing will ever separate you
from My love again.
Romans 8:38-39

Come home and I'll throw the biggest party
heaven has ever seen.

Luke 15:7

I have always been Father,
and will always be Father.

Ephesians 3:14-15

My question is...
Will you be My child?

John 1:12-13

I am waiting for you.

Luke 15:11-32

Love, Your Dad
Almighty God[6]

Would you allow the Lord Jesus to speak to you today through the reading of His Word?

Who will separate us from the love of Christ? Will tribulation, or distress, or persecution, or famine, or nakedness, or peril, or sword? Just as it is written, "FOR YOUR SAKE WE ARE BEING PUT TO DEATH ALL DAY LONG; WE WERE CONSIDERED AS SHEEP TO BE SLAUGHTERED." But in all these things we overwhelmingly conquer through Him who loved us. For I am convinced that neither death, nor life, nor angels, nor principalities, nor things present, nor things to come, nor powers, nor height, nor depth, nor any other created thing, will be able to separate us from the love of God, which is in Christ Jesus our Lord (Romans 8:35-39).

Right now, would you receive His love and forgiveness? It's a gift, but it's not yours until you receive it. No one can do it for you. If I could,

I would. Your mom can't receive the gift of God's love for you. Your dad can't receive the gift of God's love for you. Your preacher or priest can't receive the gift of God's love for you. Only you can receive the love of God.

The following story comes from our journey into the freedom of Christ. I've asked my precious wife to share her heart with you concerning her years of secret torment, the Enemy used in our lives, to keep us from the freedom in Christ. As you read her story, it comes to you with the prayer that you will come to know Christ's love is greater than all your fears, and all your shame. God's grace is greater than the load of the guilt you've been carrying; that you have been hiding in that secret place. The only thing that stands between you and the limitless love of the Heavenly Father is the truth that has the power to set you free. Freedom in Christ is worth the journey into the secret places that so often are hiding behind the walls of unnecessary fears.

PATTIE'S JOURNEY INTO FREEDOM

Sadly, I waited for 30 years to tell my husband about an event that happened to me in college, a year before we met. During those 30 years, the Lord spoke to my heart many times to tell my husband about a date I had been on with a fellow student, a date that began in fun and ended in disgust and shame.

Through the years, I had asked myself many times why I was afraid to be open and honest with my husband. We had been honest about everything else in our lives; but, for some reason, this particular event could not be revealed. The longer I waited and the more I said no to the prompting of the Holy Spirit in my life, the harder it was to even consider telling what had happened. The Enemy would remind me how I had been dishonest in not talking to my husband. He told me that, if I confessed now, he probably wouldn't believe me and think I had held back other things. The Enemy would torment me with my guilt and shame as he would replay his accusing lies that had worked so well with my fears. "If your husband really knew about this, he wouldn't love you anymore." And not only would I not have his love, but our children would be so embarrassed and ashamed of their mom, they would stop loving me, too. The monster in the closet kept getting bigger and bigger the longer I was afraid to face him. This horrible experience and all of the lies that surrounded it grew bigger the more I tried to ignore it.

As the years went on, my monster in the closet became bigger and bigger. Oh, he would stay there and not come out for long periods of time, but he was always ready to stick out his ugly head whenever I would make a move forward in my spiritual life. He was always there to remind me what a fake and liar I really was. I had been the wife of a church staff member, and even the wife of a pastor! We went into the ministry of evangelism, and I regularly sang about the forgiving power of Jesus Christ, but I couldn't trust Jesus with the outcome of being honest with my husband. How very sad to have lived so many years without the total freedom that Jesus Christ offers.

Our middle child had gone off to college and, at the end of his third year, came home to announce he had fallen into a dark pit. Realizing the seriousness of our son's life and death situation, my husband and I began to pray for help. God is so good to creatively put us into situations where we have to make a choice to follow him, or choose a way without him. As we prayed my husband and I began to listen to the Lord. Our loving Heavenly Father began to show us it was essential that we have an obedient and clean heart for Him to hear and respond to our prayers for our son.

One weekend, as God was working in a particularly strategic way in our lives, I will always remember Him saying to me, "If you want your prayers to be effective for your son, YOU are going to have to take care of the sin in your own life. You are going to have to be obedient to me. Disobedience is sin." Of course, I knew immediately that I had to finally face my secret sin and the fears that surrounded it. I knew I had to tell my husband this "secret" I had kept in my closet all these many, many years. This secret I had been harboring had grown into an unbelievably gigantic monster!

After going to church that Sunday night and coming home, I planned to confess it all. I remember sitting on the floor at my husband's feet. I began to hear the old lies that had haunted me all these years. "You are such a liar; he won't love you anymore! He will divorce you over this. Your children will think you are such a fake." I also heard in my heart, "I love my son more than I love myself." Oh, how I needed and longed for my prayers to be as effective as possible for my son.

Well, you can probably guess the outcome. My poor husband had imagined all sorts of things. Upon hearing my confession, he lovingly assured me my fears and years of torment had all been unnecessary. He loved me anyway and his commitment to me did not change. Our children have loved and honored me as a precious jewel. My prayer life opened up to heaven with a length and depth I had never known. Ministry has intensified and my relationship with my wonderful Heavenly Father is deeper and more intimate than I could have ever dreamed! There is nothing like freedom in Christ! It was just one act of disobedience by Eve and Adam that brought the curse of sin into the world. I have often wondered what blessings I have missed and the many prayers that have gone unanswered for my family as the result of my sin of disobedience.

My prayer for you is that if there is a hidden secret in your "closet" that has held you captive, speechless and ineffective, OPEN UP THE DOOR! LET JESUS CHRIST SHINE THE LIGHT OF HIS WONDERFUL LOVE AND FORGIVENESS INTO THE DARKNESS, AND SHOW YOU HOW SMALL THAT BIG SECRET REALLY IS:

"You shall know the truth and the truth will SET YOU FREE (John 8:32)."

Right now stop listening to the lie that no one will ever love you because of what you have done. There is someone who loves you no matter what. He knows everything that has been done in secret and still loves you. He understands your pain as a result of what has happened to you. Not only does He not want to condemn you, He loves you so much that He wants to heal your wounds and make you whole again. He knows everything there is to know about you, and He still is eager to have a relationship with you. He knows and understands it all, and loves you with an eternal love that can never fail. His name is the Lord Jesus Christ. His everlasting love for you was forever displayed on that old rugged cross where He gave His life for you. God's love is a gift that must be received before it is possessed. Will you receive his love and forgiveness right now? Would you pray this prayer with me right now?

PRAYER OF CONFESSION AND CLEANSING

My Dear Heavenly Father,

Thank You so much for loving me the way I am. Thank You for sending Your only Son, Jesus Christ, to pay the payment for my sin when He gave His life for me on Calvary. I thank You that I am worth His death. I thank You that Jesus Christ didn't waste His blood on me. Please forgive me for ever believing the lie of the Enemy that no one could ever love me if they knew the real me and what has happened to me. Please forgive me for trying to perform to be accepted. I now know I have sinned against You by believing the lies of the Enemy. Give me ears and a heart to discern the difference between Your Word and the lies of the Enemy. Thank You, Lord, for accepting me no matter what I have done or what has happened to me. I open up my hands and my heart to receive everything that is in Your heart for me. In Jesus Christ Almighty and Holy Name I pray, AMEN!

I'M DOING THE BEST I CAN.

SURELY, GOD ONLY EXPECTS ME TO DO THE BEST I CAN.

One of the most carefully crafted lies of the Evil One so often believed, even within the church, is I'M DOING THE BEST I CAN. Surely, God only expects me to do the best I can. This approach to life is one of the most effective deceits of the enemy, because it has the power to lead us into a 'self-reliance' kind of life. I submit to you, as we study this extremely effective deception, this teaching may stir up for some, faint memories of a distant past when our pulpits were filled with men of God who had one primary message in their hearts and on their lips—the Cross of Christ. Tragically, for many this teaching will seem unusually strange over the backdrop of our accepted, contemporary religious culture of today. Sadly, the message coming from many of America's leading, so-called "evangelical" churches is void of the Cross of Christ. Please understand, this author's intentions are not to point an accusing finger at those who may hold opposing religious viewpoints. This book, as you have no doubt already noticed, is not a treatise on the reoccurring religious debates within the church. However, if we are to walk in the freedom of Christ, we can ill afford to ignore the Enemy's lies that so often lead us into the many dangerous places of spiritual compromise. Please continue the journey with me as we study the Scriptures together concerning the lie: "I'm doing the best I can. Surely, God only expects me to do the best I can."

At the very moment the Enemy can get us to base our lives on his lies, his deceptions will have led us down a road that ends in destruction and death. Remember, Jesus said of Satan that he was a murderer from the beginning *(John 8:44)*. We know that the Devil's ultimate intention is to kill, steal, and destroy *(John 10:10)*. In *I Peter 5:8,* we find these words:

Be of sober spirit, be on the alert. Your adversary, the devil, prowls around like a roaring lion, seeking someone to devour (I Peter 5:8).

It is clear from the teachings of Scripture that Satan is out to kill us. Satan's work is about deception. All that he does, all his schemes, are perpetrated to cause us to believe his lies instead of the truth of God. Jesus said of the Devil:

You are of your father the Devil, and you want to do the desires of your father. He was a murderer from the beginning, and does not stand in the truth, because there is no truth in him. Whenever he speaks a lie, he speaks from his own nature; for he is a liar, and the father of lies (John 8:44).

Deception is Satan's main strategy of control and ultimate weapon of defeat. Remember, *you shall know the truth and the truth shall make you free (John 8:32).*

We must believe God, no matter how convincing Satan's arguments appear. Watchman Nee said of the Enemy's lies, "A skillful liar lies not only in word but also in gesture and deed; he can easily pass a bad coin, as tell an untruth. The Devil is a skillful liar, and we cannot expect him to stop at words in his lying. He will resort to lying signs, feelings and experiences in an attempt to shake us from our faith in God's Word. As soon as we have accepted our death with Christ as a fact, Satan will do his best to demonstrate convincingly by the evidence of our day- to-day experience that we are not dead at all, but very much alive. So we must choose. Are we going to be governed by appearances, or by what God says?"[1]

In the Apostle Paul's letter to the Colossian church we find these words of great warning:

See to it that no one takes you captive through philosophy and empty deception, according to the tradition of men, according to the elementary principles of the world, rather than according to Christ. For in Him all the fullness of the deity dwells in bodily form, and in Him you have been made complete, and He is the head over all rule and authority (Colossians 2: 8-10).

The word philosophy means the <u>love of wisdom</u>. However, in this context Paul is clearly defining the word as the <u>love of the world's wisdom</u>. Empty deception and the traditions of men clearly indicate the dangers of being deceived by the wisdom and thought processes of the world. The Scripture admonishes us:

Do not love the world nor the things of the world. If anyone loves the world, the love of the Father is not in him. For all that is in the world, the lust of the flesh and the lust of the eyes and the boastful pride of life, is not from the Father, but is from the world (I John 2:15-17).

The statement, "I'm doing the best I can" reminds me of an old joke my father used to tell:

A doctor was asked, "How did the operation go, Doc?" He replied, "The operation was a great success, but the patient died." Many determine the success of their lives on the basis of a faulty standard crafted and offered to them by the god of this world, Satan *(2 Cor. 4:4)*. The idea that all we are to do is our best is based on two extremely dangerous assumptions:

• My best is all I can do.

• Since my best is all I CAN do, God only expects me to do the best I can.

Let's take each one of these assumptions and see what the Bible has to say about this matter of doing our best.

TRUE RIGHTEOUSNESS

Why is the necessity of the Cross of Christ so important for us to understand? In Paul Billheimer's wonderful book on the ultimate purpose of creation, *Destined for the Throne,* he helps us understand the centrality of the Cross of Christ in our faith: "It is vitally important for every believer to know with absolute certainty that Calvary was an unutterably glorious triumph. Unless the believer fully understands and is immutably convinced of the infallible basis of his faith, he will be hampered by misgivings and will be unable to exercise his authority over Satan."[2] Understanding the foundations of the authentic Christian life comes only through understanding the scope of what happened on the Cross of Christ:

> *Since then the children share in flesh and blood, He Himself likewise also partook of the same, that through death He might render powerless him who had the power of death, that is, the devil (Hebrews 2:14);*

The Scriptures teach *ALL of our righteousness is filthy rags (Isaiah 64:6).* The stark reality is this…the very best we can do on our own, is fail. Put another way, if the best we can do is based on only what we can do, then all we can expect is the results of what we can do—which of course is a failure to achieve God's expectations. Our best always falls far short of the expectations in the heart of the One who created us for His glory:

> *…As it is written, "THERE IS NONE RIGHTEOUS, NOT EVEN ONE" (Romans 3:10).*

In and of the flesh there is no good thing. The Holy Spirit, through the Apostle Paul, puts it this way: *For I know that nothing good dwells in me, that is, in my flesh;...(Romans 7:18)*. That's why Jesus died for us—in the flesh. Since He was God He could have done it another way, but He didn't. He came in the flesh, because He had to die in the flesh. He had to die in the flesh so that our flesh would also die in Him. Understand this, Friend, the key to spiritual victory in our lives is based upon the Cross of Christ. He gave His life so that we can live, not in ourselves, but in Him; so that we can live, not in our power, but in His. If we continue to seek life in our own power and strength then that's all we'll end up with...a life of limited power and strength. If we live our lives based on the sacrificial life of Christ who died on the Cross and arose from the dead, then we receive his life of limitless power and strength.

In his classic book, *Calvary Road,* Roy Hession speaks to us concerning the nature and dangers of living a self-centered, self-controlled, or self-empowered life: "Anything that springs from self, however small it may be is sin. Self-energy or self-complacency in service—is sin. Self-pity in trials or difficulties, self-seeking in business or Christian work, self-indulgence in one's spare time; being too sensitive or touchy, resentment in self-defense when we are hurt or injured by others, self-consciousness, reserve, worry, fear...all spring from self and all are sin and make our "cups" unclean *(Matt. 20:22-23)*. All of them were put into that other cup, which the Lord Jesus shrank from momentarily in Gethsemane, but which He drank to the dregs at Calvary—the cup of our Sin."[3] Jesus died in the flesh for the purpose of killing it. Now that we live in Him, the flesh can-and must-be crucified in us. No one can earn a place in the Cross of Christ. It is a gift of God. Man had nothing to do with the work on Calvary; a work that provides a covering for his sin. God did it all. Man cannot earn it, but he must receive it.

In 1983, my wife and I had the wonderful privilege of traveling to the Netherlands and attending The International Conference for Itinerant Evangelists. It was a gathering of evangelicals from all around the world for the purpose of training, networking and great spiritual encouragement. Each participant attended through the invitation from The Billy Graham Evangelistic Association. Of the many amazing highlights of the conference, none was more exciting to me than to be introduced to Dr. J. Edwin Orr by my father. Dr. Orr was considered a spiritual giant is his understanding of revival and spiritual awakening. In his book, *My All His All*, Dr. Orr explains how it is that man has no part in the work on the Cross, but to receive the gift of God's forgiveness: "No one who is familiar with the Scriptures will dispute the fact that the ground of forgiveness is the Cross, though there are many who overlook the fact. Nor will any insist that there is a price the unregenerate can pay; it cannot be bought, or earned or bargained for. No one is forgiven merely on the ground of his conversion experience, for there have been outstanding instances of non-Christian conversions to righteous living, such as Mahatma Gandhi. The ground of forgiveness is the finished work of Christ on the Cross."[4] It is all a gift from God to anyone who will receive Christ as his, or her Savior.

SATAN'S GREATEST FEAR—THE CROSS OF CHRIST

Satan's greatest fear is to be faced with the Cross of Christ, for it is on the Cross that Jesus shed His blood for our sin, our selfishness, our arrogance, for all of our pride, and our self-centeredness. Go with me to the wilderness where Jesus faced the Evil One before He began His earthly ministry. Let's look in *Luke Chapter 4* at the confrontation between Jesus and Satan so we can better recognize the Devil's temptations and their evil purpose:

THE TEMPTATIONS OF CHRIST

The three areas of our lives that are vulnerable to the murderous lies of the Enemy are 1) The Lust of the Flesh. 2) The Lust of the Eyes, and 3) The Pride of Life, In these areas Satan looks for windows of opportunity to establish his murderous strongholds in our lives. We clearly see these areas targeted by the Enemy as we look at the temptations of Christ:

• **THE LUST OF THE FLESH**

And Jesus, full of the Holy Spirit, returned from the Jordan and

*was led about by the Spirit in the wilderness for forty days,
being tempted by the Devil. And He ate nothing during those
days; and when they had ended, He became hungry. And the
Devil said to Him, "If (Since) You are the Son of God, tell this
stone to become bread (Luke 4:1-3)."*

Now come on, this wasn't fair! (Satan is never fair. It's not in his
vocabulary.) Jesus was hungry. He had had nothing to eat, "Nada."
Absolutely nothing in forty days. The word hungry doesn't even come
close to the physical needs Christ faced in His body. Notice how He
handles Satan. And Jesus answered him, *"It is written, 'MAN SHALL
NOT LIVE ON BREAD ALONE'"* (Luke 4:4). Don't let the Enemy
talk you into something like: "Well, Jesus was different. Since He was
God it was easier for Him. This doesn't really apply to me." Please
understand, Jesus was fully man, as well as, fully God. He became man,
not half man. He was fully and completely man, just like you and me.
Jesus had to become man for Him to be our Savior. As the writer of
Hebrews puts it:

*For we do not have a high priest who cannot sympathize with
our weaknesses, but One who has been tempted in all things as
we are, yet without sin (Heb. 4:15).*

The Scripture leaves no doubt about the huge difference between lives
lived in the power of the flesh and a life lived in the power of the Spirit
of God:

*For those who are according to the flesh set their minds on the
things of the flesh, but those who are according to the Spirit, the
things of the Spirit. For the mind set on the flesh is death, but the
mind set on the Spirit is life and peace (Romans 8:5-6).*

In Jesus' answer to the Devil's temptation aimed at Christ's fleshly
needs, we get a glimpse of the huge difference between the spiritual
answers to our needs and the physical answers to our needs. In this
temptation, Satan's desperation is evident. Satan's temptations imply,
"Go on and eat the bread, just don't go to the Cross." Put another way,

"Give into the desires of your flesh, just don't go to the Cross. If You die in the flesh on Calvary, then everyone who is crucified with You will have the supernatural ability to live free from the flesh." Next we have the temptation of the Enemy aimed at the Savior's vulnerability through the lust of the eyes:

- **THE LUST OF THE EYES**

  And he led Him up and showed Him all the kingdoms of the world in a moment of time. And the Devil said to Him, "I will give You all this domain and its glory for it has been handed over to me, and I give it to whomever I wish. Therefore if You worship before me, it shall all be Yours (Luke 4:5-7)."

One might ask, "Could Satan have given to Christ all the kingdoms of the world? Were they Satan's to give?" The answer is, Yes! Through sin and disobedience, man abdicated his God given authority of dominion over the world to Satan (See *Gen. 3*). Therefore, the Devil was, in fact, able to offer the kingdoms of the world to Christ. However, the deal was offered only if Christ would receive them in exchange for not going to the Cross. It is not surprising that Satan tried to use the lust of the eyes on Jesus to try to make Him fall. Jesus said of the eye:

  "The lamp (λύχνος—illuminator, reflector) of the body is the eye; if therefore your eye is clear, your whole body will be full of light (Matt. 6:22)."

The significance of our eyes in the spiritual battles with the Evil One cannot be overstated. Cicero, the Roman statesman, rightly stated, "The eyes are the window to the soul." Not only do our eyes let into our hearts what is around us in our environment, good or bad, but our eyes reveal what is in our hearts, as well. They illuminate what is going on in our souls, good or bad. As the song we used to sing as little children reminds us, "Be careful little eyes what you see!" Notice again with me Jesus' answer to Satan's temptation to the lust of the eyes:

And Jesus answered and said to him, "It is written, 'YOU SHALL WORSHIP THE LORD YOUR GOD AND SERVE HIM ONLY (Luke 4:8).'"

No matter what it looks like. No matter how alluring or pleasing to our eyes, no matter how logical it may look, or reasonable it may seem, we must never allow anything to take the high place in our lives but God alone. It is as though Satan is saying, "I'll give you everything you can see, just don't go to the Cross. Live only for what You can see with your physical eyes. Don't go to the Cross and die for everyone. Then everyone who is crucified with You, their eyes will be spiritually opened to the truth."

• THE PRIDE OF LIFE

And he led Him to Jerusalem and had Him stand on the pinnacle of the temple and said to Him, "If you are the Son of God, throw Yourself down from here; for it is written, He will give His angels charge concerning You to guard You, and on their hands they will bear You up, lest you strike Your foot against a stone (Luke 4:9-11)."

Now let's take a good look at Satan's temptation of Jesus as he appealed to His self-centered pride. My good friend, Dr. Jim Logan—who has for so many years prayed with those who have fallen into the deceptive clutches of the Enemy—shared his experience in dealing with the spiritual issues that stem from pride: "In my week long counseling sessions with people who are under the influence of the Enemy, there's usually a major turning point. The neon light goes on and begins to flash the shiny word: PRIDE. They realize that pride has become the source of the problem, the base from which Satan has been able to launch his attacks."[5] Notice with me again how our Lord Jesus answered the Evil One's temptation. He used the living Word of God. The Word of God always works against the Enemy's scheming treacherous lies. For the Word of God is truth. In Jesus' priestly prayer for believers we find these words:

"Sanctify them in the truth; Thy word is truth (John 17:17)."

And Jesus answered and said to him, "It is said, 'YOU SHALL NOT PUT THE LORD YOUR GOD TO THE TEST (Luke 4:12).'"

Satan knows that if you and I will believe the truth of God, he doesn't stand a chance to win the battle for control of our lives. His murderous schemes are spoiled through the truth of God's Word. Satan is saying to Jesus, "Exalt yourself now, just don't go to the Cross. If You go to the Cross then everyone who is crucified with You will be given the supernatural ability to humble themselves, and walk in the supernatural power of God." It is important to note that this was only the first of Satan's attempts to try to keep Jesus from going to the Cross:

And when the devil had finished every temptation, he departed from Him until an opportune time (Luke 4:13).

Satan's attacks never cease. What doesn't work in our lives today, he thinks just might work tomorrow. Maybe, if he keeps trying, he will find us in a weaker place, and then we will give in to his lies. Now here's what we all must understand. All temptations are designed to get us to establish our lives short of the Cross of Christ. If Satan can get us to establish our marriages and our families short of the Cross of Christ, he will have won in bringing us into his pit of defeat. If the Devil can get us to establish the ministries of our churches outside of the Cross of Christ, he will have won in bringing us to defeat. If Satan can get us to establish our walk in this world short of the Cross of Christ, he will have succeeded in bringing us into death and defeat. Satan was—and is—only defeated at the Cross of Christ:

And when you were dead in your transgressions and the uncircumcision of your flesh, He made you alive together with Him, having forgiven us all our transgressions, having canceled out the certificate of debt consisting of decrees against us and which was hostile to us; and He has taken it out of the way, having nailed it to the cross. When He had disarmed the rulers and authorities, He made a public display of them, having triumphed over them through Him (Col. 2:13-15).

Jesus died on Calvary as the Sacrifice for our sins. He rose from the dead to give us two kinds of life. Both are offered in *John 3:15-16*:

• **Everlasting Life**: (quantitative life) Everlasting life is life that lasts forever.

• **Eternal Life**: (qualitative life) The life of God here and now. Eternal life is life like God has.

If the Devil can talk us into settling for what we are able to do void of the supernatural work of Christ, we will never experience this eternal life. God knows that in and of ourselves, we are failures. That's why He sent His Son to die for us, to become our Savior. All deeds performed in our own power, ability, and strength are corrupted by our sin. Sin separates us from the God who created us for His glory. No matter how noble our task, no matter how seemingly unselfish our motivation, the truth is—the best we can do on our own and in our own strength is less than what God can do in and through us.

THE DEATH OF THE FLESH AT THE CROSS

Jesus came to give us His life, His mind, and His power to do the Father's will on earth as it is in Heaven. Let's take each one and see what the Bible says:

• His life: *"The thief comes only to steal and kill and destroy; I came that they may have life, and have it abundantly (John 10:10)."*

• His Power: *"Now to Him who is able to do far more abundantly beyond all that we ask or think, according to the power that works within us, to Him be the glory in the church and in Christ Jesus to all generations forever and ever, Amen (Eph. 3:20-21)."*

• His Mind: *"Have this mind in you which was also in Christ Jesus (Phil. 2: 5)."*

• His Ability: *"For it is God who is at work in you, both to will and to work for His good pleasure (Phil 2:13)."* Look at what God says to us today, concerning His power given to us. *"I can do all things through Him who strengthens me (Phil 4:13)."*

Please let's take a careful look at the other assumption in the statement, "I'm doing the best I can. Surely, God only expects me to do the best I can." Is it true that God only expects us to do the best we can? Our opinions are just opinions. Everybody has one. We will be judged not by what we think is true, but by what is true. Jesus makes an amazing statement below. Notice how He places the standard of the Christian walk in the supernatural realm. Not only does God not expect us to do our best, God expects us to do greater works than even Jesus did:

> *"Truly, truly, I say to you, he who believes in Me, the works that I do shall he do also; and greater works than these shall he do; because I go to the Father (John 14:12)."*

You might be wondering, "Now, how could this be possible? I could never walk on water, or heal sick people, or ever raise the dead." Of course, you can't. That is, in your own power. Notice what the Angel Gabriel said to Mary when he was delivering God's message concerning the baby to whom she was to give birth:

> *"For nothing will be impossible with God (Luke 1:37)."*

Why does the Bible teach that we will give an account of every idle word in *Matt.12:36* if the Lord only expects us to do the best we can? Why does the Bible teach that we are expected to live a life of holiness, if God only expects us to do the best we can?

> *...but like the Holy One who called you, be holy yourselves also in all your behavior; because it is written, "YOU SHALL BE HOLY, FOR I AM HOLY (1 Peter 1:15-16)."*

My Friend, the Word of God is clear. Not only has our Lord called us to a life of holiness, but He has also made a way for us to live a life of holiness through the power of the living Lord Jesus. It has been correctly stated, "It is not difficult for man to live the Christian life, it is a sheer impossibility!" That is, without Christ it is impossible. Listen to the testimony from the heart of the Apostle Paul as he weighed in on the matter of living the Christian life:

> *"I have been crucified with Christ; and it is no longer I who live, but Christ lives in me; and the life which I now live in the flesh I live by faith in the Son of God, who loved me and gave Himself up for me (Gal. 2:20)."*

THE SUPERNATURAL POWER OF THE CHRISTIAN LIFE

In Jesus' discourse about the relationship between the vine and the branches, He provides an explanation of how the supernatural power of God is available to every believer. Without this supernatural power of God, we can do nothing on our own—that is, what is in God's heart for us to accomplish:

> *"Abide in Me, and I in you. As the branch cannot bear fruit of itself, unless it abides in the vine, so neither can you, unless you abide in Me. "I am the vine, you are the branches; he who abides in Me, and I in him, he bears much fruit; for apart from Me you can do nothing (John 15:4-5)."*

There is only one man who has ever lived a successful Christian life. That man is Jesus, and this same Jesus abides in the life of every believer for the purpose of living the Christian life. In the classic book, *The Key to Triumphant Living*, Jack Taylor summarized the key to living the Christian life: "There is a simple secret to the Christian life. It is, in fact, so simple that millions miss it. There is a dynamic so mighty that no life can remain the same after discovering it. It is the SECRET, THE KEY, THE SUPREME DYNAMIC, THE GLORIOUS SECRET of the Christian life. True Christianity is simply 'Christ-in-you-ity' and 'Christ-in-me-ity.'"[6] "The Christian life can be explained only in terms of Jesus Christ; and, if your life as a Christian can still be explained in terms of you—your personality, your willpower, your gift, your talent, your money, your courage, your scholarship, your dedication, your sacrifice, or your anything- then although you may have the Christian life, you are not yet living it!"[7] Let me say it again, if the Devil can talk you into settling for a life that is empty of the power of Christ; if Satan can talk you into a life of what you can do in your own strength, he will then have set the stage for your destruction. You can start turning out the lights, because the party may be over!

The truth is—the best we can ever do will never be good enough! That's why Jesus died and rose from the dead for us. He wants to come into our lives and give us the supernatural ability to be and, therefore, do what the Heavenly Father has expected of us when He created all of mankind—to reflect His glory. Did you know that all the good works that God has for us to perform in our lifetime were established before the foundation of the world? Look in your Bible with me. Read *Eph. 2:8-10*, see for yourself what God says about the works we are to perform:

> *For by grace you have been saved through faith; and that not of yourselves, it is the gift of God; not as a result of works, so that no one may boast. For we are His workmanship, created in Christ Jesus for good works, which God prepared beforehand so that we would walk in them (Eph. 2:8-10).*

God doesn't expect us to do the best we can. He knows that the best we can do could never be good enough to meet the expectations He has set for us. No, God expects us to bow in humility, yielding ourselves to Him, all the while trusting His work on Calvary. This work of Christ on Calvary is as necessary for each of us today in our everyday living as it was when many of us gave our lives to him long ago. This new life in Christ is not what we can do. This new life in Christ is a life of supernatural power; a life of victory over the powers of darkness and their lies, so that the ultimate glory will go to Almighty God. God expects us to do more than we can do on our own and has given us the supernatural ability, through the living, resurrected Lord Jesus, to accomplish His will. Not only is the power to do His will given to us by a supernatural act of God, but also the desire to do His will is given to every believer—by a supernatural act of the person of Christ who dwells within us:

> *...for it is God who is at work in you, both to will and to work for His good pleasure (Phil. 2:13).*

Through this supernatural strength, we can love each other the way He has loved us. Through His supernatural strength, we have the ability to forgive those who have hurt us through the forgiveness we have received through Calvary. Through His supernatural strength, we have been given the ability to care and sacrifice for others the way He has sacrificed for us. Through His supernatural strength, we have the ability to serve Christ in His church no matter what has happened to us. My Friend, stop listening to the lie of the Enemy that says, "God only expects us to do the best we can." This dangerous lie has the ability to keep us living a life of defeat, and ultimate death.

THE FLESH LIFE vs. THE CHRIST LIFE

The Holy Spirit has provided for us two lists that clearly reveal to us the difference in the life that is lived by the power of God and the life that is lived in our own power. The Bible calls a life lived in our own power—the flesh. The best we can do and have, as a result of living in the flesh, are these:

> *Now the deeds of the flesh are evident, which are: immorality, impurity, sensuality, idolatry, sorcery, enmities, strife, jealousy, outbursts of anger, disputes, dissensions, factions, envying, drunkenness, carousing, and things like these, of which I forewarn you, just as I have forewarned you, that those who practice such things will not inherit the kingdom of God (Gal. 5:19-21).*

In Christ, by yielding our lives to the Spirit and power of Almighty God, there is a much different result. Look with me at the following verses:

> *But the fruit of the Spirit is love, joy, peace, patience, kindness, goodness, faithfulness, gentleness, self-control; against such things there is no law (Gal. 5:22-23).*

Why do you think God's Word says, *"Mortify the deeds of the flesh?"* Why do you think God's Word says, *"Say no to the ungodly deeds of the flesh?"* Why do you think God's Word says, *"Crucify your flesh?"* Why does the Word of God teach us to *"Die to self?"* When you and I allow the flesh to control our lives, we are living a life that leads to death and destruction:

> *For the one who sows to his own flesh shall from the flesh reap corruption, but the one who sows to the Spirit shall from the Spirit reap eternal life (Gal 6:8).*

As a student at Baylor University, I attended a Bible conference held by the church I was attending. The guest Bible teacher was an internationally known Bible teacher from Scotland. Major Ian Thomas came to Waco where he taught these deep eternal truths of the God kind of life. In his wonderful book, *The Saving Life of Christ,* Major Thomas points out the impossibility of living a life of righteousness in the power of the flesh: "There is nothing quite as nauseating or pathetic as the flesh trying to be holy! The flesh has a perverted bent for righteousness—but such righteousness, as it may achieve, is always self-righteousness. The Devil doesn't mind whether you are an extrovert or an introvert, whether you succeed or whether you fail in the energy of the flesh, whether you are filled with self-pity or self-praise, for he knows that in both cases you will be preoccupied with yourself and not Christ. You will be self-centered and not God-centered."[8] Major Thomas continues as he points out the distinct differences between a life lived in the power of the flesh and a life lived in the power of Christ: "To be in Christ—that is redemption: but for Christ to be in you—that is sanctification! To be in Christ—that makes you fit for Heaven: but for Christ to be in you—that makes you fit for earth! To be in Christ—that changes your destination: but for Christ to be in you—that changes your destiny! The one makes Heaven your home—The other makes this world His workshop!"[9]

THE IMPARTATION OF THE SUPERNATURAL POWER OF CHRIST

You may ask, "How does a person receive this supernatural power to be used of God?" First, you need to be born of the Spirit. You must, as Jesus said, *be born again (John 3)*. You need to give your life to Christ and receive Him as your Savior. Secondly, if you are already a child of God and you don't see this supernatural power of God being manifested in and through your life, it's time for you to submit your life completely to the Lord. Ask Him today to fill you with His Spirit. Would you hear and obey the Word of God right now?

> *But all things become visible when they are exposed by the light, for everything that becomes visible is light. For this reason it says, "Awake, sleeper, And arise from the dead, And Christ will shine on you." Therefore be careful how you walk, not as unwise men but as wise, making the most of your time, because the days are evil. So then do not be foolish, but understand what the will of the Lord is. And do not get drunk with wine, for that is dissipation, but be filled with the Spirit (Eph. 5:14 -18).*

Let's look closer at this passage of Scripture to gain an even better understanding of how we receive this supernatural power of God's life that is in us. We see in this passage, that it is a wise man who chooses to live a life in the power of the Spirit of God. Why? Because *"the days are evil."* The days are evil because they have a curse of time upon them due to our sin. Sin's curse has caused our days to be numbered. There are just so many days we will draw breath; just so many opportunities to witness for Christ, and just so many days to allow our Lord to perform His work in and through us. Therefore, the admonition to each believer is this: don't be foolish and live in the flesh, but live a life that is continually being filled with the Holy Spirit of God. I want us to look at three important truths concerning the life that chooses to be filled with the Spirit of God.

• **The Mystery of the Filling of the Spirit**

The Apostle Paul refers to Christ indwelling the life of anyone who will accept Him as Savior, a mystery. It is a mystery that has now been revealed:

> *...to whom God willed to make known what is the riches of the glory of this mystery among the Gentiles, which is Christ in you, the hope of glory (Col 1:27).*

Although this wonderful mystery *"Christ in you, the hope of glory"* is now revealed, it is still mysterious. It is mysterious because it's not natural. It is supernatural. We're talking about the very Spirit of God coming into our lives and taking control. The Lord Jesus came to earth to die for our sin. He rose from the dead to defeat death for every believer. He ascended to the right hand of the Father in the place of all authority. Jesus is Lord! Listen to His words as He was leaving to go to the Father explaining what was to come for His followers:

> *"But I tell you the truth, it is to your advantage that I go away; for if I do not go away, the Helper shall not come to you; but if I go, I will send Him to you (John 16:7)."*

> *"And I will ask the Father, and He will give you another Helper, that He may be with you forever; that is the Spirit of truth, whom the world cannot receive, because it does not behold Him or know Him, but you know Him because He abides with you, and will be in you (John 14:16-17)."*

The Spirit of Christ is in us as believers. Can you imagine it? The very person of Christ—in all His power, authority, and glory—is living in our human, mortal bodies:

> *Or do you not know that your body is a temple of the Holy Spirit who is in you, whom you have from God, and that you are not*

your own? For you have been bought with a price: therefore
glorify God in your body (1 Cor. 6:19-20).

He has come into our bodies to manifest—to produce—everything that
is in God's heart. Not only does He come to produce it IN us, but it
is also His desire to produce it THROUGH us. How can this be? It's
supernatural. It's a "God thing." There's nothing in this life to which
we can relate this wonderful relationship we have with God through
the indwelling Holy Spirit. No experience or relationship you have ever
known is like Him. No love, no peace, nothing ... nothing is like our
wonderful Lord Jesus. Just because it is different in kind, doesn't make
it any less true. The very person of Christ dwells in our bodies so that
the glory of God, in all its fullness, may be manifested through our
lives. Watchman Nee clarifies for us what living in the Spirit means: "I
trust the Holy Spirit to do in me what I cannot do myself. This life is
completely different from the life I would naturally live of myself. Each
time I am faced with a new demand from the Lord, I look to Him to do
in me what He requires of me."[10]

What does a Spirit-filled life look like? Is it weird and spooky?
Does is make us unfit for earth? No! The life of the Spirit-filled believer...looks like Jesus. What takes place when the Holy Spirit is in
control of the life of a believer? It always looks like the Book of Acts.
The Book of Acts is not the Acts of the Apostles, in truth it is the Acts of
the Holy Spirit through Christ's body—His Church. God is performing
through the believer His miraculous works so that through the witnessing of these supernatural acts—what Paul calls "signs and wonders"—
the world comes to know Jesus is Lord.

Just the other day a young man came to me with a broken heart.
His wife had taken their two children and had left him. She was sick
and tired of his relentless critical rants coming from his heart of bitterness, his anger, and horrific rage. After several days and many hours of
the Holy Spirit's working in this precious man's life, he called me and
said his wife wanted to talk to me. When she arrived at our home, she
told me that this was the day she had decided to go to the courthouse

and file for divorce. When asked what changed her mind she said, "It is because of the change I see in my husband." It is through the 'seeing'— observing the manifestation of this supernatural work of Holy Spirit— that people come to know our blessed Lord Jesus.

- **The Practicality of the Filling of the Spirit**

   Notice with me the last sentence of this most important passage:

   And don't get drunk with wine, for that is dissipation, but be filled with the Spirit (Eph. 5:18).

Have you ever wondered, "Why would the Holy Spirit use the imagery in the Bible of being drunk with wine to express to us the significance of being filled with the Spirit?" My great aunt married a good and kind man. The only problem was he was an alcoholic. He would go for months and years at a time without a drink, and then seemingly out of nowhere something would take over his life. The siren song of the destroyer he could not ignore. My uncle would disappear for weeks at a time and waste everything they had in a drunken binge.

Maybe you have painfully witnessed this kind of evil transformation in the life of an alcoholic. When they are sober, they could not be more kind, but when they are drinking, they turn into some kind of an evil monster. When under the influence of alcohol it may be difficult to even recognize your friend, or loved one. There has been a total transformation of the personality. Something, or more likely "someone" else, has taken control of the person's emotions, of their mind, and even the consequences of their torn life. It is just like that, my Friend, when a believer is filled with the Holy Spirit. God takes over. It is His personality that overrides ours. It is His love, His mercy, His grace, and His forgiveness; His power that permeates our whole being. That's what it means to be filled with the Spirit. We are no longer in control of our own lives. It is the precious Holy Spirit who now is in charge of our lives.

How does this transformation take place? How does the Holy Spirit take control of our lives? Is it automatic, since the believer has the Holy Spirit within? In many circles within the church the words baptism and fullness of the spirit are used synonymously. Dr. John Stott in his book *Baptism and Fullness*, helps us understand the difference between baptism and the fullness of the Spirit: "It should be noted, there is a significant difference between the baptism of the Holy Spirit and the filling of the Holy Spirit. What happened on the day of Pentecost was that Jesus "poured out" the Spirit from Heaven and thus baptized with the Spirit the first 120 and then the 3,000. The result of this baptism was that they were all filled with the Holy Spirit *(Acts. 2:4)*. Thus, the fullness of the Spirit was the consequence of the baptism of the Spirit. The baptism is what Jesus did. The fullness is what they received."[11] Dr. J. Edwin Orr succinctly said it this way: "Indwelling must not be confused with full possession. The indwelling Spirit has His place in the home of the Christian soul, but every room in the house is available to Him in the home of the Spirit filled believer. One may say that every true Christian is regenerated, indwelt, assured, sealed, guaranteed, and baptized by the Spirit, but he may or may not be filled with the Spirit."[12]

We must not think of gaining the Spirit-filled life as a program to follow, or a religious pattern to repeat. We do not come into the fullness of Christ by checking off a list of do's and don'ts. There is no one formula that, when followed, the Holy Spirit is forced, or somehow obligated to respond. The filling of the Spirit is available to every believer, but the only believer who finds this holy way of living is the one who comes to the end of himself or herself. What God is asking of us is simply to surrender all to Him. That's right—everything. Continue to hang on to just one old sin, and your life will be void of the Holy Spirit's power. Many want the Spirit's power, but not the Spirit's purity. The Holy Spirit does not rent out his attributes. His power is never separated from His glorious self.[13]

Why do you think God says *Crucify your flesh?* Why does the Word of God teach us to *die to self?* If we continue to live in and live for the desires of the flesh, we will never be able to fulfill the desires of the Spirit. Jesus said:

"Truly, truly, I say to you, unless a grain of wheat falls into the earth and dies, it remains by itself alone; but if it dies, it bears much fruit. (John 12:24)." And He was saying to them all, "If anyone wishes to come after Me, let him deny himself, and take up his cross daily, and follow Me. For whoever wishes to save his life shall lose it, but whoever loses his life for My sake, he is the one who will save it (Luke 9:23-24)."

The Apostle Paul mirrored this eternal truth when he said:

"For those who are according to the flesh set their minds on the things of the flesh, but those who are according to the Spirit, the things of the Spirit. For the mind set on the flesh is death, but the mind set on the Spirit is life and peace (Romans 8:5-6), "for if you are living according to the flesh, you must die; but if by the Spirit you are putting to death the deeds of the body, you will live (Romans 8:13)."

This teaching is so different than what we learn and hear from this old world, our flesh, and the Devil. Why is this Cross so important that we are to carry it daily? The Cross is the place of death. The Cross is what you die on. Here is why the preaching of the Cross is essential to the true Gospel of Christ. It is only at Calvary we come to understand, that if we are to become all that God created us to be, it comes to us only through the work of Christ on Calvary. If we are to be victorious over the powers of darkness, we cannot fight them in our own power. They are defeated only through the power of Holy Spirit as He takes over our lives through the death of our old ways of the flesh. This is only possible through the work of Christ on the Cross. Any other way of living offered without the Cross of Christ is a lie of the Enemy and will lead to destruction and death. Any other way of life offered without the dying of self in Christ on the Cross is a pitiful counterfeit, lacking the power of God:

For the love of Christ controls us, having concluded this, that one died for all, therefore all died; and He died for all, that they who live should no longer live for themselves, but for Him who died and rose again on their behalf (2 Cor. 5:14-15).

Through the writings of Watchman Nee, we have great insight to this supernatural union with Christ to which we have been joined as believers: "Now the vital question arises: 'How do I die?' The preciousness of our Lord's work comes in right here: *you also were made dead to the law through the body of Christ (Romans 7:4).* When Christ died, his body was broken, and since God placed me in Him *(1 Cor. 1:30),* I have been broken, too. When He was crucified, I was crucified with Him. In the sight of God, His death included mine. On the hill of Calvary it was forever done."[14] How is it possible we can reckon and consider ourselves dead to sin? It has already happened on the Cross of Christ. It's a done deal. The work of Christ for our sin is finished. In Christ we are dead to the flesh, but we have been made alive in the Spirit because of His resurrection. Sins are forgiven at the Cross. Wounds are healed at the Cross. Devils are banished at the Cross. Sickness and disease are healed at the Cross:

> *Surely our griefs He Himself bore, and our sorrows He carried; Yet we ourselves esteemed Him stricken, Smitten of God, and afflicted. But He was pierced through for our transgressions, He was crushed for our iniquities; The chastening for our well-being fell upon Him, And by His scourging we are healed (Isaiah 53:4-5).*

The blood of Jesus was shed at the Cross of Calvary. Without the Cross there is no power for the believer. Praise God! All you have ever needed has been supplied through the work of Christ on the Cross! Whatever you need today, take it to the Cross. It is at the Cross of Christ you will find everything you need. God has already handled your need for you. He has provided it for you through the death of His Son on the Cross.

It is an awesome thing to be used of God to accomplish what is in His heart. To share in this "Divine Dance," to be used of God to bring His Kingdom on earth as it is in Heaven, to share in the miraculous signs and wonders of the Holy Spirit, we must submit our lives to be lived in one place. That place is on an old rugged hill called Calvary. According to a great Scottish Evangelist, James Stewart, there are four truths concerning how God uses the believer that we must come to understand and receive:

1. Whatever God claims, we must yield.

2. Whatever I yield, God accepts.

3. Whatever God accepts, He fills.

4. Whatever God fills, He uses.[15]

- **The Necessity of the Filling of the Spirit**

We must truly acknowledge and allow this truth to sink in, that is—only through the filling of the Holy Spirit is the work of God accomplished. We can't heal anyone in our own strength. Jesus wants to heal through us. We can't save anyone, no matter how much we long for them to be saved. Jesus wants to save them through His working in us (*1 Cor. 6:1-2*). We can't deliver anyone from the tormenting of the powers of darkness in our own power and strength. Jesus wants to deliver those in bondage through our lives totally submitted to Christ. Through the yielded life of the believer, empowered by the Holy Spirit, we are only then able to bring His Kingdom on earth as it is in Heaven. Please hear me when I say… try as we can, the most dedicated Christian cannot manifest God's holy presence to this old sick world that so desperately needs Him. Christ can only manifest Himself through our lives as we humbly yield our control over to the life and control of Christ.

Please don't settle for this old—but, oh, so effective—lie of the Enemy, "I'm doing the best I can. Surely, God only expects me to do the best I can." Right now, determine in your heart to trust the work that Jesus accomplished for you on Calvary's Cross. Through humility and brokenness reckon yourself dead to the flesh. Ask the Holy Spirit to come and take control of your life. Isn't it time to get off the road of destruction? Isn't it time for Heaven's purposes to be manifested in and through your life?

Would you join me in praying the prayer of the great evangelist D.L. Moody?

Our Heavenly Father, we come to wait on You for the gift of Your Holy Spirit for service. Oh God, give us the Spirit. Empty us of self and self-seeking. Oh God, bring us down in the dust before You, so that we may be filled with the Holy Spirit, so that we may have power with God and with man! Oh God of Elijah, we pray that a double portion of Your Spirit may come upon us today, that we may be anointed for the work You have for us to do; we know we have but a little while to stay here!

Oh, God, help us to bear fruit while we live! May we no longer be toiling day after day and month after month, and seeing no fruit. Oh Jesus, Master, You have gone up on high; You who has led captivity captive; You are at the right hand of God, and You have power. Oh, give us power; You can give us a fresh anointing. We pray that You will do it today. We pray that You will breathe upon us as a breath from Heaven. Grant that we may know what it is to have the Holy Spirit resting upon us for service…We ask it all in the Name and for the sake of Your beloved Son, Amen![16]

ALL I NEED IS TO GET BACK IN CHURCH.

It's essential that we understand Satan's lies are good ones. God's Word tells us in *Gen 3:1,* Satan is the most cunning and deceptive creature ever created. As a result of Satan's fall and subsequent judgment *(Isaiah 14:12-15),* he has become the leader of a kingdom of rebellion whose purpose is to oppose God and His Kingdom on earth. One third of all the angels as Jude puts it, *"who left their first estate" (Jude vs. 6),* joined Satan's rebellion. We know them as demons. They are fallen angels who are on assignment to steal, kill, and destroy as their rebel leader orders them. We must understand, Satan has had thousands of years to perfect his murderous crafting of lies.

As we continue our journey into the biblical study of LIES THAT KILL, I want to bring focus on what I believe to be one of the greatest deceptions of the Evil One. This lie is so deceptive and dangerous, it has the ability to keep people from knowing and walking in Christ. This lie is reflected in the statement, "ALL I NEED IS TO GET BACK IN CHURCH."

Now I want you to carefully study with me what is in this chapter so there will be no misunderstandings. I've been preaching the Gospel of

Christ for over 30 years. Believe it or not, I have had some folks hear what I don't say. As you have already found out in this book, the Enemy doesn't want you to understand the truths that hold Christ's power to set you free. Of all of Satan's lies, the lie that "if I just get back in church, everything will be O.K." may be the most wicked. The lies of the Devil that have a covering in the cloak of religious rituals and traditions are by far some of the most deceptive and therefore powerfully destructive.

Would you allow me to pray for us right now that Holy Spirit will come and teach us His truth that can set us free? Dear Lord Jesus, I bring my Friend and myself to You and ask that You put us into the circle of Your blood. In Jesus' mighty Name, I ask that You will be our guide into all truth as You promised You would be in *John 16:13*. Bind the liars' tongues in the Name of our blessed Lord Jesus Christ of Nazareth. Give us hearts not only to hear and consider Your truth, but give us hearts to receive Your truth. May the light of Your glory shine on the truth that can set us free in You. As a result of Your imparted Word, do the greatest work in our lives for Your greatest glory! In Jesus almighty Name I pray, Amen.

Please understand, I'm a churchman. My schooling and experience has been to serve the people of God. I have spent my life in churches. I've often joked how I was probably born in a bow tie and a three piece suit. Since my Father was an itinerate evangelist, our family was not only in church on Sundays, we were in church most every day of every week. For over thirty years I have traveled around the globe conducting evangelistic services, primarily through the invitation of churches. This has been my life's work. So please understand as you read this chapter, I'm not opposed to the church; I have given my life to serve the people of God through churches. I love the church. I am as committed to the church today as I have ever been.

WHAT AND WHO IS THE CHURCH

At the outset, it is important to clear up the false notion that the church is that local institution that houses an organization that commonly carries the name church. There is a huge difference between the true church and what many folks *call* the church. The true church is the body of Christ. We, as believers, are the church *(1 Cor. 12:27)*. Every born again child of God has been baptized by the Spirit of God into the body of Christ *(1 Cor. 12:13)*. Christ established His church on the basis of Peter's confession that Jesus was the Christ—the Son of the Living God *(Matt. 16:18)*. Everyone who has come to confess Christ Jesus as Lord and Savior becomes the body of Christ *(Romans 10:9-10)*. Although the institutions that have been established and upheld by men may be the structure in which the church functions, in and of themselves, they are not the church. Which is to say, not every institution that claims to be a church is the church. However, it is important to recognize that it is through a local body of believers that Christ manifests His presence to the lost and corrupt environment in which our Lord has placed us *(Matt. 18:19)*. Every child of God has been given the authority of God, as Jesus put it—*the Keys to His Kingdom*. Please study with me the Scripture concerning the true church:

> *He said to them, "But who do you say that I am?" And Simon Peter answered and said, "Thou art the Christ, the Son of the living God." And Jesus answered and said to him, "Blessed are you, Simon Barjona, because flesh and blood did not reveal this to you, but My Father who is in heaven. And I also say to you that you are Peter, and upon this rock I will build My church; and the gates of Hades shall not overpower it. I will give you the keys of the kingdom of heaven; and whatever you shall bind on earth shall be bound in heaven, and whatever you shall loose on earth shall be loosed in heaven (Matt. 16:15-19)."*

This authority over the powers of darkness has been given to every believer as a result of their relationship with Christ. The Bible refers to this union with Christ, *in Christ*. Look at what the Bible says to us concerning this supernatural power that God has given all believers:

> *And what is the surpassing greatness of His power toward us who believe. These are in accordance with the working of the strength of His might which He brought about in Christ, when*

He raised Him from the dead, and seated Him at His right hand in the heavenly places, far above all rule and authority and power and dominion, and every name that is named, not only in this age, but also in the one to come. And He put all things in subjection under His feet, and gave Him as head over all things to the church, which is His body, the fullness of Him who fills all in all (Eph 1:19-23).

THE WORK OF JESUS THROUGH HIS BODY

When Jesus went to his home town of Nazareth, He went into the Synagogue on the Sabbath Day. He was given a scroll of Isaiah to read. He turned to a passage of Scripture that I'm certain was familiar to all those in the sound of His voice that day. The passage He read publicly was *Isaiah 61:1*. What He said next, resulted in Him getting not only thrown out of the Synagogue that day, but in a mob-like reaction, Jesus was also cast out of His own home town *(Luke 4:28-29). And He began to say to them, "Today this Scripture has been fulfilled in your hearing"* *(Luke 4:21).* What Jesus said that day to those in his home town was that He was the Messiah. He was the One that God had promised over 750 years ago would come to take away their sin. He was the long anticipated One—God's Messiah. Notice with me in this promise of God how they would recognize the true Messiah when He came:

The Spirit of the Lord GOD is upon me, because the LORD has anointed me to bring good news to the afflicted; He has sent me to bind up the brokenhearted, to proclaim liberty to captives, and freedom to prisoners; To proclaim the favorable year of the LORD, and the day of vengeance of our God; to comfort all who mourn (Isaiah 61:1-2).

As we read in *Luke 4* and all through the Book of *Acts* we see it is always the same. When Jesus ministers His work in and through the lives of His people three things always take place: 1) He saves the lost; 2) He heals the sick; 3) He delivers those in bondage.

For several years now I have had the privilege to minister to the wonderful people of Jamaica. On one of the last trips I made to this little

Caribbean Island, our group was asked to minister in a church that was really not on our original schedule. Our team leader, who is Jamaican, asked me to preach that night. I preached a message on the three things I believe Jesus does when He comes into our presence. I asked that if anyone needed to be saved from their sins to come forward. Those who responded, I sent with our team leaders who were very capable of leading folks to faith in Christ. Next I asked if anyone needed a healing in their body to come forward. I sent these folks with the doctors and nurses on our team who had come to Jamaica to minister to the sick folks. Finally, I asked those that needed to be set free from spiritual bondage to come forward. These I met with as we walked through the process of spiritual freedom in Christ.

From the end of my sermon until we left to get on the bus to return to our hotel we were praying with these wonderful people about an hour and a half. Once we were on the bus one of the team members who was an elder in a prominent church in Dallas, Texas, turned to me and said,

"Brother Rob, I need to talk to you."

I asked, "Do we need to talk in private?"

He said, "No, we can talk as we ride back to the hotel." Then he shared with me, "The pastor of the church, where I am an elder, would never allow anything to go on like we just witnessed in this service."

I asked him, "Why not? Have we experienced anything funny or weird tonight?"

He quickly replied, "No, God met us tonight and did a great work among us." Then he said, "I guess my pastor is afraid of losing control."

Wow! What an indictment. It's the Lord's church. We should never allow anyone to be in control of God's church except Jesus. He bought the church with His own blood. He hasn't abdicated His authority over His church to us. He shares His authority with us, yes, but that shared authority is always underneath His Lordship. He is the head of His church *(Eph. 5:23)*.

In a time of great change and uncertainty, what kind of church should we be looking to invest our lives in as we approach the coming of our Lord? Is it a church with a certain worship style or format? Is it a church with a rich tradition of formalism, or meaningful spiritual ritual? Is it a church committed to a denominational structure, or one who has jettisoned its denominational past? In the days our Lord has given us, what kind of church should we seek? In what type of church can we best serve our Lord Jesus? Consider the following truths concerning God's true church:

• **The Work of Jesus through His Word Based Church**—A Church that practices what the Scriptures teach. It is one thing to say we believe in the authority of Scripture. It is something altogether different to discipline one's walk and practice according to the Word of God. The church that is effective for Christ is one whose members become much more than those who merely carry the labels of theological conservative, or fundamentalist. It will be a church that is characterized by those who have disciplined their lives not only to say they believe, but believe enough to practice the Word of God to the working it out in their lives.

• **The Work of Jesus through His Worshipping Church**—A Church worthy of our lives is one that encourages the people of God to worship Christ in any and all the ways that would honor Him. Genuine worship is never man centered. We do not determine its parameters. It is through our intimacy with Christ, born out of a grateful heart to Christ, that true worship is offered. A grateful church allows no limits to its gratitude for the work of Christ in and through His body. A Church that is effective for Christ is one where the sweet aroma of communion of her people with God is always welcomed and encouraged.

• **The Work of Jesus through His Welcoming Church**—The church to be effective for Christ must be a people who welcome not only any and all people with all their many needs, but readily welcome any and all of the works of Jesus. As we study the Word of God, we see the ministry of Christ through His church manifests itself in three ways: Jesus saves the lost, He heals the sick, and He sets the captives free. The Prophet Isaiah gave us three clear signs as to how the Christ, our Messiah, would be recognized *(Isaiah 61)*. Only Christ can perform these wonderful works of God.

Not long ago I was visiting with a Director of Missions in North Central Texas. As preachers often do, we were sharing our hearts concerning what we perceived to be the spiritual needs of the church. I told him what I believed to be the main spiritual need of so many of the churches in which I had served over the years. Most of the churches I had observed were not willing to invite Jesus to do His work among us. My friend bristled and said, "What do you mean?" I shared with him that although the history of our denomination reveals a mighty work of God at various times, few of us in our generation have seen Christ come in genuine supernatural revival power. We seem to be more interested in <u>how we talk about the work of Jesus</u>, rather than actually <u>inviting Jesus to do His work</u>. After a few seconds the truth hit him and he said, "Rob, I'm afraid you're right." Please understand my heart when I say that we—the church of the living God, must stop just 'talking' about the work of Christ, and begin to welcome Christ to do His work among us. When our world sees the work of Christ through His body, it is then they will desire to put their trust in Him. What can we expect from Jesus if He comes to do His work in and among His people? It will always look like the Book of Acts. The Book of Acts is not the Acts of the Apostles. It is the Acts of the Holy Spirit manifesting Himself in and through the church—the body of Christ:

> *And all the more believers in the Lord, multitudes of men and women, were constantly added to their number; to such an extent that they even carried the sick out into the streets, and laid them on cots and pallets, so that when Peter came by, at least his shadow might fall on any one of them. And also the people from the cities in the vicinity of Jerusalem were coming together, bringing people who were sick or afflicted with unclean spirits; and they were all being healed (Acts 5:14-17).*

What I want us to understand is that the place of worship many call the church may not be functioning as the body of Christ. Many are trying to function as the church, without the presence and power of God. Although this is not a new problem, it is <u>our</u> problem. Many in the Corinthian church had accepted a religion of "talk" instead of the manifest "power" of God:

> *For the kingdom of God does not consist in words, but in power (1 Cor. 4:20).*

If at your place of worship you hear things implied like, "The supernatural manifestations of God were only for the Apostolic Age, or "This is the 21st Century, the Bible doesn't apply to us today the same way it did in Bible times." If you hear things like, "That's our church," or "We can't do things like they did it in the Bible." Please hear my heart's cry for you and your family. You need to decide in your heart that for your spiritual heath and the spiritual health of your family, you need to get out of there. Don't allow your emotions, or attachments, to a spiritually sick church be used of the Enemy to keep you in spiritual bondage. Take your family and go to a place where the Kingdom of God is understood as a place where Christ is welcomed to do what He wishes. Go to a place where the Word of God is not just talked about. Go to a place of worship where the church welcomes the work of Christ, through the presence of Christ.

Once again, Satan has had thousands of years to perfect his lies. If they are not effective lies, we can be certain they are not Satan's lies. If he can get us to accept a counterfeit religious system to which we seek to comfort our flesh, he will have succeeded to set up a murderous system in our lives that one day will take us out. Even if it's spiritual or religious flesh, it's still flesh. We must understand it is the flesh which the Enemy uses, on which to build his murderous strongholds.

DEMONIC COUNTERFEIT RELIGIOUS SYSTEMS

My major in my undergraduate work was in religion. Please understand religion has never brought anyone to Christ. Religion can be a false demonic counterfeit which becomes a deterrent from the life and work of Christ. The demonic diversion of religion often leads us away from the Christ who can save, heal, and deliver. I would like to stop right here and make the observation that the most vicious demons I have run into are religious demons. Yes, religious demons. For when they are exposed they attempt to respond with a furious anger that is rarely seen in other demonic systems. When Christ directed His most vehement judgment and anger it was to the religious leaders. Religious demons are often permitted to do their murderous work without ever being discovered or uncovered. Think about it. What better cover could a demon have than a religious cover? Religious demons usually get a "pass" to do their destructive work.

How amazed and horrified are we when we hear of the many children who have been molested by the clergy? So-called spiritual leaders in whom they have put their solemn trust. Many of us know the painful stories of how those in ministry have had to forsake their ministries in shame because of the spiritual bondage they refused to allow Jesus to break. I learned just the other day of a broken family full of wounded souls because their father who was a leader in church was living a double and secret life of sin. What we need to understand is everything that man worships, or exalts other than Christ, a demon will attach himself. This blasphemous evil spirit is ever present behind its religious cover to steal any and all worship of the true and living God. It is time for us to recognize that Christ alone is to be exalted and manifested in and through our lives. Then and only then will our lost and dying world come to know our wonderful Savior.

Religious systems are often nothing more than demonic counterfeits to keep us from Christ. Many of them are old traditional counterfeits that look good, feel good, and often dress up like they come from God. When carefully scrutinized by the Word of God and the Spirit of God, they are nothing more than an attempt by the Evil One to divert us from Christ. Satan does not care which religious counterfeit system works, just so long as it works. Some of the most obvious religious systems used by Satan are:

• **False Religious System of Music**—Today many churches have fallen victim to this carefully crafted scheme of the Enemy. To get people in the pews, many in church leadership have led the church down a dangerous path of accommodation. In this system, the end justifies the means. This faulty religious practice gives folks what they want. Remember, even if it's spiritual flesh, it's still flesh. It is not uncommon to see churches who are enduring an arbitrary split between "traditional" worship and "contemporary" worship. So called "worship wars" have raged within the church, leaving casualties of burden-bearing believers feeling betrayed and abandoned. What we must see is that anything that causes the body of Christ to be wounded and ultimately divided can't be of Christ. Instead of asking what people want, should not we be asking what it is that God wants? After all, it is His church. Dr. Paige Patterson, President of Southwestern Baptist Theological Seminary made the point in a recent chapel message: "The Bible speaks of making melody in our hearts to God. Music is a critical and crucial component of worship, but the lyrics are more important, by far than the music. The participation of the whole congregation is the most important expression of musical worship."[1] You see, there are very powerful evil spirits assigned to music. Yes, and especially to religious music. Their assignment (among others) is to keep our attention on ourselves and away from our great and loving God. You see, it's O.K. with Satan if we worship—just so long as our worship is diverted away from the only One and True God who is worthy of worship...the Lord Jesus Christ.

• **False Religious System of Prayer**—(See Chapter 10, The Prayers God Answers, pg. 232.) How often have prayer meetings been held only for the purpose of telling God what we want Him to do without any consideration of the desires of His heart? So called "prayer meetings" are held where all that is done is talking without listening to God. The greatest prayer work accomplished in the Heavens is through listening and cooperating with Holy Spirit. After all isn't that what prayer is all about? Jesus said, "Pray, then, in this way:

"Our Father who art in heaven, Hallowed be Thy name. Thy

kingdom come. Thy will be done, on earth as it is in heaven (Matt 6:9-10)."

• **False Religious System of Preaching**—Those of us who are preachers delight in the sermon presentation of the gifted preacher. Some years ago my family was blessed to have for our preacher one whom some said was the greatest preacher in our lifetime in the State of Texas. People would marvel with great amazement at the ability of this gifted preacher. His sermons were brilliantly crafted. His presentation was polished and powerfully delivered. When he preached, it sounded like a brilliantly crafted manuscript. People would come from all around to hear this man preach. He was often the most requested and admired preacher at the State convocations of churches and church leaders. Even the late W.A. Criswell said of this amazing preacher, "To this day, I still believe he is the best preacher you'll ever hear."[2] There was only one problem. He was living a double life. Because of his lack of spiritual discipline, this preacher lost his marriage and his renowned position in shame. His preaching power was not Holy Spirit power. His gift was no doubt given by God, but the power in which the sermons were delivered was void of the power of the Holy Spirit. Notice in contrast, how the Apostle Paul refers to his preaching ministry:

"And my message and my preaching were not in persuasive words of wisdom, but in demonstration of the Spirit and of power, that your faith should not rest on the wisdom of men, but on the power of God (1 Cor. 2:4-5)."

Too often we settle for the *image* of preaching rather the manifest *power* of God in and through the life of the preacher. Why wouldn't Satan work with our spiritual flesh to keep us from experiencing the authentic work of God?

• **False Religious System of Compliance and Compromise for the sake of Unity**—Today we see a spiritually sick and compromised church as a result of an epidemic of placating our fleshly desires. How often have the folks in the church compromised the purposes of God so as to not offend anyone? I call it a "Rodney King Religion." One that says, "Can't we just get along?" NO! We must never try to "just get along" at the expense of the work of Christ. We must decide. Are we going to please men, or please God?

> *"For am I now seeking the favor of men, or of God? Or am I striving to please men? If I were still trying to please men, I would not be a bondservant of Christ (Gal. 1:10)." But Peter and the apostles answered and said, "We must obey God rather than men (Acts 5:29)."*

At the instant the thought of compromise arises a red flag of danger ought to rise within our spirit. Through accommodation and compromise of the work of the Spirit of God in and through the church, the Enemy so often accomplishes his murderous work.

False Religious System of Giving—Many times it seems, the motivation for giving is nothing more than to ease our pain for one more week, or season. The offering plates are passed as a regular ritual at the same time during the church service—to which we are so familiar. Many believers have succumbed to the notion that since they are giving their offerings to the Lord then they are no longer responsible for the misuse of those funds by the carnal leaders of the church. We are responsible to Christ to plant our spiritual seed into the good soil.

New Testament giving is an act of obedience and sacrifice to God. Satan doesn't care how much we give as long as we don't give it to the Lord. When we give to the Lord as He directs us, our gifts pass from this earthly kingdom into the hands of God, where they then are blessed and set a part for the purposes of Heaven. Once our gifts are blessed by the hands of God they become an instrument for the supernatural work of God *(Luke 9:13-17)*. Many churches build magnificent buildings so it will look like spiritual things are happening, when in fact, nothing of Heaven is really happening. These edifices so often become monuments to our filthy spiritual, and religious flesh.

• **False Religious System of Leadership**—Anyone who stands between you and your relationship with Christ is a false religious leader. No one has any more of Christ in them than you do, as a child of God. Today's religious power brokers crave the large congregations (and with them, the large salaries), the biggest ads in the papers, the prominent names on the church marquees. They make sure that people "tow the line" and obey the leadership, no matter what. If criticized, they are quick to rebuke others for "touching the Lord's anointed" (which, by the way, referred in the Old Testament to a government leader—a king—not a religious leader!).[3]

As one reads the accounts of the survivors of the 1978 Jonestown Massacre, it is clear they never believed that to follow their religious leader Jim Jones would have led to the untimely death of over 900 of their family members and friends. In the early days of People's Temple Phil Kerns writes, "Jones was a man who loved people. He was a man who cared about justice. He was a man who talked about faith and hope. It was all exhausting and quite bizarre, but a lot of good could come out of it. Certainly there could be no harm."[4] Through the sacrifice of Christ every believer now has direct access to God. The veil of the temple into the Holy of Holies has been torn by God *(Matt. 27:51)*. Through the sacrifice of Christ every believer has now been given direct access to God. Leadership is important, but we must never allow those in leadership to take the place of Christ. All clergy as well as laity alike, are under the lordship of Christ. He is Lord! When leadership speaks for Christ it must always be tested by Scripture. We must never allow anyone to take the ruling place of our lives except The Lord Jesus Christ. When we do, demons go to work.

It must also be noted that God's Name must never be used to justify our personal, ambitious agendas. To attribute the works of our flesh to the work of Christ is to use God's Name in vain. This is an extremely dangerous practice and is forbidden by God in *Deut. 5:11*. We are walking into dangerous territory when we say that God is at work when, in reality, we may be using the work of the church as a platform for our own self-centered, religious works. Even if the works of our religious flesh (the writer of Hebrews calls *dead works—Hebrews 9:14*) are dressed up in a traditional religious counterfeit cloak, they are still nothing more than lifeless works which the Holy Spirit will not use. However, the Enemy of our souls exploits every dead work to advance his own kingdom's work to steal, kill, and destroy.

CHRISTIAN MATERIALISM

Much of the Christian world in America has been seduced by one of a strategically crafted deception of the Evil One called Christian Materialism. This deception is a compromised religious system that leaves the believer powerless in the supernatural war with the powers of darkness. It is an attempt to give religious justification to our selfish desires to possess and then use those possessions for the purpose of illicit personal power and control. Christian Materialism is a toxic brew of worldly philosophies and practices mixed with religious traditions and Christian-like verbiage, purposely crafted to make it acceptable to its vulnerable carnal target. It is a carefully crafted cover for the invasion of a false god called Mammon. This chief demon seeks to bring us into spiritual bondage through the offering of this alluring false religious system as a substitute for our worship of the Lord Jesus Christ. As in any false religious system, Christian Materialism looks good, it sounds good, and of course, it feels good. Tragically, however, when it's covering of religious traditions and ecclesiastical rituals are removed, we find a deadly demonic scheme whose purpose is to steal, kill, and destroy. The only way to clearly recognize the Enemy's deceptions is to measure them against the truth God has revealed to us in His Word.

One of the false tenets of Christian Materialism is ***God wants you to have money; therefore the possession of money is a sign of God's favor and blessing.*** Of course, money may be an indicator of God's blessings, but not always. Why would God, who is wise and good, give riches to someone who was not spiritually mature enough to honor Him with those riches? *(Luke 16:10-13)* We can observe the influence of this false religious system in many church practices. One such practice is the choosing of leaders based on their worldly possessions. The Bible warns us about this dangerous practice. Jesus said, in *Matt. 23:10-12*:

> *And do not be called leaders; for One is your Leader, that is Christ. But the greatest among you shall be your servant. And whoever exalts himself shall be humbled; and whoever humbles himself shall be exalted.*

Instead of looking to those who might help finance our selfish agendas, we should be looking—first and foremost—to those whose lives manifest the Spirit of Christ with a humble servant's heart for positions of leadership. Jesus said of Himself, *"...the Son of Man did not come to be served, but to serve (Matt. 20:28),..."*

Many a pastor's spiritual integrity has been compromised because he has embraced—at some level—the crafty deception of Christian Materialism. Instead of shepherds, Jesus calls them hirelings *(John 10:12-13)*. Does not the stark contrast of the scriptural record speak clearly of the incompatibility between true Christianity and materialism? There is a constant warning throughout the Bible concerning putting our trust in riches for temporal and selfish purposes *(Prov. 30:8, Matt. 6:21, James 5:1-6)*. Jesus called riches deceitful *(Matt. 13:22)*. We must always be reminded that the one we call the "rich young ruler" wanted eternal life but never received it because He could not obey the Lord with regard to his great riches *(Luke 18:18-25)*. The Christ of Calvary we have decided to follow was a man of virtually no worldly possessions. Jesus had no place to lay His head *(Matt. 8:20)*. He was buried in a borrowed tomb. He said of His ministry that the Spirit of God had anointed Him to preach the gospel to the poor *(Luke 4:18)*. Peter had neither silver nor gold *(Acts 3:6)*. Paul, as an itinerant evangelist, lived in places he did not own. Today, he might even be considered homeless. By the standards of Christian Materialism, Christ, Peter and Paul all would be disqualified for leadership in many churches today.

The Bible also gives a clear warning concerning such prejudice with regard to the favoring of the wealthy over the poor in the church *(James 2:1-5)*. Just as a counterfeit dollar is rarely recognized except by those familiar with the authentic bill, this counterfeit religious system of the Enemy can only be exposed through the authentic truth of God's Word. It is also critically important to ask, "Where does the money come from?" Some chosen for leadership in the church today have and are receiving their riches by disregarding and disobeying God's Word. In Christian Materialism, the end justifies the means. It doesn't matter how you get money. Since "God is all about you having money," just get it. Selfish gambling practices, crooked and corrupt business deals, and some have even received their wealth through the sorrow and pain of the neglected and vulnerable *(2 Tim. 3:6-9)*. Even in the face of the teaching of Scripture concerning the prohibition of usury practices among those in the family of God *(Deut. 23:19-20)*, many churches have chosen their leaders among the ranks of the scripturally disobedient. You see, if the money (or anything else we possess) has been received from a wicked or ungodly source or through the disobeying and disregarding of God's Word *(2 Tim. 3:6-9, Deut. 23:19-20)*, it may have unholy and demonic attachments to it for the purpose of stealing God's glory. In such cases, it must be spiritually cleaned up through prayer and repentance while dedicating it to the glory of the Lord Jesus Christ alone, or it may need to be discarded *(2 Cor. 6:14-18, Acts 19:18-19)*.

Another false tenet of Christian Materialism is **prosperity is the result of the abundance of money and worldly possessions**. "Dr. Randall," you ask, "Don't the Scriptures teach prosperity?" Of course, they do! In *3rd John verse 2* we read: *"Beloved, I pray that in all respects you may prosper and be in good health, just as your soul prospers."* Here is the problem. We have allowed our worldly environment, instead of Scripture, to falsely define prosperity. There are eleven words in the Bible that are translated prosper or prosperity. Not one, that's right, not one is necessarily related to money. These words given to us by the Holy Spirit translated <u>prosperity</u> mean <u>to go on well without hindrance</u>. Prosperity means to go in peace.

You may be thinking, "Are you saying that money is evil?" Absolutely not! It is not money that is evil. **For the love—the worship of money** *is a root of all kinds of evil, and some by longing for it have* *wandered away from the faith, and pierced themselves with many a pang (1 Tim. 6:10).* The question is not whether we do or do not possess money. The question is better asked, "Does money possess us?" What is our attitude, the condition of our heart, concerning money? Some of the most selfish people I have ever known were those without money. On the other hand, some of the most spiritually poor people I have ever known had great worldly wealth. On the other hand, some of the most spiritually rich people I have ever known had great wealth. Because of their commitment to Christ, their wealth could not possess them. Is it the desire of your heart to honor the Lord Jesus in the handling of whatever He has given you? If not, there is a spiritual rat in the wood pile.

And whatever you do in word or deed, do all in the name of the Lord Jesus, giving thanks through Him to God the Father (Col. 3:17).

True Christian stewardship comes down to ownership and gratitude. It is Christ who is Lord of ALL *(John 3:31, Eph. 1:20-22, Phil. 2:9-11).* Everything belongs to Him. *The earth is the Lord's and all it contains, the world, and those who dwell in it (Psalm 24:1).* He is Jehovah Jireh—Our Provider. He is the God of our provision. It is His nature to provide for His own *(Matt. 7:9-11, Phil. 4:19).*

Blessed be the God and Father of our Lord Jesus Christ, who has blessed us with every spiritual blessing in the heavenly places in Christ (Eph. 1:3).

In *James 1:17* we are told:

Every good thing bestowed and every perfect gift is from above, coming down from the Father of lights, with whom there is no variation, or shifting shadow.

As the Heavenly Father allows us to share in His provision, it is to be used in gratitude and glory to Him. Do you see it? ALL THINGS exist for God's glory alone *(Col. 1:16).* When we allow anything or anyone other than our Lord Jesus Christ to receive the glory for what He has done and for which He alone deserves, we become accomplices in Satan's rebellion. Here is what all of us must face hopefully sooner rather than later. We can't have it both ways. No matter what we have been taught through the false religious system of Christian Materialism, no one has ever been or will ever be able to serve God and Mammon— Riches *(Matt. 6:24)*. When the two are bundled together by the strands of false religious practices, the result becomes a convoluted contaminated counterfeit used by the Enemy.

We're not off the hook just because Christian Materialism is a crafty deception. Each of us must look carefully at any area where we might have believed the lies of the Enemy rather than the truth of God's Word. Our very freedom in Christ is at stake. No matter how many times we say it or how hard our flesh wants to believe it, God will not contradict His Word. Remember, all the Enemy needs to invade the church and bring his evil corruption upon her is our disobedience to the Word of God. In the practice of Christian Materialism, one will discover an absence of the manifestation of God's power, which always results in spiritual defeat. To renounce all the workings of the powers of darkness within your life as a result of any involvement in Christian Materialism and to receive God's cleansing see: Renunciation of Mammon, Chapter 10, pg. 266.

LEGALISM

It is impossible to do a study on the subject of religious counterfeits without addressing the damnable practice of legalism. Though the law of God is "holy and righteous and good" *(Romans 7:12)*, trying to keep it in order to be accepted by God is unholy, unrighteous, and leads to destruction. Man was never designed- nor expected- to keep God's commandments on his own, nor was strict adherence to law ever God's way of making man righteous. It has always been by faith.[5] Nothing gets my blood boiling faster than seeing those in the church that are functioning under the demonic religious system of legalism. Do spiritual rulers (demonic powers, *Eph. 6:12*) have a hand in designing, developing, and defending legalistic systems? *In Colossians 2:15-22* the Apostle Paul makes it abundantly clear that they do:[6]

When He had disarmed the rulers and authorities, He made a public display of them, having triumphed over them through Him. Therefore let no one act as your judge in regard to food or drink or in respect to a festival or a new moon or a Sabbath day— things which are a mere shadow of what is to come; but the substance belongs to Christ. Let no one keep defrauding you of your prize by delighting in self-abasement and the worship of the angels, taking his stand on visions he has seen, inflated without cause by his fleshly mind, and not holding fast to the head, from whom the entire body, being supplied and held together by the joints and ligaments, grows with a growth which is from God. If you have died with Christ to the elementary principles of the world, why, as if you were living in the world, do you submit yourself to decrees, such as, "Do not handle, do not taste, do not touch!" (which all refer to things destined to perish with the using)—in accordance with the commandments and teachings of men (Col. 2:15-22)?

There may be no more deceptive demonic scheme of the Enemy than legalism. Obeying Christ is not legalism. Trusting the Word of God is not legalism. True Christianity must not ever be confused with legalism. Legalism is the attempt by man to set up his own "moral" standards to gain the approval of men, or of God. The approval of God is only gained through what Jesus did for us on Calvary. That's why legalism is such an attack on the gospel. Legalism sets up its own laws only to focus on the keeping (or not keeping) of those laws. No matter what laws man sets up for himself, he can in return break those laws. Legalism always fosters rebellion, as it leads to spiritual bondage. In *Jeremiah 17:5*, God pronounces His curse on the sin of legalism, like so many other sins at work in many sections of the church:

Thus says the LORD, "Cursed is the man who trusts in mankind and makes flesh his strength, and whose heart turns away from the LORD (Jeremiah 17:5)."

In this context—as in many other passages of Scripture—the word flesh does not denote the physical body. Rather it denotes the nature each of us has received by inheritance from our common ancestor, Adam. Adam did not beget any children until he himself had transgressed God's commandment. The essential motivation of his transgression was not so much the desire to do evil, as the desire to be independent of God. This desire is at work in every one of Adam's descendents. It is the distinctive mark of the "flesh." In the field of religion, it seeks to perform religious acts without depending on the supernatural grace of God.[7]

It has been my privilege as an evangelist to hold chapel services in many Christian schools. At the end of my message, as has always been my practice, I give a public invitation for the students to come and publicly confess their faith in Christ. On several occasions, the response has been overwhelming. In one such school in the Houston area, over half of the students in the school gave their hearts to Christ. Several of the teachers were stunned as they came to me privately and asked, "Why do you think so many of the students are just now giving their lives to Christ as their Savior?" I told them just because we teach our children creationism, or just because we make them memorize Bible verses, these things—although important—do not necessarily help them know Christ as Savior. Just because we make them cut their hair and wear dresses over their knees (or whatever other religious rules are imposed upon them), none of these necessarily represents Christ's love for our children. In fact, the message that many of them receive is a counterfeit that pushes many of them away from Christ.

Christianity is not a way of life based upon not smoking, not drinking, not carousing, not cursing and the like. If it is, then a man that doesn't do these things can think he's pretty good. Sin is not an issue of breaking man's rules. Sin is a matter of breaking God's laws. If the Christian life were based upon our deeds—good or bad—then a man could conclude: "As long as I provide for my family, as long as I am faithful to my wife, as long as I do my best, God will be pleased with me." As logical as this thinking may seem, the Bible tells us something much different:

All our righteousness is like filthy rags (Isaiah 64:6, KJV).

There is none righteous, no not one (Romans 3:10, KJV).

Please, don't misunderstand me. I am not a proponent of antinomianism. That is, against all law. Some say, "Now you are saved, anything goes." As a result of this way of thinking, God's grace becomes a license for all kinds of disobedience. Please understand, Jesus did not come to abolish the law, but to fulfill it *(Matt. 5:17).*

What shall we say then? Are we to continue in sin that grace might increase? May it never be! How shall we who died to sin still live in it (Romans 6:1-2)?

It is not the rules that keep us doing the right thing. It is our daily walk with Holy God. It is our daily dying to our old sinful flesh and its desires that enables us to live holy and righteous lives. It is in Christ alone that the law of God has been fulfilled. It is only in the new birth, through this new relationship with the Holy Spirit, that the Christian is able to "live out" God's will. God's will is not done by meeting so-called standards set up by men in the Name of Christ. No matter how we set up rules by which to live, only the righteousness of Christ in us and through us can bring true Christianity. Legalism is <u>NOT</u> Christianity! The authority, as we shall see, has been set in the heavens. Sin is an attitude of challenging the one true authority, God's Word, not the breaking of man-made rules.

THE LAW OF GOD vs. THE LOVE OF GOD

When one lives by law, absent of the love and grace of God, untold damage is done to the body of Christ and our witness to the world. Look with me at *Gal. 2:16-3:28.* In the church at Galatia there were those who came into the church after the Apostle Paul had preached the Gospel of Christ. These false preachers taught that the work of Christ was not sufficient for salvation. They taught that religious traditions and rituals were also necessary to follow to receive God's salvation. The Apostle Paul was livid. The most piercing response to false religion in the New Testament other than Christ's is recorded in Paul's letter to the church in Galatia:

> *I am amazed that you are so quickly deserting Him who called you by the grace of Christ, for a different gospel; which is really not another; only there are some who are disturbing you, and want to distort the gospel of Christ. But even though we, or an angel from heaven, should preach to you a gospel contrary to that which we have preached to you, let him be accursed (Gal. 1:6-8).*

When one speaks of the Law we mean the conditions, requirements, or standards that must be met to gain the approval of man, or God. The Pentateuch, or the first five books of the Old Testament, are referred to as the books of the law. In them we find the rules or conditions set by God for His people. "If we do thus and such, then we will be blessed. If we don't, certain consequences will follow." More specifically, the Ten Commandments are referred to as the Law of God. You may be wondering, "If we do not have to DO or KEEP the law to find favor and grace with God, then why was the Law given? Was it given as an encouragement to the people of God? Was the law given as a suggested way to live better with all mankind?" NO, not at all! The Law was given to show God's people that they were sinners. It was provided like a mirror (*Rom. 3:20*), in which we would be able to see that in our sin we are not capable of living up to God's perfect standard, His LAW. In it we see our sinful condition. Therefore, the Law of God was given to show us that in and of ourselves, no matter how hard we try, we would never be able to meet God's standards. Dear Friend, if we are incapable of meeting God's laws, then we are surely unable to gain His approval. That is why Jesus came to die for you and me. He died for us—while we were still in our sins (*Romans 5:8*), because He loves us *(John 15:13)*. The law of God was fulfilled by the love of God:

> *He who knew no sin, became sin for us, that we might become the righteousness of God in Him (2 Cor. 5:21).*

In dying for our sins, Jesus fulfilled God's law. All of God's requirements, standards and conditions were met in Him. Therefore, when any one of us puts our <u>faith</u> in Christ, we become <u>in Christ</u>. He clothes us in <u>His</u> righteousness. Not by our works, but through the work of Christ now that we are in Him, we can fulfill God's perfect law *(Eph. 2:8-9)*. Here's where the problem of religious legalism creeps into our hearts, minds, and ultimately into God's church. It is in the thinking that we want to be saved by grace, and yet continue to live by the law. When someone has fallen short of our expectations we struggle and find it hard, sometimes impossible, to forgive them. When someone has hurt us, we desire (sometimes, demand) judgment for what they have done (See Chapter 9). When we fail, it is often times too difficult to forgive ourselves. We want to receive the love and forgiveness of God, but so often we don't want to give that same love and forgiveness to others. You see we claim salvation by grace, but so very often, we demand a religious lifestyle that must be acceptable by the law.

THE DANGERS OF LIVING BY THE LAW

- LIVING BY THE LAW FRUSTRATES THE GRACE OF GOD

The Purpose of God. What is the purpose of God? **Salvation!** To redeem and restore everything the Enemy has stolen:

> *I do not nullify the grace of God; for if righteousness comes through the Law, then Christ died needlessly (Gal. 2:21).*

Look with me carefully at the words of the Apostle Paul. We find him addressing the church of Galatia concerning the danger of living by the law:

> *For as many as are of the works of the Law are under a curse; for it is written, 'CURSED IS EVERYONE WHO DOES NOT ABIDE BY ALL THINGS WRITTEN IN THE BOOK OF THE LAW, TO PERFORM THEM (Gal. 3:10).'*

If man tries to earn his salvation through abiding by the law and doing good works, he will end up with no salvation at all. Dear Friend, please understand if even ONE man can earn his salvation through his own good deeds and keeping of God's laws, then the horrendous death of Christ was needless and His Father would owe Him a great divine apology.

• LIVING BY THE LAW FALSIFIES THE PROMISES OF GOD
The Promise of the Spirit of God. The work of God is only done through the power of the Holy Spirit: (See Chapter 5.)

> *...in order that in Christ Jesus the blessing of Abraham might come to the Gentiles, so that we might receive the promise of the Spirit through faith (Gal. 3:14).*

If we can do this on our own; if we can live the Christian life in our own ability in keeping the law, then there is no reason for the Holy Spirit.

The Promise of the inheritance of God. Our inheritance in Christ is a gift that cannot be earned through keeping the law:

> *For if the inheritance is based on law, it is no longer based on a promise; but God has granted it to Abraham by means of a promise (Gal. 3:18).*

We, who are in Christ, are joint-heirs with Christ. Everything that the Heavenly Father has given Jesus is the legal inheritance of every believer. Victory over sin, a home in Heaven, victory over devils, a new way of living in the resurrection power of Christ, everything Christ has been given has been given to every believer. If God's work in our lives is based solely upon our ability to keep the law then the Scripture is not true when it says:

> *But the Scripture has shut up all men under sin, that the promise by faith in Jesus Christ might be given to those who believe (Gal. 3:22).*

• LIVING BY THE LAW FRAGMENTS THE PEOPLE OF GOD
  (Galatians 3:28)

Trying to be righteous by living by the law only fragments the people of God. It creates a division between a class of so-called "super Christians" who begin to think they are better than others, and everyone else. They are deceived and develop a pious belief system from which they operate, one that arrogantly proclaims: "since we abide by the law, our 'stuff' doesn't stink. Even though you are my brother in Christ, you cannot possibly be as 'good' as we are. Why, we don't do 'this and that'; we always do 'this and that', and we always do it 'just this way.' Which, we might add is 'THE RIGHT WAY.' To do 'this and that' 'YOUR WAY'...well, 'it is just SINFUL.'" The truth is man knows he is a sinner and needs a Savior. If and when, he goes to church and hears a distorted message of living by the law, he will leave disappointed and often times angry. How many times have you and I heard this sad statement? "The folks at that church think they're better than everyone else. I don't need that." The world knows that they are condemned by their sin. The Bible says no one will ever be able to point an accusing finger in God's face and say, "I just didn't understand:"

> *For the wrath of God is revealed from heaven against all ungodliness and unrighteousness of men, who suppress the truth in unrighteousness, because that which is known about God is evident within them; for God made it evident to them. For since the creation of the world His invisible attributes, His eternal power and divine nature, have been clearly seen, being understood through what has been made, so that they are without excuse (Romans 1:18-20).*

When the lost sinner finally darkens the doors of a "gospel preaching" church, he wants to hear a message of hope in an atmosphere of love and hope. Hope for him in his sin; hope for a home hereafter and a life of freedom here and now. He does not want to drag himself to a place that is supposed to provide love and hope and find a cauldron for hatred and judgment.

WHY BELIEVERS ACCEPT RELIGIOUS COUNTERFEITS

• **Sadly, it is all that most believers have ever known**—Change in our lives, however necessary it may be- is <u>always</u> uncomfortable. Freedom in Christ is often tragically unfamiliar and unknown territory. Beth Moore says it well, "I believe the church suffers from a strength-sapping case of unbelief; but we've had the ailment so long, we don't know how good authentic belief feels."[8] One of my dear counselor friends put it this way, "Getting free is easy. Staying free is the hard part." Why? Because we have to walk in the freedom of Christ. Freedom will always take us into the places we have rarely, if ever known. For many, the demonic religious counterfeit carries a weird comfort. Sadly, it is all they have ever known.

• **The Demonic Religious Counterfeit enables us to keep our secrets, secret**—Satan will offer you anything just so you won't decide to live a life in truth. The truth of God has the power to set the captives free *(John 8:32)*. The demonic religious counterfeit cries out to the flesh, "Don't come clean. You don't have to confess. Act like everything is O.K. What was done in secret must stay in secret. Everyone has problems. Just go to church and keep doing what you're doing." (See Chapter 4.)

• **It exalts our flesh and its accomplishments**—The demonic religious counterfeit not only appeals to our flesh, but it also allows the exaltation of our flesh. Remember, Friend, Satan doesn't care who is worshiped just so long as we do not worship the Lord Jesus Christ. In the demonic religious counterfeit there's not only room for self-praise and self-worship, it's encouraged.

• **The Demonic Religious Counterfeit allows life without the Cross**—(See Chapter 5.) The cross is what you die on. The cross is the place of death. Jesus said if anyone would choose to follow Him, they would have to take up their cross daily *(Luke 9:23)*. Our flesh hates the idea of dying. So often we choose the religious counterfeit, because it offers a life without sacrifice. The religious life, on the other hand, is life without the Cross of Christ. Since Christ is life, life without His sacrifice on the Cross for our sin always leads to destruction and death.

• **Religion allows us to stay in control**—Oh, how we want to stay in control! Jesus said, *"For whoever wishes to save his life shall lose it; but whoever loses his life for My sake shall find it (Matt 16:25)."* In the insecurity of the flesh man will always fight to stay in control. Our fear of losing control may be one of the greatest tools of the Enemy to keep us in spiritual bondage. Dear Friend, Jesus is Lord! A man cannot serve two masters *(Matt. 6:24)*. The demonic counterfeit religion tricks us into believing that we are in control. Please understand, if we stay in control of our lives, then Jesus is NOT. If we are in control—no matter what our religious tradition allows—we are living a life of sin and disobedience.

• **It's hard to admit we've been wrong**—Genuine humility is the most difficult thing for the flesh to obtain. Without it, you and I will never see God. Humility is not an option, if we are to walk with God:

> *But He gives a greater grace. Therefore it says, "GOD IS OPPOSED TO THE PROUD, BUT GIVES GRACE TO THE HUMBLE." Submit therefore to God. Resist the devil and he will flee from you. Draw near to God and He will draw near to you. Cleanse your hands, you sinners; and purify your hearts, you double-minded. Be miserable and mourn and weep; let your laughter be turned into mourning, and your joy to gloom. Humble yourselves in the presence of the Lord, and He will exalt you (James 4:6-10).*

Humility is not what God does for us. We are in charge of our hearts. So many believers remain in bondage simply because they refuse to humble themselves, admit they have been wrong, and surrender to God.

NO! Just getting back in church will not fix what is broken in your life. Only Jesus can heal your wounds. He is Jehovah Rapha—the God who heals. I want to say again, I'm not opposed to the local church. I've given my life to serve Christ through the church. But what we all must face is this truth from the Scripture—the local church must never become a substitute for the working of Christ in your life. The local church must never be allowed to become a substitute for the precious presence of Christ. Reject the lie that anything can heal you but Jesus. Reject the voice that would say, "I just need to get back in church." You may need to go to church, but the church will never have the power to heal your wounds. Only Christ Jesus can heal your wounds. The church can't bring you to God. Only faith in Christ can bring you into the presence of God. The church might make you feel better for a little while, but it does not have the power to save, to heal, or to deliver you from bondage. Only Jesus can save, heal, and deliver. Please don't be passive and allow the church to become a substitute for your walk and intimacy with the living Lord Jesus. I know of no more hideous demonic trick than to lead someone into believing that going to church will fix what is broken in their lives. Yes, you may need to go to church. You will not find what you need by merely going to church. It is through the ministry of Christ, you will find your needs will be met.

Would you join me today in a time of prayer as we confess our sin of cooperating with any false demonic religious system? Let's call it what it is. It is sin. We must repent of any and all involvement. Won't you do that right now!

Prayer of Cleansing from Demonic Religious Counterfeits
(I John 5:20-21, Matthew. 4:10, Exodus 20:3,
Matthew 22:37, Rev. 2:4-5, Deut. 5:7-8)

Dear Lord God, Please show me any place or any time in my life when I have sought after religion instead of You to meet my needs. I have allowed my religious traditions to be more important than You. I am so sorry I have offended You and Your Word when You so clearly said that I "shall have no other gods" before You. I confess to You that I have not loved You with all my heart and soul and mind. Because I have sinned against You, and violated the first and greatest commandment, I repent and turn away from seeking comfort in religion and now choose to return to You, and You ONLY, Lord Jesus, as my first love. Please forgive me for not trusting and loving You.

Please forgive me for going through the motions of worship without submitting my heart to You. Please forgive me for not cooperating with You to be used of Your Spirit in worship and ministry. I repent of ever accepting the counterfeit of religion in the place of Your work in and through my life. I repent for not believing Your Word as true for today. I renounce each way I have cooperated with the lies of the Enemy; and, in so doing I cancel out any and all ground Satan may have gained in my life. In the Name of the true and living God, the Lord Jesus Christ, I renounce my worship of any and all false gods of religion.

Please forgive me when I have sought my answers except from Your truth, I have sinned against You. Please forgive me for believing Satan's lies. I choose to worship only You, Lord. I ask You, Father, to enable me to keep my going to church in its proper place in my life. I choose to seek first the kingdom of God and Your righteousness. You and You alone are Lord. There is one Lord! You are He! I call on You, Lord Jesus, to come and set this captive one free.

Thank You that You have come to destroy the works of the Devil in my life. All cover spirits will come to attention and be removed by the finger of God. I ask You Lord Jesus by Your blood, by Your Spirit and according to Your Word, to cut all the demonic ties at every level. All demons under the assignments of Baal must come to attention in the presence of the Lord Jesus. I put all demonic assignments in the circle of the blood of Jesus Christ and declare them null and void. I ask that all assignments and evil spirits sent by Your Enemy would be cast out of my life. There will be no manifestations except the manifestation of the Holy Spirit. You will not separate. You will not divide. You will not get reinforcements. You must face the judgment of the Lord Jesus Christ both now and eternal judgment. I bind every spirit under the assignments of Baal with the three-fold cord that cannot be broken in the Name of the Father, Son, and Holy Spirit. You must go where Jesus tells you to go, when Jesus tells you to go. Thank You, Jesus, for my victory in You. Thank You, for Your wonderful work in my life for Your greatest glory! Amen.

CHRISTIANS CAN'T HAVE DEMONS.

A most effective, but dangerous lie of the Enemy so often heard and implied in our religious culture is "CHRISTIANS CAN'T HAVE DEMONS." In many church traditions, it has been assumed, if not openly taught, that if a person has a demon he must not be saved. Hastily, the conclusion is drawn that Christians can't have demons. To presuppose that Christians can't have demons is not only to ignore the teaching of Scripture, but it leaves the believer helpless and vulnerable to the attacks of the Enemy. Whatever we have been taught, or have chosen to believe must pass the test of a careful study of the Word of God. The presumption of automatic safety from demonic powers based upon our salvation is simply not biblical. Although we may be saved, we are not automatically safe.

It's amazing how the subject of Christians and their relationship to the darkness becomes a point of contention within the church. It would seem to me that, if there was ever an area where we would work toward a biblical agreement, it would be this one. The Enemy knows if we stay in the area of argument and division, we will not look for the truth that sets people free. So the reality is this, instead of studying for the sake of truth, we draw our self-centered conclusions and wrap them up in our "spiritual platitudes" and scurry to the nearest place of so-called personal safety. Paralyzed by our willing ignorance, we are unable to help those around us—those we love, and those who remain in spiritual bondage. Although the issue of the Christian and demonic activity is a hot button, we can't afford to ignore it, nor can we retreat to the safety of the standard answers. It is interesting to note that man has an innate fear of demons. We may speak of the Devil or Satan regularly; however, when one mentions demons, fear begins to enter the conversation. Many believers have adopted the fallacious idea that if they ignore Satan and his strategies, he will ignore them. Scripturally, such a position is indefensible.[1] Remember, Paul says, *"in order that no advantage be taken of us by Satan; for we are not ignorant of his schemes (2 Cor. 2:11)."* Paul may not have been ignorant of Satan's schemes, but I must admit, I was. I simply had not studied the matter biblically.

In facing the real horrifying possibility of buying a casket to bury our son, it became evident that the spiritual pit into which he had fallen was not completely of his own doing. If it had been, he could have delivered himself out of the demonic darkness that had overcome him. As his father, I needed to discover what was going on that had caused my son to come to this dangerous place of hopelessness and despair. Although I knew the struggle was spiritual, I had no idea how it could be that demons could have been assigned to my family. Like so many, I had concluded that Christians can't have demons. I believed that we as believers could be harassed and hindered at times, but my theological training had no place for the concept that a believer in Christ could in fact have demons.

Out of necessity to dig for the truth, I went out and bought a new Bible. I told the Lord that He would have to be my guide into all truth as He promised in *John 16:13*. With a red highlighter, I marked every passage in the New Testament that had any reference to the supernatural battle with the powers of darkness. When I was finished, I was amazed! I had a red Bible! Passage after passage, page after page, Scripture verse after Scripture verse, there it was. The New Testament is the story of God's great victory in Christ over the supernatural dark world of sin and Satan.

THE NEW TESTAMENT WORLDVIEW

• In the Gospels—*Matthew*, *Mark*, *Luke* and *John*—we see Jesus revealed as the Son of God. He declared His deity through supernatural encounters of performing miracles and confronting demonic powers.

• In the book of *Acts* is the record of the church. So filled with Holy Spirit power were the early saints that they were constantly confronting their pagan culture through supernatural power encounters with the powers of darkness.

• The wonderful book of *Romans* explains how this new life in Christ is offered to everyone who will receive Christ as Savior. Through submission to the supernatural power of God this new life in Christ offers freedom from sin and its destructive consequences.

• In the letters to the Church in Corinth we find the dangerous results of cooperating with the supernatural world without spiritual discipline.

• In the book of *Galatians* we have a clear condemnation of both the message and its messenger who would attempt to add human effort to the supernatural salvation of Christ.

• In *Ephesians* we are provided understanding about the rights of every believer to cooperate with the supernatural authority and power of God in Christ to dispose of supernatural powers of darkness.

• In the book of *Philippians* we find the supernatural picture of how Christ's Name is above all other names in power and authority. In the ages to come every knee will ultimately bow to Him as Lord.

• In the letter to the Church at Colossae we discover how God supernaturally has delivered everyone who believes in Christ as their Savior

from the supernatural Kingdom of Darkness into the supernatural Kingdom of God's beloved Son.

• In *First* and *Second Thessalonians* we have the record of how Satan
supernaturally hindered the work of the Apostles. We see the promise of how one day Jesus is supernaturally coming for every believer
in Christ. Until the coming of Christ for His church, the supernatural
power of Satan and his Anti-Christ is at work in our world.

• In the letters from Paul to his son in the ministry, Timothy, we have
the clear warning concerning the supernatural teachings of demons that
are believed by those who are not spiritually vigilant. We also find in
Timothy the sad reality of the deceived who hold to a form of godliness,
but all the while denying its supernatural power.

• In the little books of *Titus* and *Philemon* we discover how leaders,
as well as members, of the church are to live by the supernatural power
of God as we look to the supernatural coming of Christ.

• In the book of *Hebrews* we find how Jesus is the supernatural heir
of all things. How His Name is greater than the supernatural kingdom
of angels, and how the sacrifice of His blood was accepted by God to
supernaturally pay the price for all sin. The writer of *Hebrews* also tells
us that the Word of God is supernaturally able to pierce through the
division of soul, spirit, and body and supernaturally judge the thoughts
and intentions of the heart. He also tells us that faith is a supernatural
act of obedience to the supernatural Word of God.

• In the book of *James* we find the explanation of how the Evil One is
supernaturally involved in temptation that leads us into sin; how we are
to submit to a supernatural God and resist a supernatural Devil.

• In the books of *First* and *Second Peter* we discover how fleshly
lusts supernaturally war against the soul, how we are supernaturally
healed by the wounds of Christ, and how a supernatural Devil and his

evil angels prowl about *like a roaring lion, seeking someone to devour,* is ultimately judged by God and cast into a supernatural hell.

• In the epistles of *First, Second* and *Third John* we discover that light and darkness are in a supernatural conflict and how sin is cooperating with a supernatural Devil. We see the necessity of testing of the supernatural spirits.

• In the book of *Jude* we find how God's judgment is certain against all who rebel against God including the supernatural judgment of the supernatural evil angels, the supernatural judgment of wicked cities, and the supernatural judgment of evil men.

• In the book of The *Revelation* we find an amazing supernatural glimpse into the future of the last great battle between the supernatural forces of darkness and the supernatural power of Almighty God. A time is foretold when the kingdoms of this world will ultimately and supernaturally become the kingdom of our Lord and Savior Jesus Christ.

• God's Word is so clear as to the reality of the spirit world around us. Look carefully with me at these words of the Holy Spirit through the pen of the Apostle Paul:

> *"...while we look not at the things which are seen, but at the things which are not seen; for the things which are seen are temporal, but the things which are not seen are eternal (2 Cor. 4:18)."*

The supernatural world is the real and eternal world. Everything we see, everything we know and experience in our physical world happens as a result of what's going on in the spiritual world. I know this idea of the supernatural world is mostly foreign to our western materialistic worldview. It is however, the teaching of the Bible. We see it in our Lord's Prayer when He taught us to pray:

> *Thy kingdom come, Thy will be done, on earth as it is in Heaven (Matt 6:10).*

Without question the Bible is a supernatural book about our supernatural unseen world. It is impossible to believe what the Scriptures teach without believing in the reality of the supernatural. You see, I was taught to believe the Scriptures, but I was not provided instruction on engaging the powers of darkness by the supernatural power of God. Because of my son's spiritual condition, I found myself in desperate need to find how the teachings of this supernatural Bible could impact the supernatural battle in which we found ourselves.

THE SCHEMES OF THE ENEMY—TO CONTROL

I have come to learn that the schemes of the Enemy to attack and ultimately control the believer are totally different than schemes he uses to control the nonbeliever. While the results of the battle look the same in both—death and destruction—the process, which leads to this horrific end is very different. When it comes to God's people, evil spirits are spirits of influence. That's not true for unbelievers in the world. They're held firmly in Satan's grasp, under his control, blinded in their hearts and minds; utterly dead to spiritual truth until quickened by the Holy Spirit. They're members of his kingdom of darkness *(Ephesians 2:2)*. Conversely, Christians are already "possessed" (owned) by the Holy Spirit, so demonic possession in the sense of ownership is never the issue. The issue then for the believer is the influence the Evil One can exert on us. It becomes problematic for believers when we underestimate the powerful influence Satan can have in the life of any believer.

Only eternity will reveal the number of believers who have led unproductive, frustrated lives of spiritual defeat. All of us can make a long and painful list of those in ministry that have had to forsake their ministries because of attacks of the Enemy. This happens in spite of the very clear New Testament warnings concerning demonic activity—all addressed to believers.

In discussing demonic spiritual warfare on the personal level, Dr. Scott Moreau, Assistant Professor of Missions and Intercultural Studies at Wheaton Graduate School, explains, "One general principle must be noted on the onset: demons can only influence believers to the extent that we allow them to do so. The act of giving or allowing Satan to take any amount of control in our life is referred to as giving ground *(Eph. 4:27).*"[2] Dr. Clinton Arnold, Professor of New Testament Language and Literature and Director of the Master of Theology program at Talbot School of Theology, describes the process and how to resist in this way: "It is likely that any sinful activity that the believer does not deal with by the power of the Holy Spirit can be exploited by the Devil and turned into a means of control over a believer's life. Therefore, Christians need to resist. For Paul there is no middle ground. There's no nominal Christianity. Believers either resist the influence of the Evil One who works through the flesh and the world, or they relinquish control of their lives to the power of darkness. Giving in to those temptations does not just confirm the weakness of the flesh; it opens up the lives of believers to the control of the Devil and his powers. We need to recognize the supernatural nature of temptation and be prepared to face it."[3]

It is critical that we all understand our vulnerability to demonic influence, and acquire an adequate biblical answer for any situation we face. Those who don't understand their vulnerability will likely blame themselves, or God, for their problems. If we blame ourselves, we feel hopeless because we can't do anything to stop what we're doing. If we blame God, our confidence in Him as our benevolent Father is shattered. Either way, we have no chance to gain the victory that the Bible promises us. Then there is the tendency of the church in the Western world to attribute all of Satan's activities to the flesh. This also leaves us with no way to resolve spiritual conflicts.[4]

Whole books have been written on this subject of the relationship between Christians and demons. Let me refer you to a complete work on this subject by C. Fred Dickason entitled *Demon Possession and the Christian*, Crossway Books, Wheaton, Ill., 1987. To come to a consistent biblical view we must study the Scriptures carefully and prayerfully. When I first seriously considered the question of Christians and demonization, I, like so many, could not understand how this could be. Through faulty deductive reasoning I had come to two conclusions that, in my mind, I believed to be theologically correct. Then working from my comfortable conclusions, I worked backwards to prove them.

TRADITIONAL ARGUMENTS

We must resist the temptation to resolve the conflict intellectually without resolving it spiritually and biblically. Spiritual problems demand spiritual answers. Willing ignorance lock many believers in defeat; unknowingly we remain just outside a walk in the victory of our Lord. Ignorance, however comfortable, is not bliss—especially in the battle with the forces of darkness. It's dangerous and can lead us to destruction. My conclusions were the same as many today who reject the possibility that Christians can have a demon. These arguments assert: 1. Demons cannot be in the same place with the Holy Spirit. 2. Once bought by the blood of Jesus, the believer becomes God's own personal possession. Therefore, a Christian cannot be possessed (owned) by any devil. Let's take each one and study the Word of God thoroughly.

Let us take the first argument and carefully look at it: demons cannot be in the same place with the Holy Spirit. This is a theological presupposition. It is not a biblical certainty based on scriptural exegesis. Not a single verse of Scripture states that the Holy Spirit cannot, or will not, dwell in a human body or any other area, where demons are present.[5] This argument is based more upon a syllogism of logic rather than sound biblical interpretation. Although, this argument seems logical, the question should be, is it biblical? The following syllogism represents this argument:

- **The major premise**: Every Christian is indwelt by the Holy Spirit.

- **The minor premise**: The Holy Spirit cannot dwell with demons.

- **Conclusion**: Christians cannot have demons.

In any syllogism, if any premise is false then the conclusion cannot be true. The verses of Scripture that are most often quoted are *2 Corinthians 6:14-18, James 3:11-13* and of course *I John 5:18*. When understood in context of the rest of Scripture it is clear that none of these verses teach that the Holy Spirit cannot or will not dwell in the same location with a demon. My Father taught me as a boy, "Text without context can be pretext."

Earnest B. Rockstad, for many years was a pioneer in the area of warfare counseling, he poured out his life ministering to the spiritually sick and afflicted. He and his precious wife opened up their home to many of the "castaways" of society. Through trial and error, the Lord used Brother Rockstad to bring deliverance to the captives. Out of the crucible and encounters with the darkness, came a careful study of these matters. Through his taped memoirs and teaching outlines we are able to learn much concerning the realities and relationship between the Christian and demons. He states, "It rather amazes me that men can be so sure that the Holy Spirit will not dwell in the same body with an evil spirit. They must have a higher estimate of the human nature in themselves and others than what the Bible teaches. The depravity of the human heart is such that it is difficult to see how the Holy Spirit deigns to enter in the first place. Think what He has been subjected to in the life of every one of us!"[6] Let's face it, the Holy Spirit dwells within us, and according to the Scriptures, *the heart is deceitful above all things and desperately wicked, who can know it (Jeremiah 17:9,* KJV).

We also find in the Scriptures many occasions when the Devil is in the presence of Holy God. In the study of Job we see that Satan is summoned by God into His presence. One of his names is *"Accuser of the Brethren."* Satan spends much of his time in the presence of God accusing Christians before God, the Righteous Judge. Satan is the god of this world and *"the prince of the power of the air (Eph. 2:2)."* Thus, Satan and his demons are present in the atmosphere of this world, but so is the omnipresent Holy Spirit. This means that they must coexist.[7] Sound biblical interpretation demands that Scripture must be taken in light of all Scripture.

Let's look at the second argument most often used. Once bought by the blood of Jesus, a Christian cannot be owned, or "possessed," by a devil. The difficulty is the presupposition based on the definition of the King James translation "possessed or possession." Once again I had drawn my conclusion and sought to prove it on the basis of my presupposition. The word "possession" clearly implies ownership. The Scriptures do clearly teach ownership of the believer by the purchase through the blood sacrifice of Christ:

Be on guard for yourselves and for all the flock, among which the Holy Spirit has made you overseers, to shepherd the church of God which He purchased with His own blood (Acts 20:28).

In Him, you also, after listening to the message of truth, the gospel of your salvation having also believed, you were sealed in Him with the Holy Spirit of promise, who is given as a pledge of our inheritance, with a view of possession, to the praise of His glory (Eph. 1:13-14).

Clearly one cannot mistake the truth of the Scriptures that once a person has been saved he or she becomes God's personal possession. It is here we have our dilemma. The word in the New Testament is *daimon*. In fact, the very term "demon possession" itself is a part of the problem. It is used in most English versions of the Bible to translate a single Greek word, yet it may not be the best translation at all. Dr. Timothy Warner writes, "The use of the word possession to translate the expressions used in the Greek New Testament to indicate the relationship between demons and people is unfortunate, if not unwarranted. We obtain our English word demons by translating the Greek word *daimon*. We should have done the same with the Greek word *daimonizomai* a verb form of the same Greek root. It would then come into English as demonize and we could then speak of the degree to which a person could be demonized rather than being limited to either—or options imposed by the possessed—not possessed view."[8] I believe Warner is correct when he concludes, "spiritual possession clearly implies ownership and would seem to include the control of one's eternal destiny. It would be impossible to be owned and controlled by Satan and have a saving relationship with Christ at the same time." So if the question is, Can a Christian be demon possessed? The answer is clearly, NO![9] A born again, born of the Spirit Christian CANNOT BE POSSESSED by the

Devil! So the question then is not, Can a Christian be possessed, but rather, Can a Christian be DEMONIZED?

WHAT THE BIBLE SAYS CONCERNING DEMONIZATION AND THE BELIEVER

Let us look at the Word of God together. The following is a list of just a few scriptural examples of God's people being demonized. It is necessary to look at all of the Word of God to glean the eternal truth of this most serious matter:

• Case of King Saul *(1 Sam. 9-31)*. He was a true Old Testament believer. He was filled by the Holy Spirit on more than one occasion. On three occasions an evil spirit entered his life, causing dramatic personality changes when the demon was in manifestation.

• Case of Israel as a rebellious nation *(Hos. 2:13,17)*. It is altogether possible that most of the adult Jews who had given themselves to gross spirit-idol worship were demonized when God sent them into captivity. The prophets describe in shocking detail their total surrender to the spirit world. Israel united the cult of Baal with the worship of Jehovah. The result was a deplorable syncretism, which soon led Israel to reject the Law of her God. She was, in turn, rejected by God *(Hos. 4:1-10)*. Israel had become ensnared by the Devil. The people became as demonized as the Baal worshippers they had joined *(Hos. 9:1,7-10, 15 Chapter 10:2* with *1 Cor. 10:18-22; 1 Tim. 3:6-7, 2 Tim. 2:26)*.

• In the New Testament we have vivid case studies of Jews, regular synagogue attendees, who were severely demonized *(Mark 1:21-28:39)*.

• The case of the demonized daughter of Abraham (Abraham—The Father of the Faithful) *(Luke 13:10-17*; see *John 8:33-35; Gal.3:29)*. She was a true Jewish believer. Her sickness was caused by an evil spirit from which Jesus set her free.

- The case of the demonization of Peter *(Matt. 16:23, Mark 8:33, Luke 4:8)*. Notice Jesus does not rebuke Peter by name. He rebukes Satan who was able to so invade Peter that his mind and voice were used for evil.

- The case of the early church being demonized *(Acts. 5:1-10)*. It is clear that Ananias and Sapphira were true believers, but Satan filled the heart of Ananias. To fill is to control, the same expression used for the filling of the Holy Spirit.

- Paul's thorn in the flesh in *2 Cor. 12:7*. He refers to the source of it as a *messenger of Satan*. This word is <u>*aggelos,*</u> or better translated, <u>*angel*</u>. Most of the time this word is translated in the New Testament as <u>angel</u>.

WARNINGS CONCERNING THE DANGERS OF BELIEVERS BECOMING DEMONIZED

- Paul cautions against the potential demonization of bishops, elders, and pastors *(1 Tim. 3:6-7)*, Bible teachers, preachers, and prophets *(2 Cor. 11:3-4, 13-15; 1 Tim. 1:19-20* with *2 Tim. 2:14-26; 1 Tim. 4:1, I John 4:1-4)*. There is the enigma of demonized "deaconesses" *(1 Tim. 5:9-15),* and the danger of demonized gifted Christian leaders and miracle workers *(I John 4:1-4* with *Matt. 7:13-29; 2 Thess. 2:1-17; Rev. 13)*.

- James teaches that there are two different kinds of wisdoms available to every believer. One is from God, and the other is from Satan. Bitter, jealous, selfish, ambitious, arrogant, lying, and cursing believers who receive this unholy wisdom can become demonized *(James 3:9-15)*.

- Paul's concern of his new converts *receiving another spirit (2 Cor. 11:4)*.

- *Neither give place to the Devil (Eph. 4:27, KJV).* The warning to Christians about the danger of giving an area of their lives (knowingly or unknowingly) over to the occupancy by Satan. In the study of the Armor of God, a warning is clearly implied that a Christian without the Lord's armor can be penetrated by Satan *(Eph. 6:10-18).*

- In the passage that warns the Christian of the danger of Satan as a *roaring lion,* it is also implied that the believer can be destroyed—or *gobbled up*—by his adversary, Satan *(I Peter 5:8).*

Dr. Neal Anderson observes, "The fact that a Christian can be influenced to one degree or another by the god of this world is a New Testament given. If not, then why are we instructed to put on the armor of God and stand firm *(Ephesians 6:10)*, to take every thought captive to the obedience of Christ *(2 Corinthians 10)*, and to resist the Devil *(James 4:7)*? What if we don't put on the armor of God, stand firm, assume responsibility for what we think; and what if we fail to resist the Devil? Then what? We're easy prey for the Enemy of our souls."[10]

Be sober, be vigilant for your adversary the Devil is like a roaring lion seeking whom he may devour (1 Peter 5:8, KJV).

What does it mean to be devoured by Satan? Would God warn us of that which is not a possibility? The word *devour* means to gobble down quickly. The Bible clearly states that the Devil was a murderer from the beginning. *The thief comes only to steal, kill, and destroy (John 10:10).* Satan is not just trying to irritate or intimidate us. Satan is trying to kill us. It is clear that all of the warnings given in the New Testament concerning the dangers and potential destruction by the Enemy are given to the Church. In the light of this, the believer must understand that although our victory is secure in the finished work of our Lord Jesus at Calvary *(Col. 2:13-15)*, we are in a fierce battle *(Eph. 6:13-18)*. The battle is from without and sometimes from within. In the same way we can lose our peace, love, joy, etc. (although we possess it in Christ). We can lose the victory, if we continue in sin and rebellion against God and the working of His Holy Spirit within us. The habitual ignoring of the work of the Holy Spirit in the believer's life will lead to habitual sin and rebellion against God. Any rebellion against God joins the believer to Satan's rebellion and can allow a *stronghold* (*topos* Eph. *4:27*, a place for the Enemy to work) in the believer's life. This stronghold will ultimately render the believer hopeless and powerless in the battle, and will ultimately bring defeat.

TWO PRIMARY WAYS A BELIEVER CAN BECOME DEMONIZED

There are two primary ways by which a believer can become demonized. First, they were demonized before their conversion. All demons do not always automatically leave the body of demonized unbelievers when they turn to Christ. While most of us have been taught that they will, the New Testament nowhere teaches such a doctrine. To affirm otherwise is a theological presupposition, not a biblical certainty. Second, believers become demonized after their conversion by traumatic blasphemous sins they commit or these most serious sins committed against them. Satan and his evil spirits will attach themselves to sin areas of a believer's life. They will work continually to increase their control over these areas. That control is only partial, however, never total. Thus, demonized believers are able and responsible to turn against the demons attached to their lives. If these believers do not learn the way to victory in the warfare for their thought life, they will begin to form evil habits of imagination and fantasy. This, in turn, leads to the beginning of loss of control over their thought life. Over a period of time, loss of thought control inevitably leads to bondage to evil fantasies, which soon leads to evil actions. The end can be almost total control by certain compulsive forms of sin.[11] Remember, *as a man thinketh in his heart, so is he (Prov. 23:7,* KJV).

Usually demonically troubled believers battle in four primary sin areas:

• Illicit sexual practices or fantasies out of control.

• Deep-seated anger, bitterness, hatred, rage and rebellion, often leading to destructive and/or self-destructive impulses (Preoccupation with Rock Music).

• A sense of rejection, guilt, poor self-esteem, unworthiness, and shame (Alcohol and or drug abuse).

• Strange attraction to the occult and to the spirit world, often, but not always, with a desire for elicit power over circumstances and other people.[12]

After many years of careful study of the Word of God and through his experiences in praying with those in darkness, Dr. Chuck Swindoll, former President of Dallas Theological Seminary and world renowned radio Bible preacher, weighed in on the question, "Can a Christian be Demonized?" "For a number of years I questioned this, but I am now convinced it can occur. If a 'ground of entrance' has been granted the powers of darkness (such as trafficking in the occult, a continual unforgiving spirit, a habitual state of carnality, etc.), the demon(s) sees this as a green light—okay to proceed. Wicked forces are not discriminating with regard to which body they may inhabit. I have worked personally with troubled, anguished Christians for many years. On a few occasions I have assisted in the painful process of relieving them of demons."[13]

There is also the matter of <u>generational</u> or <u>ancestral sin</u>. The believer is most vulnerable in the area of familial sin. Generational sin is sin judgment that moves through the family line. It is called by various other names such as transference, inheritance, or familial sin. An ancestor who gives place to Satan not only hurts himself, but he opens the door of grave harm to his children, grandchildren, and on down the line. This ground of transference would seem to account for little children having to endure this invasion of the powers of darkness.[14] Satan and his demons are "legalists." That is, they do not have to leave unless the covenant—or contract—made with the Devil is broken. Only the blood of Jesus, which is the New Covenant, has the power to cancel out the covenant of sin and death *(1 Cor. 11:25)*. The ground that the Enemy has taken through generational sin must be discovered and denounced. A clear commitment to Christ through confession of these specific sins brings the blood covenant of the Lord Jesus to bear. Once the ground has been taken back through confession demons must leave, for they have no other place to go within the life of the believer.

Also, there is an area that is extremely controversial within some circles. However, it is an area that is widely being discussed and accepted in the area of clinical psychology, as well as many deliverance counselors. That is the matter of *alters*—alternative personalities, known in counseling circles as Multiple Personality Disorder (MPD), or what is now referred to as Dissociative Identity Disorder (DID). Some in this complex world of Christian counseling call the splitting of the personality *fragments*. I call them *fractures* because of what has happened to create the disorder. Multiple Personality Disorder usually begins in childhood because, unlike adults, children can't run from abuse. The only place they can hide is inside their heads. As the victim grows older, the separate personalities become ever more autonomous, and each has its own special way of functioning in the everyday world.[15] Wherever one finds the fragmentation of a personality, you will always find the work of the Enemy. The personality of the believer can be split—fractured—because of unhealed damage. Our Lord has wonderfully created every human whole, not fragmented. Alternative personalities (or fragments) are the work of the Enemy. Whenever you find a personality that has been split through emotional or physical trauma, you will find demons. When dealing with fragments one must not only have deliverance from evil spirits that have attached themselves to the broken parts of the personality, but there must also be a work of healing and restoration. Jesus offers wholeness, as well as healing *(John 5:1-6)*. We are so quickly diverted to our places of so-called "comfortable" conclusions. So often we run to these conclusions without making certain that they line up with the truth of the Word of God.

THE FINAL END OF SATAN AND HIS DARK KINGDOM

We must understand Satan is the god of this world. He controls the world's systems and all who are in the world who have not come to know Christ as their Savior. However, Satan's rule is only for a season. One day which I believe is coming soon, Jesus will come to stop the madness, insanity, and death. Satan and his demons are on a short leash and their season of deception and destruction is coming to an end. Hallelujah!

> *These will wage war against the Lamb, and the Lamb will overcome them, because He is Lord of lords and King of kings, and those who are with Him are the called and chosen and faithful (Rev. 17:14).*

And in *Rev. 20:1-3*—What a wonderful day our Lord has promised!

> *Then I saw an angel coming down from heaven, holding the key of the abyss and a great chain in his hand. And he laid hold of the dragon, the serpent of old, who is the devil and Satan, and bound him for a thousand years; and he threw him into the abyss, and shut it and sealed it over him, so that he would not deceive the nations any longer, until the thousand years were completed; after these things he must be released for a short time.*

Then in vs. 7, we see recorded the final demise of Satan:

> *When the thousand years are completed, Satan will be released from his prison, and will come out to deceive the nations which are in the four corners of the earth, Gog and Magog, to gather them together for the war; the number of them is like the sand of the seashore. And they came up on the broad plain of the earth and surrounded the camp of the saints and the beloved city, and fire came down from heaven and devoured them. And the devil who deceived them was thrown into the lake of fire and brimstone, where the beast and the false prophet are also; and they will be tormented day and night forever and ever.*

What a great and glorious day that will be! It's not time yet for Satan's total destruction. Satan has been given amazing supernatural powers to rule this world and its systems. But make no mistake, his time is coming to an end. Praise the Lord!

The Christian has been given the power to walk in the victory bought for us when Christ shed His blood on Calvary. It is the believer, and only the believer, who can have any genuine hope. In *Col. 2:15*, Jesus conquered Satan at Calvary. Only those of us who have entered into the blood covenant of Calvary can walk in His wonderful victory. Please understand, if you are a believer your freedom has been paid for by Christ, It is a free gift to everyone who believe in Christ, but it is not automatic.

Christians cannot be possessed—owned, if you will—by a devil. However, Christians can have demons. If there is anything in your life that is stealing, killing and destroying then according to Jesus, the Enemy is at work in your life *(John 10:10)*. If you are witnessing the Enemy's destructive work, then he is there. We need to stop focusing on where they are and recognize the results of their evil work.

THE RELATIONSHIP BETWEEN THE FLESH AND DEMONS
SIN—THE HIGHWAY DEMONS TRAVEL

To understand the truth concerning the relationship between Christians and demons, we must look to the Word of God:

> *Let no one say when he is tempted, "I am being tempted by God"; for God cannot be tempted by evil, and He Himself does not tempt anyone. But each one is tempted when he is carried away and enticed by his own lust. Then when lust has conceived, it gives birth to sin; and when sin is accomplished, it brings forth death (James 1:13-15).*

Here the Bible teaches there is a process, a progression that leads us into death. Sin is the avenue, or highway, demons travel. Let's look more closely at this passage. What is the deadly progression of sin?

1. Temptation: The thought of evil

2. **Carried away,** Drawn away: Lured from safet

3. **Enticed:** Caught by bait

4. **Lust:** Craving what the thought represents; self over others

5. **Lust conceived:** Yielding of the will; sin is birthed

6. **Sin:** The act is committed—We own it!

7. **Death:** The evil in the heart of Satan has had his way

Where do these evil thoughts come from? Who is the tempter? All evil comes from the heart and mind of Satan. He is the Evil One. For a season, Satan has the world in his control.

> *For all that is in the world, the lust of the flesh, and the lust of the eyes and the boastful pride of life, is not from the Father, but is from the world (I John 1:16).*

If Satan can influence us to sin, and we cooperate with him, then his plan of destruction and death will be accomplished. We don't seem to recognize the supernatural evil power behind the temptation to sin. Behind every temptation, behind every thought that would lead us to disobey God's Word there are very powerful spirits. They are ever vigilant at working and watching for even a fracture—all they need is a small window of opportunity to invade and build their strongholds for the purpose of taking us out.

To ignore the Enemy of our souls by believing his lies that *"when we are saved we are automatically safe"* is to give Satan a distinct advantage in the spiritual battles of life and death. To believe the lie that *"Christian's can't have demons"* can get you killed. Satan is real! Yes, and demons are real! Demons are on a real mission, a mission to steal, kill, and destroy. Demons have a specific target...the believer! Christians can, and often do, fall into their deceptions, which can lead to an untimely death.

Dear Friend, if you do not know Christ as Savior, trust Him today. Right now, ask Him to be your Savior. Receive the sacrifice of God's Son, for the forgiveness of your sin. He is your only hope from total death and destruction. If you are a believer in Christ, receive all He has for you today. He has come to set you free. Receive Christ's freedom right now.

IF IT'S CONSENSUAL, THEN IT'S OK.

As we continue our journey into the LIES THAT KILL—Dangerous lies that when believed, have the power behind them to lead to a life of destruction and ultimate death. Let's bring into focus the lie so often used by the Enemy to bring us into spiritual bondage. That is, IF IT'S CONSENSUAL, THEN IT'S OK.

THE DANGERS OF CONSENSUS

May I first say a word concerning the dangers of living life based on consensus? Webster's Dictionary defines _consensus_ as 1) Group solidarity in sentiment and belief; 2) Collective opinion.[1] So, consensus is an opinion based upon a group decision. Simply put, consensus is a position rooted in peer pressure. Many aspects of life are based on consensus. Even with only a casual observation of the political process, whether in government, on school boards, or even in church governance, one will find the practice of consensus. Consensus looks to satisfy the pleasure of those involved. It is, in reality, a way to the path of least resistance. In the practice of consensus, the end most often does justify the means.

Margaret Thatcher, former Prime Minister of Great Britain, was reported to have said, "Whenever you find consensus, you will find the lack of leadership." The problem with making decisions based on consensus is that truth is rarely, if ever, found through consensus. The truth may be on the right or the left of a matter. If we settle for anything less than the truth of God, we have invited the powers of darkness into our lives. It is the truth that has the power to set us free from the bondage of the Evil One, not just our opinions *(John 8:32).* We must always be careful with whom we fall into agreement. We must never look to the places of the Devil's compromises to get the approval for our behavior. Looking to demonized persons and their ruling principalities for our approval and for the standard by which we live is extremely dangerous. It can be catastrophic and ultimately lead to death.

Although there are many dangerous areas where the practice of consensus can bring us into spiritual bondage, allow me to focus our attention on the most obvious area. That is, the area of sex. Just because the issues surrounding sex are of a sensitive nature, we can ill afford to neglect this most important area so often corrupted and compromised by the process of consensus. To ignore the biblical study concerning sex gives the Enemy of our souls an advantage in the spiritual battles and can hinder our journey into spiritual cleansing.

SEX IS A GOD THING

Sex is a wonderful thing, because sex is a God thing. It is man who has tarnished the holy purpose of God for sex through his disobedience and selfishness. The great tragedy is that so many today have no real understanding of sex except through the corruption and distortion of Satan's counterfeit. They have never seen a good and holy relationship in the sacrificial love of God shared between a man and a woman. The whole idea of sex came from the mind and heart of Holy God. God created men and women with the need for intimacy. When God created man, He said, *"It is not good for the man to be alone; I will make him a helper suitable for him (Gen 2:18)."* God never intended man to be alone so He did something wonderful to fix man's aloneness. He made woman:

And the LORD God fashioned into a woman the rib which He had taken from the man, and brought her to the man. And the man said, "This is now bone of my bones, and flesh of my flesh; she shall be called Woman, because she was taken out of Man." For this cause a man shall leave his father and his mother, and shall cleave to his wife; and they shall become one flesh. And the man and his wife were both naked and were not ashamed (Gen 2:22-25).

He created man and woman with a blessing and a purpose. Not only did God have a wonderful plan for them, but He blessed them so they could accomplish His purpose for them:

And God created man in His own image, in the image of God He created him; male and female He created them. And God blessed them; and God said to them, "Be fruitful and multiply, and fill the earth, and subdue it (Gen. 1:27-28);"

God's created purpose for them through this wonderful intimacy was to be fruitful and multiply. What a tragedy so many have fallen prey to the Enemy's counterfeits as opposed to godly sex. Few seem to understand that sex is a good and godly thing. Even the very mention of the word <u>sex</u> can often bring up images of the <u>taboo</u>, of dark and ugly secrets. Why do you suppose this is? Perhaps it is because few have seen or experienced the real thing. Sex—a gift created by God is to be a holy, wonderful, and a blessed intimate experience between a man and a woman.

In *1 Cor. 6:16*, the Holy Spirit, through the pen of the Apostle Paul, repeats the truth found in *Genesis 2:24*. That is, the marriage union between a man and a woman is a "one flesh" relationship. God said that the two (man and woman) will become *ONE FLESH*. Most of us have heard the reference to *ONE FLESH* as we have witnessed a couple taking their vows in their wedding ceremony. Certainly, a reference in Scripture to "one flesh" has greater meaning than a mere reference used in a ritual of a wedding ceremony. What does it mean to be *ONE FLESH*? Paul refers to this one flesh union between the husband and his wife as a *mystery*. Think of it. This relationship of intimacy and trust between a man and a woman is not just a natural relationship. It's a supernatural relationship, because it's of God:

> *FOR THIS CAUSE A MAN SHALL LEAVE HIS FATHER AND MOTHER, AND SHALL CLEAVE TO HIS WIFE; AND THE TWO SHALL BECOME ONE FLESH. This mystery is great; but I am speaking with reference to Christ and the church (Eph. 5:31-32).*

THE DEVASTATION OF DIVORCE

So few of us today have a true understanding of the seriousness of this supernatural relationship between men and women. Why is that? It is my conviction that we "just don't get it." We seem to have forgotten (assuming we ever knew it) that the relationship between a man and a woman has spiritual realities and carries with it supernatural consequences. Could it be that this is the primary reason so many marriages fall under the sad gavel of the divorce court? According to Jennifer Baker of the Forest Institute of Professional Psychology in Springfield, Missouri, 50% of first marriages, 67% of second, and 74% of third marriages end in divorce. The sadness of divorce is not just the damage done to the souls of the marriage partners, but the carnage of the broken lives of the children of divorced parents. Of all children born to married parents this year, fifty percent will experience the divorce of their parents before they reach their 18th birthday.[2] William Bennett, author of the *Book of Virtues*, recognized back in 1994 in a speech to the Christian Coalition's national convention: "If you look in terms of damage done to the children of America, you cannot compare what the homosexual movement has done to what divorce has done to this society. In terms of the consequences to children, it is not even close."[3] Is it any wonder why God hates divorce *(Malachi 2:16)*?

In Daniel Henderson's book, *Think Before You Look*, he states the chilling reality of what has happened to the American marriage vow: "No doubt, Americans have lost a sense of the power of the marriage vow. It seems that for many of us, marriage has become more of an experiment in social fulfillment than a life-time commitment for better or for worse."[4] Everywhere we look, marriage vows are broken as if they did not matter. The sexual exploits of President Bill Clinton set a new low in the credibility of the marriage vow. Many were troubled when Christian artist Amy Grant and her new beau, Vince Gill, disposed of their current spouses to take new "vows." We've all been jolted by George Barna's figures indicating that professing Christians have moderately higher rates of divorce than the general population, including atheists and agnostics.[5]

Dr. Rick Perrin, Senior Pastor of Cornerstone Church (PCA) in Columbia, South Carolina, observes: "A theology of marriage must be more than a sundry list of Scripture verses on the subject. We must develop and draw from a comprehensive understanding of God's creation of male and female, why and how '*the two become one flesh.*' How this '*mystery*', as Paul calls it, is so significant as to represent Christ's relationship with His church."[6] The church of Jesus Christ is referred to in Scripture as His bride, and Jesus is referred to as the bridegroom *(Rev. 18:23)*. Look with me at the beauty of this holy relationship between Christ and His church:

> *And I saw the holy city, new Jerusalem, coming down out of heaven from God, made ready as a bride adorned for her husband. And I heard a loud voice from the throne, saying, "Behold, the tabernacle of God is among men, and He shall dwell among them, and they shall be His people, and God Himself shall be among them (Rev. 21:2-3).*

Those who have accepted God's sacrifice for their sins have entered into a special, supernatural and eternal relationship with Christ. This wonderful and holy relationship is pictured in the Bible as the intimate relationship between husbands and their wives.

While a student at Baylor University, I fell in love with Pattie Reese from Silver City, New Mexico. In the aftermath of my parent's horrific divorce, I was deeply troubled with the nagging question as to how I could be faithful to anyone in marriage for the rest of my life. I was determined not to go through anything like my parents had gone through. At all costs, I was determined to avoid such tragedy even if it meant my staying single. My Father had asked me to lead the music for a revival meeting he was conducting in Kansas. While traveling down the interstate, I expressed to him that I was in love with Pattie, and how I was considering asking her to marry me.

I asked him, "Daddy, how can you know for certain that no matter what you can be faithful to your wife?"

He quickly responded, "Son, are you serious?"

"Deadly serious," I replied. "Daddy, if I can't be certain, I'm not going to get married."

That day my Father gave me the truth God used to set me free from my paralyzing fears. He said, "Son, when you go to the altar to make your marriage vows, you're not just committing your life to Pattie. The wedding vows you make are to God. He is faithful, not you. It is the Lord who puts the power within you to keep you faithful. Son, if you are faithful to keep your relationship fresh and healthy with Jesus, He in return will keep you faithful to your wife."

Well, let me tell you, Jesus is faithful! His power works! Pattie and I have been married for 36 wonderful years (and counting)!

THE MYSTERY OF THE "ONE FLESH" RELATIONSHIP
Let's look closer at the biblical meaning of *ONE FLESH*:

Do you not know that your bodies are members of Christ? Shall I then take away the members of Christ and make them members of a harlot? May it never be! Or do you not know that the one who joins himself to a harlot is one body with her? For He says, "THE TWO WILL BECOME ONE FLESH." But the one who joins himself to the Lord is one spirit with Him. Flee immorality. Every other sin that a man commits is outside the body, but the immoral man sins against his own body. Or do you not know that your body is a temple of the Holy Spirit who is in you, whom you have from God, and that you are not your own? For you have been bought with a price: therefore glorify God in your body (1 Cor. 6:15-20).

Notice with me, this reference to *ONE FLESH* is directly related to sexual relations between a man and a prostitute. What this tells us is this: in the spirit world when two have had sexual relations, they share much more than a physical natural relationship. They share a supernatural relationship. That's right, any sexual relationship in which the two people involved become *ONE FLESH*, they also become *ONE FLESH* in the spirit world. Sex is not merely a physical act. It is a spiritual act, as well. There are supernatural principles that everyone needs to be aware of concerning the sex act.

Sex is a means by which demons may be transferred from one person to another. We know from countless testimonies of those who have been ritualized in the Occult practices of Satanic Rituals, many have been involved in horrific sexual perversions. These acts are so physically and emotionally painful that the person who is being abused (often a child) chooses to disassociate from the pain and trauma of the abuse. At this spiritually vulnerable time, an alternative personality is enabled to take control to blot out the indignities and the pain. Acceptance of such a personality subsequently makes the person vulnerable to other influences from the world of darkness.[7] During a seminar on Ritual Abuse at The University of California at Berkeley, one of the conference speakers, Eliana Gil, stated statistics revealed that 98% of those suffering from Multiple Personality Disorder (MPD) have been sexually abused; most of them on a repeated basis.[8] Through these gross perverted rituals, demons have been assigned to the broken pieces of the lives of these wounded victims.

We find the same supernatural practice in Ephesus through the worship of Diana—Artemis is her Greek name in *Acts 19*. We know from Jewish and Roman historians that the Temple of Diana was lined with Temple prostitutes who were for hire to aid in these most vile sexual acts for the purpose of transferring demons to the practitioners of these temple rituals. Both priests and priestesses had to sacrifice their fertility to the goddess (Diana) in their own way.[9] What we must all understand and make certain that our children understand—the sex act is not merely a physical act. It is a supernatural act. Be careful with whom you have sex. Knowingly, or more likely unknowingly, you may receive demonic attachments through a sexual act with demonized partners. Now let me make it very clear; as has already been stated, God is the one who created male and female. When dedicated to Him, the act of sex is a holy and beautiful thing:

> *Let marriage be held in honor among all, and let the marriage bed be undefiled; for fornicators and adulterers God will judge (Heb. 13:4).*

One thing is for certain, God is concerned about who is having sex with whom. Sex outside of marriage, especially in this day and time, is a dangerous practice physically. Sexually transmitted diseases have proliferated in recent years—diseases just waiting to destroy your life. However, sex outside of marriage is also a dangerous practice because of how it affects us spiritually. Those of you who have had sex education in school learned that having sex with someone is not just having sex with that person. It is as if you are having sex with every partner in that person's sexual exploits. Let's put that truth into a spiritual context: when you have sex with someone who has had sex with someone, who has had sex with someone, etc. you are very likely cavorting, or cooperating, with everyone's demons. In other words, having sex is a means by which the sharing of the supernatural is experienced.

Dr. Jim Logan points out: "When one engages in pre-marital or extramarital sex, our bond of fellowship with God is broken because we sin. In its place, people form all kinds of unnatural bondings. We call them _soul ties_. These soul ties can be incredibly powerful. That's why a woman will go back time and again to a man who beats her. There's some kind of an unnatural tie to that person that has to be broken by the power of God. Remember what *Proverbs 5:22* says? *He shall be holden with the cords of his sins.* There are people who have God's life in them, but they are bound up with all kinds of sins. Somehow, when it is sexual, it seems to be worse."[10]

The Bible links the act of sex outside the sacred bonds of marriage to the practice of witchcraft. Yes, witchcraft. I fear most people have never read the following passages of Scripture:

All because of the many harlotries of the harlot, the charming one, the mistress of sorceries, Who sells nations by her harlotries and families by her sorceries. "Behold, I am against you," declares the LORD of hosts; "And I will lift up your skirts over your face, and show to the nations your nakedness and to the kingdoms your disgrace. I will throw filth on you and make you vile, and set you up as a spectacle (Nahum 3:4-6)."

In *Exodus 22:16-18* look with me at what the Bible says concerning having sex outside of marriage:

And if a man seduces a virgin who is not engaged, and lies with her, he must pay a dowry for her to be his wife. If her father absolutely refuses to give her to him, he shall pay money equal to the dowry for virgins. You shall not allow a sorceress to live (Exodus 22:16-18).

In *Revelation 21:8,* we find these words concerning the matter of having extramarital sex:

But for the cowardly and unbelieving and abominable and murderers and immoral persons and sorcerers and idolaters and all liars, their part will be in the lake that burns with fire and brimstone, which is the second death (Rev. 21:8).

Notice what the Bible (KJV) calls people who practice immorality—*whoremongers*, and whoremongers are listed right next to *sorcerers*. The truth is, when two people have engaged in sex, they are sharing with each other everything in their spiritual lives, as well. That is the reason why God's Word is so precise in its condemnation of sex outside the boundaries of marriage. Notice, for those who are conceived outside of marriage, God's Word tells us that illegitimate birth carries with it a ten generation curse *(Deut. 23:2)*. This curse, as in all curses, is only broken through the blood covenant in Christ Jesus. All sin and disobedience is only forgiven at the Cross of Christ. Praise His Holy Name, through Christ we have the forgiveness of all our sin *(Col. 1:13-14)*.

> *Christ redeemed us from the curse of the Law, having become a curse for us—for it is written, "CURSED IS EVERYONE WHO HANGS ON A TREE (Gal. 3:13)."*

THE SPIRITUAL DAMAGE OF ABORTION

It is a risk I must take to deal with the spiritual issues of abortion. Because abortion has been so politicized in our day, I fear we have lost the ability to see the real spiritual devastation left in the wake of this horrific practice. Abortion will never be settled in the court rooms of our justice system. Even if abortion were to be declared illegal today, selfish mothers and fathers would still find a way to dispose of their unwanted children. Ultimately, God is not just looking to the judges of our courts to determine the matter of abortion. God is looking in at the court rooms of the hearts of mothers and fathers to find the expression of His love concerning the creation of these precious children.

If we would dare to open our spiritual eyes, we would see the untold number of wounded and hopeless people all around us. The broken lives of parents are all around us as the result of the carnage of abortion. For no reason of their own, their unborn babies have become the victims of the brutal theft of their God-given destinies. These innocent precious children were murdered simply because they were in the way of the sexual exploits of their self-centered parents, each believing the Enemy's lie that consensual sex made it O.K. Millions and millions of the dead innocent children cry out for justice from their bloody graves. No less ravaged by the Enemy are the mothers who have aborted their babies. Through their relentless pain of their unyielding guilt and deep sorrow, the Enemy is tirelessly at work to destroy these precious tormented souls. Dr. David Reardon writes concerning the connection between suicide and abortion: "A 1987 study of women who suffered from post-abortion trauma found that 60 percent had experienced suicidal ideation, 28 percent had attempted suicide, and 10 percent had attempted suicide more than once, often several years after the event."[11]

In the pews of our churches, sit the broken and wounded needing the spiritual cleansing and healing of our Lord. It could very well be this is the primary reason most of our churches, not to mention our families, are spiritually sick and lifeless. Those of us who have been sexually active in our earlier years have tried to ignore the spiritual damage that has been done through our sexual exploits. Many have married their sexual partners thinking that marriage would cover up our sins. There is but one remedy for our sin—the blood of our precious Lord Jesus. If we have ever tried to cover up our sin without going through the cleansing blood of Jesus through confession and repentance, we have cooperated with Satan's deadly deceptive lies.

THE PERILS OF PORNOGRAPHY

No study of consensual sex would be complete without looking carefully at the epidemic and spiritual devastation that is brought about as the result of pornography. Worldwide, pornography revenue in 2006 was $97.06 billion. Of that, approximately $13 billion was in the United States. Every second $3,075.64 is spent on pornography, 28,258 Internet viewers are viewing pornography, 372 Internet users are typing adult search terms into search engines, and every 39 minutes, a new pornographic video is made in the United States.[12] From Hollywood's obsession with the worship of beautiful women, to the myriad of vulgar ads that feed our culture of materialism, not to mention the gateway to Hell we have intimately come to know as the internet, the god of this world has been more than effective in bringing destruction and death upon our country, our families, and the church's witness for Christ.

On the morning of April 23rd, 2010, the national news program, *ABC's Good Morning America*, reported that 31 top officials working for the SEC (The Securities and Exchange Commission) from 2008— 2010 had an addiction to porn. This is the government agency whose responsibility it is to keep watch over the corruption and fraud in our nation's banking system. "These guys in the middle of a financial crisis are spending their time looking at prurient material on the internet," said Peter Morici, a professor at the University of Maryland and former Director of the Office of Economics at the U.S. International Trade Commission.[13] Just think, the financial meltdown in America that almost brought America to financial ruin was overseen by highly demonized individuals addicted to the illicit demonic power of porn. I submit to you that this was not just dirty guys behaving badly. This was a carefully devised evil scheme of the Enemy. He strategically placed highly wounded and demonized agents of evil to aid in inflicting Satan's damage and destruction to our nation and to steal the hard-earned wealth of our people.

The word <u>pornography</u> comes from two Greek words, *πορνεία—porneia—fornication—idolatry* and *γραφή—graphe—writing*. Let's look more closely to the word *porneia* so we can understand what we are dealing with in the practice of pornography. We find the word in *Galatians 5:19-21, 1 Cor. 6:9, 18, and 2 Cor. 12:21.* Each time it refers to the act of sex outside of the vows of marriage. The act of <u>pornea</u> is fornication—immoral sex outside the marriage vows:

> *Now the deeds of the flesh are evident, which are: <u>immorality</u>, impurity, sensuality, idolatry, sorcery, enmities, strife, jealousy, outbursts of anger, disputes, dissensions, factions, envying, drunkenness, carousing, and things like these, of which I forewarn you just as I have forewarned you that those who practice such things shall not inherit the kingdom of God (Gal. 5:19-21).*

> *Or do you not know that the unrighteous shall not inherit the kingdom of God? Do not be deceived; neither <u>fornicators</u>, nor idolaters, nor adulterers, nor effeminate, nor homosexuals, nor thieves, nor the covetous, nor drunkards, nor revilers, nor swindlers, shall inherit the kingdom of God (1 Cor. 6:9-10).*

I am afraid that when I come again my God may humiliate me before you, and I may mourn over many of those who have sinned in the past and not repented of the impurity, <u>immorality and sensuality</u> which they have practiced (2 Cor. 12:21).

Pornography is a mind/imagination fantasy game. It is the mental lusting after women, of which Jesus condemns:

You have heard that it was said, 'YOU SHALL NOT COMMIT ADULTERY'; but I say to you, that everyone who looks on a woman to lust for her has committed adultery with her already in his heart (Matt. 5:27-28).

That's right, you can commit adultery in your heart and the spiritual consequences are the same as if you have committed the act of adultery. It is not only possible, but sadly common for folks to have affairs of the heart. Billy Graham has rightly stated, "In the battle between the imagination and the will, the will loses every time." Pornography involves the cherishing of sinful desires. Like any good bait, there is a hook behind pornography waiting to enslave and destroy its prey. Addiction to pornography is as destructive as any other addictions. Whether work, alcohol, drug, food, or any other tormenting addictions, pornography can lead to a loss of total control of a person's life.

Not so long ago, I was asked to preach in the church where I had grown up from childhood through my teen years. This is also the church where Pattie and I reared our children. What a blessing it was to preach the Word of God to so many precious people that have been so instrumental in our lives. At the end of the service, I opened the altar for specific prayer needs. I asked if anyone needed to receive Christ as their Savior so they could be set free from their sin, to meet me at the front for prayer. Next I asked if there were those who needed to be set free from the ravages of pornography, to come to the piano side of the auditorium for a time of prayer. Next, I called for those who needed physical healing. I asked them to meet underneath the balcony for a prayer meeting. God moved powerfully that night as many were saved, healed, and delivered.

The next morning, I received a phone call from the Office of Pastoral Ministries of the church. The secretary said, "Brother Rob, I have a man who was in attendance in last night's service who has asked permission to e-mail you. Is it O.K. if I give him your e-mail address?" I told her, of course it was. This man who contacted me was named Jim (for the sake of confidentiality I'll call him Jim). Jim had been a very well-known and successful pastor. Because of his addiction to porn, he had lost his ministry, his good name, his 20-plus-year marriage and, of course, his children. Jim had lost it all. He told me how he had turned himself over to a ministry that specialized in sexual addictions with the hope of being able at some point to see the restoration of something of what the Enemy had stolen. With great joy, he shared with me how the Lord spoke to him through the service in which I had ministered. The Lord led Jim to humble himself and publically denounce his sin through confession. He told me when he came forward and confessed his sin something wonderful happened to him that night. He said, "Dr. Randall, I've been set free. My demons that have so ravaged and tormented my life are gone!"

This horrific story of Jim's loss is tragic enough. However, the reality is that pornography addiction has become all too common for pastors and church leaders. According to Christianity Today's Leadership Survey of December 2001, 51% of pastors say cyber-porn is a possible temptation, 37% say it is a current struggle. Roger Charman of Focus on the Family's Pastoral Ministries reports that approximately 20% of the calls received on their Pastoral Care Line are for help with issues such as pornography and compulsive sexual behavior.[14] Wherever one finds spiritual bondage to pornography, the destruction left behind is always beyond horrific. The greatest tragedy is that these horrific loses are all unnecessary. Jesus came to give us a life of freedom:

It was for freedom that Christ set us free; therefore keep standing firm and do not be subject again to a yoke of slavery (Gal. 5:1).

Simply put, when someone is <u>out</u> of control, someone else is <u>in</u> control. Who is this someone who comes to take control of our lives through the sin of pornography? Remember sin is the highway demons travel. Jesus said in *John 8:34, "Truly, truly, I say to you, everyone who commits sin is the slave of sin."* Look carefully with me at these chilling words given to us by the Holy Spirit concerning how sexual sin is cooperating with demons:

> *having eyes full of adultery and that never cease from sin, enticing unstable souls, having a heart trained in greed, accursed children; forsaking the right way they have gone astray, having followed the way of Balaam, the son of Beor, who loved the wages of unrighteousness, but he received a rebuke for his own transgression; for a dumb donkey, speaking with a voice of a man, restrained the madness of the prophet. These are springs without water, and mists driven by a storm, for whom the black darkness has been reserved. For speaking out arrogant words of vanity they entice by fleshly desires, by sensuality, those who barely escape from the ones who live in error, promising them freedom while they themselves are slaves of corruption; for by what a man is overcome, by this he is enslaved (2 Peter 2:14-19).*

In the biblical counselor's prayer room, three primary causes have been found to be the roots of the ravages of pornography addiction:

• **Sexual abuse in childhood**. When a child is sexually abused, he/she become easy prey to the lies of the Enemy. Lies like, "No one really loves you, since they didn't protect you" or "Sex must be the same as love, since the one who abused you was the one responsible to show you love." The truth is, since a child cannot protect himself, he is an easy target for the Enemy. Without proper spiritual covering from their parents or legal guardians, children are at great risk for demonic attachments.

• **Bondage to pornography in adolescence**. It is uncanny how many men who are addicted to pornography can remember in graphic detail the first pornographic picture they saw in adolescence.

- **A sense of powerlessness that led to a lust of illicit power**. When a man has been robbed of his manhood (his authority), he is tormented by a sense of powerlessness. Think of it…at the click of the mouse, the pornographic model is always ready at his beckoning. He picks the time, he picks the place, he picks his pleasure, and in his mind, she is always ready to perform for him. More than the sex, the victim to pornography addiction craves the <u>power</u> and <u>control</u> his <u>fake world</u> provides. Both of which his <u>real world</u> has stolen from him.

The consequences of sexual addictions are as horrific as the addiction itself. Dr. James Dobson's interview with serial killer, Ted Bundy, is a powerful reminder of the ultimate trap of a fantasy world. In the interview Bundy stated that every man he met in the prison system who was motivated to commit violence was deeply involved in and addicted to pornography. Bundy agreed with FBI studies that the most common interest serial killers have is pornography.[15] You might not believe it if you didn't see it for yourself, but the Bible links sexual immorality to liver problems:

> *With her many persuasions she entices him; with her flattering lips she seduces him. Suddenly he follows her, as an ox goes to the slaughter, Or as one in fetters to the discipline of a fool, Until an arrow pierces through his liver; As a bird hastens to the snare, So he does not know that it will cost him his life (Prov. 7:21-23).*

As in the passage mentioned above, *2 Peter 2:14-19* also mentions the names of two very powerful demons connected with the lust of undisciplined eyes:

> *Sheol[16] and Abaddon are never satisfied, nor are the eyes of man ever satisfied (Prov. 27:20).*

Beyond the addictions that leave souls wounded and bleeding, what else is at stake when sexual appetites are fed that are beyond that which is sanctioned by the Creator? Fellowship with Holy God is at stake. Even though we may be saved, sexual addiction will separate from the

One who gave His life so that we might live in the victory of Christ. Sexual immorality blinds us so that we are unable to see God. Jesus said it this way:

Blessed are the pure in heart, for they shall see God (Matt 5:8).

Like in any other spiritual battle, this battleground is fought primarily in the mind. To break the bondage of sexual addictions and their wounds, the victim must be found and brought to Christ through repentance and faith. We must believe the truth when God says in His Word that He forgives, that He does not condemn, that His power is greater than ALL sin, and that His cleansing is available to everyone who will receive it. If we can't believe the truth, we can't live the truth.

TAKING BACK THE GROUND OF SEXUAL ADDICTION

Once spiritual cleansing has occurred for those who have been in the storm of sexual addiction, the ground that the Enemy has stolen through our sin and disobedience must be reclaimed for Christ. Just as we learn to run from a venomous snake, we need to learn to run from sexual immorality. We must be vigilant to be aware and sensitive to every thought that would enter our minds to disobey God. When they come, we must be prepared to go into battle mode. We must recognize that behind the thoughts to disobey God are the very Powers of Darkness that must be rebuked by the Name and authority of Christ Jesus:

Flee immorality. Every other sin that a man commits is outside the body, but the immoral man sins against his own body (1 Cor. 6:18).

To be rid of the demonic system of death that accompanies sexual sin, there must be a radical commitment to holiness. Anything less will not be adequate for the spiritual battle that will ensue. Sexual sin is so serious and so destructive that Jesus teaches it must be radically amputated. Notice how Jesus teaches how to handle sexual immorality:

...but I say to you, that everyone who looks on a woman to lust

*for her has committed adultery with her already in his heart.
"And if your right eye makes you stumble, tear it out, and throw
it from you; for it is better for you that one of the parts of your
body perish, than for your whole body to be thrown into hell.
"And if your right hand makes you stumble, cut it off, and throw
it from you; for it is better for you that one of the parts of your
body perish, than for your whole body to go into hell (Matt.
5:28-30).*

My counsel to everyone who comes to me for help with pornography
addiction is:

• **Burn it all!** Every magazine, every picture, every remaining vestige of darkness must be eradicated and destroyed. Pray over it. Give
the whole mess to Christ. Take it to Calvary—destroy it all!

• **Put filters on all computers to which you have access.** Going on
the internet without a filter is not only foolish, it is dangerous. Just as a
drunk can't go into a liquor store, those who are battling sexual addictions cannot go on a computer without an effective filter.

• **Set up an accountability system.** Ultimately, I believe that if you
are married, your accountability partner needs to be your spouse. Remember, the sin of pornography has not only been committed against
God, it an offense against your own body and a sin against your spouse.
The greatest fear of any woman is that the man she has picked to be
her husband cannot be trusted. If she doesn't feel safe for whatever the
reason(s), the damage done to her heart is incalculable. Both partners
will need spiritual cleansing. The trust that has been lost can only be
reclaimed through the expression of a genuine brokenness, the kind of
contrition that leads to a consistent life of openness and accountability.

• **Learn the following seven verses and get ready to use them in
the battle against Satan.** When, not if, the evil ones return, they must
be rebuked with the Word of God just like Jesus used the Word of God

against the Enemy in *Luke 4.*

1) *And when you were dead in your transgressions and the uncircumcision of your flesh, He made you alive together with Him, having forgiven us all our transgressions, having canceled out the certificate of debt consisting of decrees against us and which was hostile to us; and He has taken it out of the way, having nailed it to the cross. When He had disarmed the rulers and authorities, He made a public display of them, having triumphed over them through Him (Col. 2:13-15).*

2) *Blessed are the pure in heart, for they shall see God (Matt. 5:8).*

3) *And do not be conformed to this world, but be transformed by the renewing of your mind, that you may prove what the will of God is, that which is good and acceptable and perfect (Romans 12:2).*

4) *For who has known the mind of the Lord, that he should instruct Him? But we have the mind of Christ (1 Cor. 2:16).*

5) *But do not let immorality or any impurity or greed even be named among you, as is proper among saints; and there must be no filthiness and silly talk, or coarse jesting, which are not fitting, but rather giving of thanks. For this you know with certainty, that no immoral or impure person or covetous man, who is an idolater, has an inheritance in the kingdom of Christ and God (Eph. 5:3-5).*

6) *For it is God who is at work in you, both to will and to work for His good pleasure (Phil. 2:13).*

7) *Finally, brethren, whatever is true, whatever is honorable, whatever is right, whatever is pure, whatever is lovely, whatever is of good repute, if there is any excellence and if anything worthy of praise, let your mind dwell on these things. The things you have learned and received and heard and seen*

in me, practice these things; and the God of peace shall be with
you (Phil. 4:8-9).

Because of the space limitations of this book, let me refer you to a
couple of wonderful books concerning how to deal with sexual temptation that lead to addictions. Daniel Henderson's book, *Think Before You*
Look, published by Living Ink Books, is a wonderful resource that is
extremely helpful. In addition, Stephen Arterburn and Fred Stoeker's
book, *Every Man's Battle*, published by Waterbook Press, has been used
of God in countless lives to help men through the minefield of sexual
temptation.

Please, do not believe, for even a moment the lie that just because
you join with others in disobedience to God and His Word all is O.K.
Just because what you engage in may have been -or is even now- consensual, does not mean your sin is O.K. Just because what you do, or
what you have done is not illegal and is accepted by your peers, does
not mean it is O.K. Just because you have participated in, or have had
perpetrated against you something pronounced or accepted as politically correct, does not mean it is O.K. Just because those around you
may say it's O.K., or how hard they may try to convince you that it is
O.K., does not mean it is O.K. In this old wicked world ruled by Satan,
the god of this world *(2 Cor. 4)*, we all must be careful where we walk
and with whom we walk, because we are all subject to fall victim to the
Enemy's murderous schemes:

> *Do not be deceived, God is not mocked; for whatever a man*
> *sows, this he will also reap. For the one who sows to his own*
> *flesh shall from the flesh reap corruption, but the one who sows*
> *to the Spirit shall from the Spirit reap eternal life (Gal. 6:7-8).*

Please hear the words of Jesus, coming from the loving heart of our
Heavenly Father:

> *"All that the Father gives Me shall come to Me, and the one*
> *who comes to Me I will certainly not cast out. For I have come*
> *down from heaven, not to do My own will, but the will of Him*

who sent Me. And this is the will of Him who sent Me, that of all that He has given Me I lose nothing, but raise it up on the last day. For this is the will of My Father, that everyone who beholds the Son and believes in Him, may have eternal life; and I Myself will raise him up on the last day (John 6:37-40)."

The question is often raised, "Dr. Randall, can any and all immorality be cleaned up though Christ Jesus?" Oh, yes! No matter what you have done, or what has been done to you cleansing and forgiveness is available to you right now. At the very moment you are willing to humble yourself and turn from your sin, through confession and repentance, all sin can be cleansed. At that moment, you can be healed and set free from everything that would continue to enslave you. The blood of Calvary covers all sin!

And when you were dead in your transgressions and the uncircumcision of your flesh, He made you alive together with Him, having forgiven us all our transgressions, having canceled out the certificate of debt consisting of decrees against us and which was hostile to us; and He has taken it out of the way, having nailed it to the cross. When He had disarmed the rulers and authorities, He made a public display of them, having triumphed over them through Him (Col. 2:13-15).

Do you want to be free today? Do you want to be free from the liars and tormentors? Won't you turn to Christ right now? He has the power to set you free through the sacrifice of His blood poured out for you at Calvary. You can be free. Only through faith in Christ's work for you on Calvary can you be free. What can wash away your sin? Nothing, but the blood of Jesus! What can make you whole again? Nothing, but the blood of Jesus! My Friend, won't you humble yourself and cry out to Him right now?

LIES THAT KILL

9

SINCE I'VE BEEN HURT, IT'S OK TO WANT REVENGE.

L et's continue our journey into the place that few people are willing to go. Would you go with me to look at what may be the lie that brings the greatest darkness in our lives? As it is true of all Satan's lies, believing them will keep us from knowing and walking in the freedom of Christ. This lethal lie, if believed, leads to death and destruction. It is the belief that it's OK to want revenge if someone has hurt you. The thinking goes something like this: "Justice is a good thing isn't it? I want justice done to the person that has hurt me."

If Satan can get you and me to hang on to bitterness, the loss of the control of our lives will follow. Most of the ground that Satan gains in the lives of Christians is due to unforgiveness.[1] Harboring prolonged un-forgiveness gives the Enemy a green light to proceed with his evil plans of destruction. If ignored, the birth of full-blown bitterness is certain to follow. Bitterness is a powerful tool of Satan to control and destroy our lives. Like a slow-growing cancerous tumor, ignoring it will not save us from its ultimate destruction. Be certain that, if we allow bitterness to remain at any time in our lives, Satan will use it to his benefit to rob us of our joy, of our faith, and ultimately our very lives.

TWO KINDS OF PEOPLE

When it comes down to it, there are really only two kinds of people: 1. Those who have been wounded and hurt, but have never experienced Christ's healing, and, 2. Those who have been wounded and hurt, but have experienced Christ's healing of their wounds. If you have been lied to, if you have been wounded, if you have been used and abused for the selfish pleasure of others, you are a part of the human race. Everyone has been hurt. *Man is born of trouble (Job 5:7).* I'm not trying to say that your hurts and wounds aren't significant, but the real issue every believer must visit is this, "Is it O.K. for me to want revenge against those who have hurt me?"

We are most like Satan when we are angry and bitter. We are most like Christ when we forgive. It was Christ who said of His murderers:

"Father forgive them for they know not what they are doing (Luke 23:34)."

It is important to note that, almost without exception, every book written on spiritual warfare has an extensive section on the issue of bitterness. Allowing bitterness to take root in our lives is to give the Devil a workshop for building places to accomplish his murderous schemes. The Bible calls these places <u>*strongholds*</u>. It is clear from the teaching of Scripture that what is at stake is our fellowship with God and His freedom, offered to us in Christ. We must trust God to do what's right to those who have hurt us. Not trusting God allows a barrier between us and God.

We can be certain that Satan is watching us very carefully. Unrelenting, day and night he is prowling like a hungry, *roaring lion seeking someone to utterly devour (1 Peter 5:8).* Look with me at how the Bible warns us about hanging on to anger for just one day:

BE ANGRY, AND YET DO NOT SIN; do not let the sun go down on your anger, and do not give the devil an opportunity (Eph. 4:26-27).

One of the quickest ways to allow Satan a stronghold in our lives is to hang on to bitterness. "Dr. Randall, you don't understand how bad I've been hurt. I can't trust anyone. The one who has hurt me has destroyed my life." It is true I may not understand your pain, but our Lord Jesus does. You can trust Him with your hurts and wounds. You can trust Him! Jesus died so you can be set free from the tormentors. Jesus was wounded to heal your wounds. Look with me at what He did for us on Calvary:

> *Surely our griefs He Himself bore, And our sorrows He carried; Yet we ourselves esteemed Him stricken, Smitten of God, and afflicted. But He was pierced through for our transgressions, He was crushed for our iniquities; The chastening for our well-being fell upon Him, And by His scourging we are healed (Isaiah 53:4-5).*

The Bible refers to God as judge. He is a good God and will always do right. *Shall not the Judge of all the earth do right? (Gen. 18:25)* He is the Righteous One. He is good, and all that He does is good. There is a clear prohibition in God's Word concerning harboring offences— taking up any kind of an offense. Look with me at the words of Jesus when He gave the Sermon on the Mount:

> *For if you forgive men for their transgressions, your heavenly Father will also forgive you. But if you do not forgive men, then your Father will not forgive your transgressions (Matt. 6:14-15).*

BITTERNESS LEADS TO A LIFE OF SEPARATION, ISOLATION, AND LONELINESS

Inevitably, bitterness leads to a life of isolation and into a place of extreme loneliness. Man was not created to be alone. He was created to receive love and to give love. Man was created by God with the need for relationships. God said when He created man, *"It is not good for the man to be alone; I will make him a helper suitable for him (Gen 2:18)."* We must not allow bitterness to keep us in isolation and separation from others. No one does well alone. There may be no greater pain in life than loneliness. People do strange things just so they won't be alone. When we refuse to forgive, God stands back and lets us cope with our problems in our own strength. The Bible says the backslider—the one who slides back, away from God—is *"filled with his own ways (Prov. 14:14)."* So when one is left to oneself and to the flesh, those unthinkable capabilities toward sin in that person are given free reign.[2] Remember, the flesh is the avenue demons travel. Not only will bitterness separate us from the sweet fellowship with God, it will also make us such a grouch that no one will want to be around us—except for those who have to put up with us, of course. Bitterness will sour our soul. It will soil our thinking. It will contaminate our life with darkness. Bitterness, if left unchecked, will rain upon our lives unmentionable sorrow through loneliness.

To the best of our ability, we must allow what has happened to us to be used of God to bring everyone who was involved to the Cross of Christ. It is at the Cross where His mercy, forgiveness and healing are limitless. Complete healing is only available at the Cross of Christ. Praise His Holy Name! Jesus' blood was shed not only for you and me, but it was also shed for all those who have caused hurt and pain in our lives. Jesus invites us to come, bring our hurts and wounds and leave them with Him. He knows the burden is too great for us to carry. We must take our hurts and wounds and leave them with Jesus. We must take our burdens to His Cross and leave them there, for our strong and compassionate God will bear the weight we cannot! He can handle it! We must never forget that God, in His loving sovereignty, has a plan to work all things that have happened to us for our good and His ultimate glory *(Romans 8:28).*

BITTERNESS LEADS TO A LIFE OF PRIDE AND SELF-CENTEREDNESS

But if you have bitter jealousy and selfish ambition in your heart, do not be arrogant and so lie against the truth. This wisdom is not that which comes down from above, but is earthly, natural, and demonic. For where jealousy and selfish ambition exist, there is disorder and every evil thing (James 3:14-16).

Resentment that results in bitterness is the full-blown manifestation of pure selfishness. One never exists without the other. Selfishness and bitterness are like conjoined twins. Bitterness freezes in time the one who is the object of our anger in time. Let me explain. We expect others to allow us to grow and move on from our mistakes. However, when we hold a grudge, when we enter into the judgment of another, we are refusing to let them grow and move on from the moment of the evil event. Our bitterness ties the person to that event in time. Essentially we are saying, "I'm not willing to allow that person to grow in the Lord and be forgiven." If we want others to forgive us, then we must offer them the same forgiveness that we expect. When we hold on to our unforgiveness and bitterness refusing to forgive, we are not allowing others the same grace that has been offered to us by Christ. Bitterness changes the rules on the playing field. If we are to expect others to forgive us, then, my brother or sister, we must let others move on from the evil that happened in the past.

Hanging on to an offense while allowing bitterness a place in your life, is not just about you and that other person who has hurt you. Everyone with whom you are in contact has to put up with your sour spirit. No matter how hard you try not to, you will project your wounded heart on others. Like any other demonic stronghold, you don't manage bitterness. It ultimately always manages you (See Chapter 3). Your hatred and anger cannot help spilling over and wounding the people you love the most. You may want to stop hurting them; but, without the cleansing work of Christ in your life, you won't be able to stop:

> *Pursue peace with all men, and the sanctification without which no one will see the Lord. See to it that no one comes short of the grace of God; that no root of bitterness springing up causes trouble, and by it many be defiled (Heb. 12:14-15);*

As Carly Simon's classic hit of the 70s so aptly states, "You probably think this song is about you, don't you? Don't you? Don't you?" It's time to get over yourself. Bitterness is never just about us. Bitterness is a scatter bomb that will destroy everything and everyone around you, even those whom you love.

BITTERNESS LEADS TO A LIFE OF REBELLION AGAINST GOD

Remember Satan's great sin was rebellion *(Isaiah 14:12-15)*. Bitterness, in its root form, is rebellion against God. God's Word says:

Never take your own revenge, beloved, but leave room for the wrath of God, for it is written, vengeance is Mine, I will repay says the Lord (Romans 12:19).

Do not speak against one another, brethren. He who speaks against a brother, or judges his brother, speaks against the law, and judges the law; but if you judge the law, you are not a doer of the law, but a judge of it. There is only one Lawgiver and Judge, the One who is able to save and to destroy; but who are you who judge your neighbor (James 4:11-12)?

The only one who has the legal right to judge is the only True Judge— Jehovah God. He is righteous. He is just. True justice comes only through Him. He will make all things right one day. All will face Him in judgment:

But you, why do you judge your brother? Or you again, why do you regard your brother with contempt? For we shall all stand before the judgment seat of God. For it is written, "AS I LIVE, SAYS THE LORD, EVERY KNEE SHALL BOW TO ME, AND EVERY TONGUE SHALL GIVE PRAISE TO GOD." So then each one of us shall give account of himself to God. Therefore let us not judge one another anymore, but rather determine this—not to put an obstacle or a stumbling block in a brother's way (Romans 14:10-13).

God sent His only Son to die for all sin. Jesus became the supreme sacrifice that God has declared is sufficient for all sin, even the sin of the one who has hurt you. When we decide that we must help God out to bring judgment upon our enemies, we have knowingly or unknowingly, joined Satan's rebellion against God. You see, God can handle these matters all by Himself. He has shed His perfect Son's blood that all sin might be cleansed and forgiven. We must never allow ourselves to sit in the seat of judgment. It's not our job. When we allow bitterness to rule our lives, we must recognize we have trespassed into God's territory. Judgment belongs in the heart and hands of God. Jim Logan, in his wonderful book, Reclaiming Surrendered Ground, helps us understand the real underlying issues behind bitterness: "Bitterness is making God accountable to me. It's also an affront to His sovereignty. In effect, we're saying, 'God, I don't like what You're doing and I want You to know it. You didn't ask my permission or check with me ahead of time and I'm angry.'"[3]

In *Matthew 7* we are commanded by our Lord not to judge. It is from the verb translated "to judge" that the English word <u>critic</u>, or <u>criticize</u> is derived. When we permit ourselves to criticize other people (especially our fellow believers) in such a way that we are pronouncing judgment on them, we are disobeying Scripture and are thus guilty of a rebellious attitude toward God. [4]

When we allow bitterness a place in our hearts, we must quickly recognize we are walking in a very dangerous place. Rebellion is as the sin of witchcraft *(1 Sam. 15:23)*. E.M. Bounds warns of the spiritual dangers of bitterness: "An unforgiving spirit invites Satan's possession. His favorite realm is the spirit, to corrupt our spirit, to provoke us to retaliation, revenge or un-mercifulness—that is his chosen work and his most common and successful device. Paul brings this device out into the open so we can thwart Satan's plans. When Satan generates an unforgiving spirit in us, then he has us, and we are on his ground."[5]

But whom you forgive anything, I forgive also; for indeed what I have forgiven, if I have forgiven anything, I did it for your sakes in the presence of Christ, in order that no advantage be taken of us by Satan; for we are not ignorant of his schemes (2 Cor. 2:10-11).

When my parents' 20-plus-year marriage ended in divorce, the hurt and pain that was leveled upon me and my family was overwhelming. It was during a time when I was extremely vulnerable to the Enemy's lies, as I was entering my teenage years. Since my Father was a well-known preacher, the hurt was even greater than you can imagine. Instead of humbling myself before God, I shook my fist in the face of God and said, "If you're the kind of God that would allow this kind of pain in my life, the deal is off. Everything I have promised, You can forget it." Although I had been saved and called to preach, through my unhealed wounds and resulting unforgiveness, I gave the Devil a place to work in and through my life. My anger against God resulted in a disastrous and dangerous time in my young life. I became sexually active. I became a thief. My life quickly filled with the trash of the world. My mouth became filthy because my heart became filthy. I joined others in playing the music of rebellion. My young life began to spiral out of control. You see, my problem was not my sex life. My problem wasn't the "rock 'n roll" life of rebellion I was living. My problem wasn't my dirty mouth. All of these sordid things were the rotten fruit, the manifestations, of my deep rooted bitterness.

God showed me through the unfailing love of others that His love never fails. With a broken heart toward my sin, I did return to Him in repentance some four years later; but the immeasurable damage was done. Even though I believed I was justified in my anger against God, the truth is I had been duped by the Devil. You see, my bitterness didn't help my parents get back together. My bitterness didn't keep the Lord from loving me. His love for me through it all stayed the same. All my bitterness did was to build a wall. Although the love of Christ was always available to me for the healing of my hurts and sorrows, this demonic barrier kept me from receiving the love and power of the Cross. Hanging on to our wounds through anger only brings us into rebellion. Dear Friend, I am here to testify that a life of rebellion is just not worth it.

BITTERNESS LEADS TO A LIFE OF BLASPHEMY

To remain bitter is to walk in the shoes of a <u>heretic</u>. Please hear me out. To allow bitterness any place in our lives is to act as though Jesus' shed blood was not enough to cover the sins of the person who hurt you. Bitterness demands more blood. Jesus blood is the full payment for your sins and for all the sins of the people who have hurt you. Stop listening to the lies. Jesus' blood is enough for all, ALL sin!

Some years ago while preaching as a guest evangelist, I began to offer prayer meetings after the revival services in the churches where I had been invited to preach. I will never forget a fateful night in Arkansas when God's forgiveness and love was manifested in a most dramatic way. I was approached by a new young father who was deeply concerned about the sin of his ancestors passing to his newborn son. We asked the Lord to come and cleanse these supernatural attachments to the evil ones that had been opened in his family through unconfessed sin. Jesus faithfully met us and cleaned up the mess. When I returned to the sanctuary of the church, I found the pastor on the receiving end of a verbal attack from a woman that had attended the services that night. I walked up to them and asked:

"Ma'am, do you need to see me?"

As quickly as the words came out of my mouth, she fired back, "I sure do!"

I'm certain the pastor was deeply relieved that the angry woman and her mess had been passed to me.

I asked her, "What's going on? Why are you so angry?"

And here it came. Like a double barrel shotgun filled with acidic, toxic filth, She said, "The woman who destroyed my life, my children's lives, and my marriage was in church tonight. How dare she come into the house of God after she has had an ongoing sexual affair with my husband! Who does she think she is coming in here after what she has done to ruin my life?"

I let her go as long as she needed to vent. I don't know how long it was, but the spewing of her venomous anger took awhile before she finally took a breath. She paused to see if I had anything to offer the conversation. I looked her in the eyes and said: "You're so full of bitterness, I bet you can't even pray." I continued, "In fact, I bet you're no longer certain that you are saved."

She sheepishly looked back at me and said, "How did you know?"

I replied, "Because that's what bitterness does to our souls. It separates us from our Lord."

Her open, festering wounds were so visible I could see the volume of hurt deep inside her. I'm convinced that, had she brought a gun to the service that night, there would have been blood on the walls of that church. I asked her if she wanted to talk it through. She said she did. We sat down on the front pew. I will never forget what ensued for the next hour or so. I made the observation and asked her:

"You want that woman dead, don't you? If you could, you would have her head on a platter, wouldn't you?"

She replied, "I sure would."

I looked her in her eyes and said, "You're a heretic."

She was startled. She looked at me as if to say, "What do you mean, heretic?"

"Jesus blood is enough for your sin, but not for hers. You want her to shed her blood for her sin. That's makes you a heretic."

That truth hit her right between the eyes. She took a spiritual pause and began to see her condition.

Finally she conceded, "I can't live like this."

I replied, "Nobody can. It will only kill you."

She said, "What can I do to get rid of this bitterness?"

I turned to *James Chapter 4*, and asked her to read aloud the following passage:

What is the source of quarrels and conflicts among you? Is not the source your pleasures that wage war in your members? You lust and do not have; so you commit murder. And you are envious and cannot obtain; so you fight and quarrel. You do not have because you do not ask. You ask and do not receive, because you ask with wrong motives, so that you may spend it on your pleasures. You adulteresses, do you not know that friendship with the world is hostility toward God? Therefore whoever wishes to be a friend of the world makes himself an Enemy of God. Or do you think that the Scripture speaks to no purpose: "He jealously desires the Spirit which He has made to dwell in us"? But He gives a greater grace. Therefore it says, "GOD IS OPPOSED TO THE PROUD, BUT GIVES GRACE TO THE HUMBLE." Submit therefore to God. Resist the devil and he will flee from you. Draw near to God and He will draw near to you. Cleanse your hands, you sinners; and purify your hearts, you double-minded. Be miserable and mourn and weep; let your laughter be turned into mourning, and your joy to gloom. Humble yourselves in the presence of the Lord, and He will exalt you (James 4:1-10).

We walked through every verse of this passage as it applied to her wounds of resentment and revenge. Then I reminded her, "Jesus loves this other woman as much as he loves you. He died for her, too." I told her before we prayed, "If our prayer was only about her and her wounds, the Lord would probably not even come into the room to do His cleansing work. If we are to expect the Lord to come and do His work, we must humble ourselves and ultimately desire what He wants to do for His glory alone." I asked her, "Are you ready to pray and get this evil stuff cleaned up?"

She said, "I'm ready. I can't live like this."

As we began to pray, I prayed first and asked the Lord to come in His great love and power. I acknowledge to God that what we needed to take place, only He could accomplish. I brought her and her family before the courtroom of Heaven and asked if Jesus would be her advocate, her lawyer (as He promises us He would be in *1 John 2:1*). I asked Him to plead her case before God who is the righteous judge. I continued to pray for a while as the Lord prompted me. Then I turned to the woman and said:

"It's time for you to pray. Just tell the Lord what is on your heart and what you want Him to do."

She began by praying for her children as only a mother can.

Then she prayed for herself, telling the Lord that she could not live with this bitterness that was killing her, any longer. All the while she prayed, I was praying silently for her… "Oh, Lord, please show her that until she can forgive this other woman the way You have forgiven her, this whole demonic system will not be destroyed." I prayed in my heart for her to see the truth as she was crying out to God. Finally, here it came from the depths of her heart: "Lord would you do a great work in her life. Let her know how much you love her. Bring her to the Cross of Christ and pour your love over and in her."

In an instant, it was all gone. After our tears were wiped away, her countenance was completely changed. The load she could carry no longer had been removed. Her life had been renewed. Her faith in the Lord had been recovered. Most of all, her intimacy with her Lord Jesus had been gloriously restored. She was transformed from a babbling, bubbling cauldron of hate and fountain of caustic bitterness to a powerful prayer warrior being used of our precious Lord.

> *But when Christ appeared as a high priest of the good things to come, He entered through the greater and more perfect tabernacle, not made with hands, that is to say not of this creation; and not through the blood of goats and calves, but through His own blood, He entered the holy place ONCE FOR ALL, having obtained eternal redemption (Heb. 9:11-12).*

> *But He, having offered ONE sacrifice for sins FOR ALL TIME (Heb. 10:12).*

It's a horrible thing not to be able to live what you claim to believe. A life of bitterness is no less than taking our Lord's Name in vain. When bitterness is manifesting through us, in essence, we are claiming one thing and living another. The very nature of blasphemy is visualized through the life of the one who is bitter. We must see the hypocritical disconnect. If we claim to have received the Lord's forgiveness even though we didn't deserve it, how much more important is it to forgive others when they don't deserve it? Bitterness that manifests through our lives is like a cloak that covers the authentic love of Christ's forgiveness. Although we claim Christ as our Savior and our Lord, everyone else sees something quite different.

For many years, my family and I have attended a cowboy camp meeting that is convened annually in the Davis Mountains of West Texas. This meeting and its subsequent camp grounds were founded by a Presbyterian circuit riding preacher by the name of Bloys. For over a century, thousands of people, who have their family ties to the West Texas ranches, come to worship and fellowship around the things of the Lord. One afternoon, rather than take a nap, like so many had chosen to do, I chose to attend the service that was held underneath the old, open-air tabernacle. The Methodist preacher, one of four others, who preached that week, had been chosen to lead the service. The text for his sermon was:

> *As you therefore have received Christ Jesus the Lord, so walk in Him (Col. 2:6).*

God spoke clearly and powerfully to me that afternoon through that wonderful Methodist preacher. He gave me a word that has forever changed my life. The last appeal of his message was: "If you have been saved by grace, why can't you learn to be gracious to others?" Wow, what a word! I have come to understand that the "litmus test" of authentic Christianity is grace—the willingness to give as our Lord has given, forgiving those who have hurt you the same way our Lord has forgiven us.

BITTERNESS LEADS TO A LOSS OF GOD'S POWER

> *And do not grieve the Holy Spirit of God, by whom you were sealed for the day of redemption. Let all bitterness and wrath and anger and clamor and slander be put away from you, along with all malice. And be kind to one another, tender-hearted, forgiving each other, just as God in Christ also has forgiven you (Eph. 4:30-32).*

It is only through our yielding and cooperating with the Holy Spirit that God's power is manifested through our lives (See Chapter 5). We shouldn't be surprised when the Holy Spirit is grieved when we cooperate with bitters one of the most frequent causes of people missing the grace of God:

> *See to it that no one comes short of the grace of God; that no root of bitterness springing up causes trouble, and by it many be defiled (Heb. 12:15);*

Grieving the Holy Spirit through anger, bitterness, wrath or other forms of human cursedness probably ruins more Christian testimonies than any other kind of sin. *Galatians 5:20-21* lists hatred, strife and wrath in the same category as murderers, drunkennesness and anger. It heads the list of the things that grieve the Spirit of God. Bitterness is an inner condition; an excessive desire for vengeance that comes from deep-rooted resentment. It became Esau's preoccupation *(Genesis 27:41).*[6] The verse ends with a sobering warning:

> *...of which I forewarn you just as I have forewarned you that those who practice such things shall not inherit the kingdom of God (Gal. 5:21).*

The reference here to the Kingdom of God is not just referring to Heaven. It is also warning us that, if we continue to cooperate with the flesh and allow these sins a place to rule in our lives, there will be a block to receiving God's Kingdom work in our lives. On the other hand, the absence of bitterness allows the Holy Spirit to be Himself in us. When we cooperate with the Holy Spirit in renouncing these works of the flesh, we become like Jesus. R.T. Kendall admonishes every believer to relinquish bitterness: "When the Spirit is grieved, I am left to myself; and I will struggle with emotions ranging from anger to fear. Relinquishing bitterness is an open invitation for the Holy Spirit to give His peace, His joy, and the knowledge of His will."[7] Bitterness not only thwarts the power of God for me in my struggle, it is also a denial of God's ultimate purpose of His work in our lives. It is through suffering that God's purifying process is accomplished in our lives. Now, I may not like this, but it's still true:

Therefore, since Christ has suffered in the flesh, arm yourselves with the same purpose, because he who has suffered in the flesh has ceased from sin, so as to live the rest of the time in the flesh no longer for the lusts of men, but for the will of God (1 Pet. 4:1-2).

This truth may fly in the face of so much of the false and self-centered preaching of self-gratification we hear today. These simple-minded preachers imply that when someone gets saved everything is going to be wonderful. Consequently, we live a clueless life, defeated when trials come because we are unaware of this one truth… Jesus did not come to make us happy. He came to make us HOLY! Christians and non-Christians go through the same life experiences, with one big difference.

God's people don't have to go through their suffering alone. Dr. Logan reminds us: "When Jesus died on the cross, the darkness surrounded Him; and He cried out in agony. Jesus went through His darkness all alone so that I don't have to go through my darkness alone."[8]

For to you it has been granted for Christ's sake, not only to believe in Him, but also to suffer for His sake (Phil. 1:29).

BITTERNESS BRINGS THE JUDGMENT OF GOD

Do not judge lest you be judged. "For in the way you judge, you will be judged; and by your standard of measure, it will be measured to you (Matt. 7:1-2).

As Jesus taught his disciples how to pray, notice the emphasis He put on forgiveness:

And forgive us our debts, as we forgive our debtors (Matt. 6:12).

We must forgive with the same heart of obedience that our Lord has given to us by forgiving us our sins. What is at stake is our fellowship with Him:

For if you forgive men for their transgressions, your heavenly

Father will also forgive you. But if you do not forgive men, then your Father will not forgive your transgressions (Matt. 6:14-15).

No one can change the spiritual laws of God. There is a law of reciprocity that is always at work in the spirit world *(Matt. 7:1-2)*. Whatever you dish out is what you get in return. When we speak curses upon ourselves or others, those very curses come back upon our own heads. If we curse, we get curses. If we bless, then we get blessings. The act of forgiving others is necessary if we are to be able to receive in return the work of God. We are able to love others because Christ first loved us. Since He gave, we give. We are able to offer love and forgiveness to others only through the gift of God's love and forgiveness. We cannot give what we do not possess. Any and all bitterness plugs up the flow of the power of God in and through our lives.

After graduation from seminary, having served several churches in various leadership positions, including serving as the pastor of a wonderful country church, I felt the urging of the Lord to enter into the ministry of vocational evangelism. I believed that the work of evangelism would give me the best opportunity to practice the gifts God had given me. At that same time, my Father was serving as the pastor of a wonderful church in Kansas for sixteen years. The Lord had been dealing with both of us to go into the ministry of vocational evangelism. So we committed the years that lay ahead for the Lord to use us as a father-son evangelistic team, for the sake of winning souls for Christ. God did give us three wonderful years together before Daddy was taken home to be with our Lord.

Now, as has already been shared earlier in this chapter, my parents were divorced. Every ugly thing that could have been said was spoken. Every accusation, every innuendo, and every nasty thing that bitterness fosters in a broken family we had witnessed. My mother had personally called every pastor in every church where my father had a meeting scheduled and made sure they cancelled the meeting. Because of the mess the denomination that my father served had no alternative but to dismiss him and terminate his work with them. After counseling with our pastor, it was determined that my Dad had to leave Texas to survive. It seemed every curse produced as the result of divorce that any family could endure, we had experienced. Daddy avoided Texas. He just never came back. After the very bitter break-up, my parents would have nothing to do with each other. Except for me and my sister's "big events"—graduations, weddings, etc., Mother and Daddy didn't want to have anything to do with one another. Quite frankly, I didn't blame them. The divorce was awful.

My father's lifelong best friend was then serving in South Texas as a Director of Missions. He insisted that we come to conduct revival meetings in several churches in his association. With much reluctance—and I'm sure struggling with overwhelming fear—Daddy agreed that we would come. Since I lived in the North Texas area and Daddy was coming from Kansas, we agreed he would pick me up as he went through; we would travel together to the upcoming revival meetings in South Texas. My mother was living with us at the time. She was in need of constant care while recuperating in our home from one of her many dangerous surgeries resulting from her diabetes. Mother and Daddy were going to have to see each other once again.

To say I was nervous about their reluctant encounter would be an understatement. I knew my Mother would be stewing in her pot of ongoing bitterness and that it would most likely explode in an ugly outburst. It seemed to me, we just had more sorrow than any family needed. I wanted to make certain, as best I could, that there would be no more inflicted wounds. Cautiously I went to my Mother's bedside to try to defuse her ticking bomb of bitterness. My Mother, being of Scottish and Irish decent, was born with a short fuse and this volatile reunion of my parents could easily blow at any moment.

"Momma," I asked, "are you nervous about seeing Daddy?"

She sat staring straight ahead, not batting even an eyelash.

I repeated my question, "Momma, are you nervous about seeing Daddy again?"

She barked her response—most of you know, too well, that

Mothers can bark—"Wouldn't you be?" She shouted! "I was married to him over twenty years. We had two children together. Wouldn't you be?"

"Yes, Mother, I guess I would be nervous, too. I just thought it would be best if you and I talked about it before He arrived, to avoid a blow up."

Then, she said something I shall never forget. "Son, who's going to pay for all the pain we have been through? Who's going to pay for the hurt you and your sister have had to endure these many years? Who's going to pay for it all?"

It was then I took my small-framed, infirmed mother in my arms; and, as we cried together, I said, "Momma, JESUS PAID IT ALL. ALL TO HIM WE OWE. SIN HAD LEFT A CRIMSON STAIN, BUT HE WASHED IT WHITE AS SNOW! That's what we've preached all over the world all these years. That's the Gospel of Christ. He carried our sin to the cross. Can't we believe and practice what we claim to believe? Can't we give all of our hurts, sorrows and wounds to Jesus? He carried them all to Calvary. There's no need for us to keep carrying them. He did it all for us!"

From that time on until my Mother's death some few years later, she was never quite the same. At that moment, in our home in North Central Texas, a light seemed to shine in my mother's heart. I believe she came to better understand what Christ did for her on Calvary. I never again saw the awful bitterness that had so plagued her life during those many difficult and dark years.

BITTERNESS ULTIMATELY LEADS TO DEATH

Let me say it again. We are most like Satan when we are bitter and angry. We are most like Christ when we unconditionally love and forgive those who have hurt us. Bitterness is a powerful chief demonic system that allows the Enemy ground to ultimately destroy everyone and everything it touches. We find this clear warning in Scripture concerning the relationship between bitterness and the Devil:

Be angry, and yet do not sin; do not let the sun go down on your anger, and do not give the Devil an opportunity (Eph. 4:26-27).

The word opportunity in the verse above is a translation from the Greek word topos. We get our word topography from this root word. It literally means ground or a place for the Devil to work in our lives. What is Satan's work? What is his ultimate purpose in gaining any influence and control of our lives? Jesus said that the Devil was a murderer from the beginning and has come to steal, kill, and destroy. He is truly as the Scriptures describe him, 'like a roaring lion seeking someone to devour' *(I Peter 5:8)*. His mission is to kill us. Bitterness opens the door and allows him to come into our lives and perform his murderous work. Bill Glass, a faithful and fellow evangelist who has ministered many years to the men and women in the prison systems across America has said, "There is one common denominator that all men on death row share." What would you guess it is? "All who sit on death row waiting for their day of execution hate their fathers." That's right, these precious souls for whom Christ died are eaten up with the Devil's principality whose name is BITTERNESS. Tragically, in these broken lives, Bitterness has accomplished Satan's evil plan of murder and subsequent death.

Not only does bitterness rot the soul, but when our soul becomes sick, the body will respond in kind. I have found that bitterness will open the door to many diseases. Many cancers, blood and metabolic disorders such as diabetes have at their root cause the spiritual destruction of bitterness. Dr. Henry Wright, Senior Pastor of The Pleasant Valley Church in Thomaston, Georgia has followed the Lord's leading in his life to pursue the connections between certain diseases and their spiritual roots. He and the people of his church have seen a phenomenal work of God through this healing ministry. Many hundreds of verifiable testimonies of God's healing power continue to come from this praying church. God continues to heal sick people from so-called "incurable" diseases through this most effective ministry of working with Christ. Dr. Wright says of the body: "You are very chemical in your creation. You are very nuclear, you are very sexual, you are very spiritual, but you are also very chemical. You have a number of organs and glands, particularly in the endocrine system, which secrete a particular chemical. It kind of goes like this; a squirt here, a squirt there, here a squirt, there a squirt, everywhere a squirt, squirt. Your Enemy knows that he can control the rate of your squirts by your thoughts and by your soul and by your spirit. Your Enemy knows that things like bitterness and guilt and fear, if allowed to remain within your consciousness, can be used of him to control you. When your spiritual dynamics are compromised by the Enemy in a manner that he can control your body and he can control your chemistry, then he can put depression or any other psychological or biological malfunction on you when he feels like it."[9]

Sid's Story

When my book, *The Invisible War—Living in Victory Over the Enemy,* was first released, I sent a copy to many of my pastor friends. On New Year's Day, 2003, I received a phone call from a pastor I had not heard from in several years. In my thirty years serving as an evangelist, Sid was by far the most effective soul-winner I had known. His greatest thrill was to lead a soul to Christ. He was the best at it I had ever seen. However, the last time I had heard from Sid he was experiencing what is commonly called "burn out." He was quitting the ministry and heading to a secret place to try to get his life back together. He told me that his nerves just couldn't take dealing with people any longer. He asked me not to try to contact him; but that when he was ready to talk, he would call me. I told him I would honor his request and would be praying for both he, and his sweet wife. When I received his phone call that New Year's Day, you can understand how happy and somewhat shocked I was to hear from my dear friend.

With great joy, Sid told me how excited he was about my book. He said, "Rob, I always knew I had bitterness in my life, but I didn't know how to get rid of it. When I read your book, it was as though you were right here holding my hand, walking me through the prayers of healing." He was so excited that he was almost shouting over the phone. "Rob," he said, "it's gone. It's finally gone. At the foot of my bed, when I cried out to God, my demons of bitterness left me. Oh,

Rob, every pastor in Texas needs this book." I told him to pray to that end, that maybe one day we could place a book in every pastor's hand in Texas! Some months went by, and I called Sid on the phone. When he answered, his voice was weak. He sounded sick.

He said, "Rob, I've been diagnosed with a fast growing bone cancer, and the doctors don't give me any hope to live long."

I said, "Sid, let me pray for you right now."

We had an old-fashioned prayer meeting on the phone that day. I mean we got a hold of Heaven. I prayed over my friend and I asked God to remove the spirit of death from him. I cried out to the Lord Jesus to give Sid more years to live so he could win many more souls to Christ. I don't know how long we were on the phone, but God came down and His power was evident. Jehovah Rapha, our Healer, came and met us that wonderful day. In all honesty, I felt the the next phone call I received would be from Sid's wife telling me about Sid's funeral. Weeks and then months went by. One day, I became curious so I called to see if Sid was O.K.. When he answered the phone, his voice was strong and full of life again.

He said, "Rob, it's gone. It's gone. I mean it's all gone. The doctors can't find any trace of the cancer."

We began to rejoice together over the phone. Through his overflowing joy, this is what Sid said: "Rob, if I had not gotten rid of the bitterness I had so struggled with all my life, I would be dead. When Jesus came and took away all my bitterness, it opened up my life to be healed."

UPDATE! I just spoke with Sid today to get his permission to publish his story. Seven years later he is still cancer free. Hallelujah, what a Savior!

GETTING RID OF BITTERNESS
FORGIVENESS DOES NOT CONDONE SIN

Pastor Henry Wright helps us to understand that forgiving others is not condoning their sin: "It is necessary to understand that, in releasing your offender, you have released yourself. You forgive others because

Christ has forgiven you. You don't have to carry someone else's sin inside of you. Their sin is their sin. God will be their judge. My Friend, your freedom does not depend upon their resolution—it depends upon your resolution. When you forgive others, you are not letting them off the hook, but giving them to God still wiggling on the hook. You're now off the hook. When you forgive someone, you continue to hate their sin; but you are commanded to love them. To forgive, you don't have to condone their sin."[10]

What I'm sharing with you next holds the keys to unlocking the secrets to the evil work of bitterness in your life. If you have made it this far, be warned—the Enemy will do everything within his power to hinder you from continuing the journey into spiritual cleansing. Please stay on course. We're almost there. My prayer for you is that you will not only be able to see how the lies of bitterness have been so effective in your life, but that you will be able to call upon Holy Spirit to destroy all the works of bitterness. May you be set free from these powers of darkness and their murderous effect they have had in your life. Getting rid of bitterness is not just agreeing with what the Word of God says about it. Of course, we must begin with the foundation of truth to experience the freedom of Christ *(John 8:32)*. My Friend, we can believe every word of the Scriptures is true and yet never know God and His wonderful work in our lives. The devils believe the Word of God is true, but look at the mess they're in:

You believe that God is one. You do well; the demons also believe, and shudder (James 2:19).

TAKING THE GROUND BACK THROUGH CONFESSION

If we confess our sins, He is faithful and righteous to forgive us our sins and to cleanse us from all unrighteousness (1 John 1:9).

Getting rid of bitterness is a two-fold process: <u>CONFESS</u> AND <u>BLESS</u>. Each is as important as the other. Each must be handled in proper order. Let's deal with bitterness through our confession first. Since bitterness is an evil spirit, it must be expelled. For an evil spirit to be expelled, the sin that opened the doorway into which it found entrance must be confessed. When the Lord Jesus was asked of his accusers what the greatest commandment was, do you remember what He said?

> *YOU SHALL LOVE THE LORD YOUR GOD WITH ALL YOUR HEART, AND WITH ALL YOUR SOUL, AND WITH ALL YOUR MIND. This is the great and foremost commandment. The second is like it, YOU SHALL LOVE YOUR NEIGHBOR AS YOURSELF. On these two commandments depend the whole Law and the Prophets (Matt. 22:37-40).*

This is big! Jesus said that the whole Law and the Prophets—the whole of the Old Testament rests upon God's revelation in these two commandments. WOW! In Jesus' response, we find the key to freedom from the Spirit of Bitterness. First, notice that there are three areas in which we can take up an offense and allow the Spirit of Bitterness access into our lives. These areas are: bitterness toward God, bitterness toward others, and bitterness toward ourselves. It is essential that we have a loving and forgiving heart toward God, and others, as well as toward ourselves. If any offense is allowed to remain, bitterness will not leave. We cannot be free from bitterness until every place we have taken an offense is recognized and confessed as sin.

Humble yourself before the Lord and ask the Lord to come and show you any offenses that you have harbored through unforgiveness that are still at work in your heart. Take a pad and a pen and get ready to write down what He reveals to you. God is more concerned about your freedom in Christ than you could ever know. Your freedom cost Him His life. Ask the Lord Jesus to shut the mouths of the accusers and liars. Say aloud, "May no other voice be heard, but the voice of the Lord Jesus." Ask the Holy Spirit to show you if you have ever been angry at God and why. Write down what He tells you and agree with Him—confess it as sin. Ask the Holy Spirit to show you if an offense is still working in your life toward anyone who has offended you and why. Write down what He tells you and agree with Him—confess it as sin. Now ask the Holy Spirit to show you if you are holding on to any unforgiveness toward yourself for what you've done. It may be an offense that is the result of things that have happened to you. Write down what He tells you and agree with Him—confess it as sin.

BITTERNESS—THE PRINCIPALITY

Bitterness is much more than just a powerful emotion, even though emotions are involved. Bitterness is like an octopus. It has many tentacles, each struggling for ultimate control and power. Notice how each of these underlings is connected to the other. Notice the progression of the 'Bitterness System' from the top of the list to the bottom of the list. Each underling, or tentacle must be removed individually before Bitterness will leave. If one of its underlings is allowed to hang on, Bitterness will hang on. Get alone with our Heavenly Father. Ask Him to silence all other voices, but His voice. Humble yourself and ask Him to tell you where any of the underlings of Bitterness listed below are still at work in your heart. When He tells you, agree with Him. Confess each one aloud. Ask Him to forgive you for cooperating with the Evil One through His demonic system of bitterness. When all areas of cooperation with the underlings are confessed before God, ask the Lord by His power, by His blood, and by His Word to remove Bitterness from you. Once it's done, ask the Lord to give you the same love for the one who has hurt you that our Lord has so freely expressed toward you in the sacrifice of His Son, Christ Jesus. It's all a gift. Receive it! Thank Him for His work in you!

THE DEMONIC SYSTEM OF BITTERNESS

Underlings:

- **Unforgiveness**- To enhance the normal feeling of unforgiveness.

- **Resentment**- Playing the record of the wrong.

- **Retaliation**- Plotting to get even for wrong done.

- **Anger/Wrath/Rage**: Physical manifestation of defilement.

- **Hatred**- Stage of elimination- Carries out the evil.

- **Violence**- Bitterness in Motion- The full-blown manifestation.

- **Murder**- The full completed work of Satan.[11]

Now that the confession of our sin and disobedience to God has been made, now that the evil spirits have been put on notice that they must leave and allow you to walk in the freedom of Christ, we must show our acts of repentance through blessing those who have hurt us.

TAKING THE GROUND BACK THROUGH BLESSING

But I say to you who hear, love your enemies, do good to those who hate you, bless those who curse you, pray for those who mistreat you (Luke 6:27-28).

For many years, my wonderful wife and I have practiced something that is extremely effective and powerful. Whenever we have run into a grouch that has been intentionally ugly toward us or our family, we bake them a cake. We call it the ministry of cake. The cake has amazing transforming powers. Almost before our eyes, the person "morphs" from a mean grouchy ogre to a prince or princess that is full of kindness. It's amazing to watch what a gift will do when blessed by God. Always remember—it is the wounded that wound others. Bitter people are the way they are because of the unhealed damage that has not been resolved at the Cross. What they need is JESUS to heal them! Only Jesus can heal them!

Please understand, I'm encouraging you to do something which the Lord prompts me to do on a regular basis. Just a few days ago I went into a prayer meeting at a conference on healing. My body was

manifesting some bad stuff as the result of some unresolved issues I had
with a couple of brothers in Christ. So, I prayed and gave my resentment
toward these guys to the Lord. In fact, I had been faced with the matter
so often it seemed I was in a constant place of declaring my forgiveness
for these men. I asked the Lord to bless them and their families. Then
the Lord said to me, "I will bless them through your blessing them.
Send them both a gift of blessing." So, I called up the florist and sent
both of them a beautiful bouquet of flowers. Now, I have no idea at this
time if the gift of these flowers meant anything to these men. I have to
leave that up to the Lord to deal with them. You see, the act of blessing
was meant to remove from my life any residue of darkness that the Enemy could use in my life. Of course, you must pray about it first. Give
it to the Lord; but, after we have given the matter to the Lord through
confession, we must also bless those who have hurt us.

Important Note:

Now that you are aware that **Bitterness** is a chief demon, it is important that you take this extremely serious. If you have cooperated
with Satan through bitterness at any time in your life like I have, it will
be important for you to revisit these areas on a regular basis to make
certain the Spirit of Bitterness has not crept back into your life. Please
understand that these areas where you have cooperated with the Devil in
the past always become the places where you are most vulnerable to the
attacks of the Enemy. Satan takes note of these places of disobedience.
Because it has worked for him in the past, he knows it may just work
for his murderous schemes again. You must stay vigilant, continuing to
allow the love and forgiveness of our Savior to rule in your heart. You
must never stray too far from the forgiving heart and the love of our
Lord Jesus. You now have the help you need—the knowledge of how to
get rid of bitterness as soon as it rears its ugly head. Immediately take
it to Cross of Calvary through confession. Practice repentance through
the act of blessing those who have hurt you.

PRAYING IT THROUGH.

TAKING THE JOURNEY INTO SPIRITUAL CLEANSING.

The methods of spiritual cleansing offered in this book are not presented as to presume that they are the only way to freedom in Christ. The words on these pages are not magic. They are not printed here so as to be used as a religious ritual. These methods and prayers are offered as a guide. In them are represented the biblical truths that God uses to set the captives free.

Unless the Spirit of God breathes His life upon these prayers, they will be nothing more than mere words on a page. The prayers in this book are a collection of prayers that when used of God have been known to help people in spiritual darkness find freedom in Christ. It is Christ alone who is our Savior. It is Christ alone who is our Deliverer. It is Christ alone who is our Healer.

Each prayer in this chapter is a declaration of freedom from spiritual bondage. It is recommended that each prayer as applied should be spoken aloud. Spirits of darkness cannot read our minds; they can only hear what we speak.

THE PRAYER GOD ANSWERS:

The effectual fervent prayer of a righteous man availeth much (James 5:16 KJV). Now to Him who is able to do exceeding abundantly beyond all that we ask or think, according to the power that works within us (Eph. 3:20).

Before any attempt to set the captives free is approached, before any confrontation with the rebel prince is launched, the believer **must** understand the eternal truths concerning the prayer that God answers.

- **God answers the Prayer that is prayed under the Sacrifice of Christ**

Since the attack on America on September 11, 2001, our nation has been in a state of shock and sorrow like we have not known in our lifetime. In an effort to heal our nation's sorrow, a prayer meeting was scheduled in Yankee Stadium. Expectantly, I watched with millions of others as the prayer meeting was broadcast on national television. Maybe you were as shocked and hurt as I was as the Name of Jesus was only mentioned once in the two hours of this so-called "prayer meeting." What a waste. Prayers can only reach the Throne Room of Heaven through the sacrifice of Christ:

*I am the way, the truth, and the life, no one comes to the Father **except by me** (John 14:6, KJV).And whatever you ask **in my name** that will I do, that the Father may be glorified in the Son (John 14:13). Truly, truly, I say to you, if you shall ask the Father for anything, He will give it to you **in my Name** (John 15:16, 16:23).*

It is only through our union with Christ, made possible through His sacrifice for our sins on Calvary, that we are able to approach the Holy of Holies with our petitions. ...and raised us up with Him, and seated us with Him in the heavenly places in Christ Jesus *(Eph. 2:6).* This passage is a direct reference to *Eph. 1:20* that tells us that only through our union with Christ, made available through His blood sacrifice for our sins, are we able to come and be received before a Holy God.

- **God answers the Prayer that is Specific**

   You have not because you ask not (James 4:2). …but in everything by prayer and supplication with thanksgiving let your requests be made known to God (Phil. 4:6).

Why are we to be specific when we pray? Isn't God omniscient? Doesn't He already know what is going on? Prayer is not an effort to get God's attention. We have His undivided attention through our union with Christ. Prayer is a time of getting our hearts in tune with the heart of God. Prayer is not some self-centered exercise of manipulating God to do what we want. Prayer is not some "name-it and claim-it, blab-it and grab-it" means by which we seek to fill our own selfish desires. No, no! Prayer is exercising our union with Christ to join our hearts with the very will and heart of our Heavenly Father. *If you ask Me anything in my Name, I will do it (John 14:14).* Prayer is working together with God to see His will accomplished on earth as it is in Heaven:

   Truly I say to you, whatever you shall bind on earth will be bound in heaven; and whatever you loose on the earth shall be loosed in Heaven (Matt. 16:19).

- **God answers the Prayer that is prayed in the Spirit**

   And in the same way the Spirit also helps our weaknesses; for we do not know how to pray as we should, but the Spirit Himself intercedes for us with groanings too deep for words (Romans 8:26).

Once again, it is through our union with the Lord Jesus that our prayers become effective prayers. The Spirit of God who dwells within each believer is the one who teaches us how to pray and what to pray. It is through this holy relationship with God that effective prayer resides. There are times in all of our lives when our hurts are so deep, our sorrows so overwhelming that we don't know if we can pray, much less know what to pray. These are the times when our prayer time becomes a time of healing and sweet communion with the Lord. It is the Holy Spirit who will take over the prayer "closet." There is no night so dark that our Lord is not present. There is no tear-stained pillow that our Lord does not share our grief *(Isaiah 53:4-5)*. It is through the precious ministry of the Holy Spirit, the One who stands beside us, the One who never leaves us or forsakes us, who enables us to be in communion with God in prayer. Even in the passage concerning the Armor that God gives us when we are engaged in a spiritual battle, we find this admonition:

*With all prayer and petition pray at all times **in the Spirit** (Eph. 6:18).*

• **God answers the Prayer that is offered in Submission to His will**

God is opposed to the proud, but gives grace to the humble (James 4:6).

Herein lies the key to effective prayer:

You ask and do not receive, because you ask with wrong motives, so that you may spend it on your pleasures (James 4:3).

If we ever expect God to hear and answer our petitions, they must be presented to Him in complete humility and submission to His will. Fasting comes into focus at this point. Fasting is not an attempt to become super spiritual. Fasting is not some kind of "work" to get into God's presence. Fasting is simply putting aside our flesh so it cannot influence our communion with the Lord. God answers the prayer that is presented in total submission to His will:

And this is the confidence, which we have before Him, that, if we ask anything according to His will, He hears us (I John 5:14).

BIBLICAL PRINCIPLES FOR SPIRITUAL CLEANSING

The ministry of spiritual cleansing is the sovereign work of grace by our Lord Jesus. He is the One who came to *set the captives free (Luke 4)*. He is the One who was *manifest that He might destroy the works of the Devil (I John 3:8)*. He is our deliverer. He taught us to pray, *Deliver us from the Evil One (Matt. 6:13)*. In simple outline form here are the principle truths that are involved in setting the captives free:

A. DISCOVER through discernment the work (or ground) of the Devil. **RECOGNIZE** the work of the Devil *(I John 3:10, James 3:11-12)*.

B. DENOUNCE the work of the Devil.
  * **RENOUNCE** *(2 Cor. 4:2)*.
  * **REPENT** Turn from sin and turn to God for forgiveness *(Acts 8:22-23)*.
  * **RESIST** *(James 4:7)*.
  * **REPLACE** the lies of the Enemy with the **TRUTH** of **GOD'S WORD** *(John 8:32)*.

C. DECLARE out loud your commitment to Christ *(Romans 8:35-39)*.
  * Your **Position** in Christ—Victor, not a victim *(Col. 2:15, Eph. 6)*.
  * Your **Posture** of victory—**Humble** yourselves before God *(James 4). Reckon yourself dead to sin (Romans 6:11)*.
  * **Proclaim** your Victory—*(Rev. 12:11)*.

D. DELIVER through **DISPOSING** the Enemy *(Luke 8:26-33)*.
  * **RECLAIM for** Christ the area stolen by the Enemy *(Eph. 4:26-27)*.
  * **REFILL** the empty area with the Holy Spirit *(Luke 11:22-26)*.
  * **RENEW** the mind through the Word of God *(Romans 12:1-2, Phil. 4:8, 2 Cor. 10:5)*.
  * **REJOICE** with all of heaven in the work of the Lord Jesus Christ *(Luke 15:7, 10, 32)*.

UNDERSTANDING SATAN'S STRONGHOLDS

"For though we walk in the flesh, we do not war according to the flesh, for the weapons of our warfare are not of the flesh, but

divinely powerful for the destruction of (strongholds) fortresses. We are destroying speculations and every lofty thing raised up against the knowledge of God, and we are taking every thought captive to the obedience of Christ (2 Cor. 10:3-5)."

A stronghold is a fortress, a "beach-head," Satan has been allowed to build within our lives. It is ground that has been given over to the Enemy through continual unconfessed sin and an unrepentant heart. Holy Scripture warns us:

Be of sober spirit, be on the alert. Your adversary, the Devil prowls about like a roaring lion, seeking someone to devour (I Peter 3:8).

Our arch Enemy, Satan, is continually looking for a place to take advantage in our lives for the ultimate purpose to *steal, kill, and to destroy (John 10:10).* Sin always separates us from a Holy God and His protection, not His grace and love *(Romans 8:35-39).* God's Word tells us:

Be angry, and yet do not sin; do not let the sun go down on your anger, and do not give the Devil an opportunity, a place (Eph. 4:26-27).

This word translated <u>opportunity</u> or <u>place</u> is <u>topos</u>. We get the word <u>topography</u> from this word. It literally means a place or ground by which the Devil can get an advantage in our lives to defeat and ultimately destroy us. Herein lies the truth concerning strongholds. They are places in our lives given to the Devil by sin, disobedience, and unbelief. Spiritual warfare is the struggle between believing the lies of the Enemy, (who is the Father of Lies, *John 8:44*), and the truth of the Word of God *(John 17:17, Psalm 119:89, 2 Tim. 3:16, John 8:32).* Think of a stronghold in the terms of how the Bible refers to it. It is a fortress. I like to think of it as a tower or a wall. It is a place given to the Enemy through believing his lies. The Enemy fortifies these fortresses through time. Behind these, the Enemy hides to do his evil work of stealing, killing, and ultimate destruction. Rarely is the demonic exposed and seen, but the evidence of their destruction is clearly seen.

(See The Pulling Down of Strongholds, The Enemy's Fortresses—Hiding Places, to help visualize the nature and function of the Enemy's strongholds pg. 238.)

The structure of these strongholds is explained on page in the Stronghold Structure Section of the Stronghold Prayer. These strongholds although invisible are real structures, real fortresses where the Enemy has been allowed by our sin and unbelief to do his evil work. Once they are torn down the evil ones will have to find another place to do their evil work. A stronghold is revealed when a person can no longer believe what God has said. All sin was completely forgiven; dealt with by God on the Cross of Christ. Through the blood sacrifice of the Lord Jesus, all Satan's power was broken and placed under the authority of the Lord Jesus Christ *(Col. 2:15)*. There is no freedom apart from Christ *(John 8:36)*. Jesus came to set the captives free *(Luke 4:18)*. If a person continues in sin and refuses to receive the only way to forgiveness for that sin, the person is essentially saying, "I don't believe God is able to forgive me. I don't believe that Jesus' blood forgives all sin. I don't believe that I can be forgiven. I have gone too far. Jesus can't forgive me. I can't forgive that person. God can't heal me of these hurts." To believe these lies is to join oneself to the rebellion in the unseen world against God, against God's will and against God's Word *(1 Tim. 2:4)*. Jesus said, *"You shall know the truth, and the truth shall make you free (John 8:32)."*

The following illustration is presented to help better understand Satan's Strongholds:

THE PULLING DOWN OF STRONGHOLDS
(Illustration C)

The following Stronghold Prayer is presented here by permission of a godly warrior, Dr. Norman Coad of Burleson, Texas. Dr. Coad received it from the Lord through working many years with the spiritually wounded. Norm and his wife Beverly learned spiritual warfare while serving 18 years as missionaries in West Africa. They now have an effective counseling ministry of spiritual cleansing and healing in North Texas where they have served the Lord Jesus for 20 plus years. This following powerful prayer tears down the strongholds (the hiding places for the Enemy to do his evil work). Each stronghold is based upon a lie that has been, or is being believed.

The Enemy's Fortresses – Hiding Places
A Stronghold is present when
someone <u>cannot believe</u> the Truth of God!

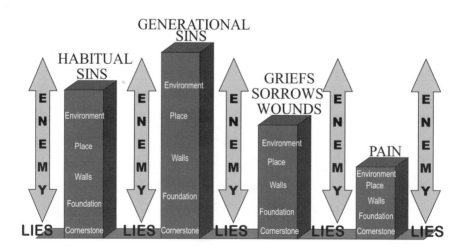

STRONGHOLD PRAYER

1. I bring the bindings, judgments, anathemas, and coverings of the blood of the Lord Jesus Christ to bear.

2. Whatever structure, level, spirits, materials, motors, batteries, light, shadow, or never.

3. Whatever the demons, demon creatures, ancestral spirits, and spirits of living flesh, animal spirits and nature spirits, or any other spirits we may not know about whatever their foundations, formations, and functions.

4. Whatever the assignments, curses, or judgments, ties, deceptions, destructions, triggers, batteries and programming, without or within us, without or within the family, without or within covens, whatever the location or place, whatever their times, foundations, formations, or functions.

5. Declaring them null and void and without effect, sending them back to their point of origin, with judgment, pain, and condemnation in the Name of the Lord Jesus Christ.

Pray the "Stronghold Prayer" over each area of the "Stronghold Structure." Think of the stronghold as a tower with its separate parts.

STRONGHOLD STRUCTURE

A. Environment (*2 Cor. 10:3-5*)   70x7x7 to 2nd*
    System of thought contrary to the teaching of the Word of God. Ideas learned as a child without biblical basis.

B. Place (topos) given to the devil   70x7x7 to 7th
    (*Eph. 4:26-27*) (Anger)
    Non-biblical ideas we act on to create sin in our lives.

C. Walls (*James 1:13-15*)   **70x7x7 to 3rd**
   Sinful thoughts, sinful emotions, sinful behaviors that hurt others and us.

D. Foundation (*Isaiah 53:4-5*)   **70x7x7 to 4th**
   · **Griefs – Normal emotions to express loss**
   · **Sorrows – Things that happen we wished had never happened**
   · **Wounds – Unhealed damage to spirit or body that is continual pain, abusive action or trauma.**

E. Cornerstone (*Isaiah 53:4-5*)   **70x7x7 to 5th**
   Iniquity (Hebrew word), way of life built on lies.[1]

*As you pray, applying by faith the truth of the Word of God in each area of the stronghold, call on the Lord to bring to bear all of the power of God needed to destroy all the works of the Enemy. These mathematical formulas represent the power of God used (as discovered in the counseling room by those in the ministry of spiritual cleansing) to break down each piece in the structure of the Enemy's strongholds.

PRAYER PREPARATION FOR SPIRITUAL CLEANSING

Spiritual cleansing is not possible unless the person is willing to confess (agree with God) concerning his or her sin. Whatever the areas of bondage are in a person's life, the will is free to choose Christ. The person must want to be free and willing to come to Christ as his only hope in receiving true freedom *(Matt. 12:43-45)*.

Prayer

Dear Heavenly Father, I choose to give my life to You. I choose to follow You only, serve You only, and believe You only. I acknowledge Your presence in this room and in my life. You are the only omniscient (all-knowing), omnipotent (all-powerful), and omnipresent (ever-present) God. As I come into Your presence, I ask You to show me any working of the Enemy in my life. Help me see the lies of Satan for what they are. Help me face the truth and believe the truth. Come and release Your creation unto Yourself. I'm dependent upon You; for, apart from You, I can do nothing. I stand in the truth that all authority in heaven and on earth has been given in the resurrected Christ; and, because I am in Christ, I share that authority in order to make disciples and set captives free. I ask You to fill me with Your Holy Spirit and lead me into all truth. I pray for Your complete protection and ask for Your guidance. Put me in the circle of the New Covenant in Your blood. In the mighty Name of the Lord Jesus Christ, I pray. Amen. In the Name and authority of the Lord Jesus Christ, I command Satan and all his evil spirits to release me and to leave my presence in order that I can be free to do the will of God. I commit myself to the will of God. I submit my body to my heavenly Father as a living sacrifice, holy unto the Lord. I refuse to be intimidated by Satan's lies or to give in to any physical harassment. As a child of God, who is seated with Christ in the heavenlies, I command every evil spirit to go where Jesus tells you to go when Jesus tells you to go. He is Lord over all things. All spirits must come to attention to face the judgment of almighty God. There will be no manifestations except the manifestation of the Holy Spirit. I belong to God and the Evil One cannot touch me. I ask that no other voice be heard but the voice of the Lord Jesus. All others must be silenced in the presence of Holy God. I ask the Lord to reveal to me His truth as the Holy Spirit will guide me.

REMOVING DEMONIC LEGAL RIGHTS
Canceling Permissions

Prayer

Father, I thank You for Jesus and for my salvation through Him. He is the Savior, and I am the sinner. I am so grateful to be washed in His blood. Because You have forgiven me, I choose to forgive others. Everyone who has hurt me, lied to me or disappointed me, I forgive. I repent of unforgiveness. I know it is sin. I forgive myself and apply Your great forgiveness to my life.

I repent of anger, bitterness and hatred; of rebellion, resentment and revenge; of envy, jealousy and strife, doubt, unbelief and skepticism; of lust, witchcraft and idolatry and all the works of the flesh. I denounce the sins of my ancestors. I totally separate myself from generational curses. I renounce all unholy vows, pledges, oaths or ceremonies, and I choose to be free from all permission of any secret societies' curse. I denounce all unholy soul ties and confess them as sin. I confess that Jesus Christ is my Savior and Lord, He's my Deliverer and my Healer, and He broke the power of all curses. I choose to be free and I will be free in Jesus' Name.[2]

PRAYERS FOR SPIRITUAL CLEANSING

The wages of sin is always DEATH. No one is exempt from this eternal truth. Unconfessed sin always leads to habitual sin. Habitual sin most often leads to spiritual bondage. People who get caught in the "revolving door" of sin-confess-sin-confess will find the instructions of *James 4:1-10* most helpful:

• Submit to God

• Resist the Devil

• Draw near to God

• Cleanse your hands

• Purify your hearts

• Be miserable, morn, and weep

• Humble yourself

It is so important to remember the following promise of God concerning the confession of our sins:

If we confess our sins, He is faithful and righteous to forgive us our sins and to cleanse us from all unrighteousness (1 John 1:9).

Confession is not saying, "I'm sorry" but saying, "I did it." Confession is agreeing with God that He is right in what He says and that you have been wrong. Only the sorrow that leads to repentance (a change of thinking, which is believing the truth of God) will bring God's spiritual cleansing *(2 Cor. 7:10)*.

Prayer for Spiritual Cleansing from False Religions, False Teachings, and Rituals
(1 Cor. 10:20)

All that the Enemy does is a carefully designed counterfeit to the work and truth of God. It is critically important to renounce (verbally reject) past or present involvement with occult practices, cult teachings, and rituals, as well as non-Christian religions. You must renounce any activity or group that denies Jesus Christ, or offers guidance through any source other than the absolute authority of the Bible. As well as any group that requires dark, secret initiations, ceremonies, promises, or pacts must also be renounced. Begin this step by praying aloud:

Prayer
Dear Heavenly Father, I ask You to bring to my mind anything and everything that I have done knowingly or unknowingly that involves occult, cult, or non-Christian teachings or practices. I pray that all of Satan's deceptions will be seen for what they are in my life. I want to experience Your freedom by renouncing the evil things in which I have been involved. In Jesus' mighty and holy Name I pray, Amen. Lord, I confess that I have participated in_____. I know it was evil and offensive in your sight. Thank You for your forgiveness. I renounce any and all involvement with_____. I cancel out any and all ground that the Enemy has gained in my life through this activity. In the Name of my Lord Jesus Christ I pray, Amen.

Prayer for Spiritual Cleansing from Idolatry
(I John 5:20-21, Matt. 4:10, Exodus 20:3,
Matthew 22:37, Rev. 2:4-5, Deut. 5:7-8)

Prayer

Dear Lord God, I have allowed other things and other people to become more important to me than You. I am so sorry I have offended You and Your Word when You have said, I "shall have no other gods" before You. I confess to You that I have not loved You with all my heart and soul and mind. As a result, I have sinned against You, violating the first and greatest commandment. I repent and turn away from this idolatry and now choose to return to You, Lord Jesus, as my first love. Please forgive me for not trusting and loving You. As I come before You, please show me anything or anyone I have allowed to become an idol in my life. I renounce each of them. In so doing, any and all ground Satan may have gained in my life through my idolatry is taken back for the glory of God. In the Name of Lord Jesus Christ, the one true God, Amen. In the Name of the true and living God, Jesus Christ, I renounce my worship of the false god of (name the idol). Please forgive me. As I have sought my answers except from Your truth, I realize where I have sinned against You. Please forgive me for believing Satan's lies. I choose to worship only You, Lord. I ask You, Father, to enable me to keep this area of (name the idol) in its proper place in my life. I choose to seek first the Kingdom of God and Your righteousness. You and You alone are Lord. There is one Lord, and You are He! I ask that all assignments and evil spirits sent by Your Enemy would be cast out of my life. I call on You, Lord Jesus, to come and set the captives free. Thank You that You have come to destroy the works of the Devil in my life. All demons must come to attention in the presence of the Lord Jesus. There will be no manifestations except the manifestation of the Holy Spirit. You may not separate. You may not divide. You may not get reinforcements. You must face the judgment of the Lord Jesus Christ. I bind every spirit involved in my idolatry with the three-fold cord that cannot be broken in the Name of the Father, Son, and Holy Spirit. You must go where Jesus tells you to go, when Jesus tells you to go.

Special Renunciations for Satanic Ritual Involvement

1. I renounce ever signing or having my name signed over to Satan. I announce that my name is now written in the Lamb's Book of Life.

2. I renounce any ritual where I was wed to Satan. I announce that I am the bride of Christ.

3. I renounce any and all covenants, agreements, or promises that I made to Satan. I announce that I have made a new covenant with Jesus Christ alone, which supersedes any previous agreements.

4. I renounce all satanic assignments including duties, marriage, and children. I announce and commit myself to know and do only the will of God and accept only His guidance for my life.

5. I renounce all spirit guides assigned to me. I announce and accept only the leading of the Holy Spirit.

6. I renounce any giving of my blood in the service of Satan. I trust only in the shed blood of my Lord, Jesus Christ.

7. I renounce ever eating flesh or drinking blood in satanic worship. By faith, I take Holy Communion, representing my Savior, the body and blood of the Lord Jesus.

8. I renounce all guardians and satanic parents that were assigned to me. I announce that God is my heavenly Father and the Holy Spirit is my guardian by whom I'm sealed.

9. I renounce any baptism whereby I am identified with Satan. I announce that I have been baptized into Christ Jesus, and my identity is now in Him, alone.

10. I renounce any sacrifice made on my behalf by which Satan may

claim ownership of me. I announce that only the sacrifice of Christ has any claim on me. I belong to Him. I have been purchased by the blood of the Lamb.[3]

Now that the stronghold of the Enemy has been broken, and now that the evil spirits are gone, ask the Lord to cleanse with His blood the areas vacated by the Enemy. Ask Christ Jesus to put a seal of His blood on that area. Now ask the Lord to fill you with His Spirit.

Spiritual Cleansing from the Work of Covens
(Eph. 5:11-14, Romans 13:12)

Satan's work is done on the earth in many different ways and through many different levels of evil. One of the avenues of perpetrating evil on the earth is through the workers of iniquity who have signed on as disciples of Satan. Through their lust for illicit power and money, they do the Enemy's evil bidding. They join groups of other highly demonized individuals called <u>covens</u>. In these covens, demonic activities are usually carried out in secret. Their function is to carry out the evil purposes of Satan on the earth as it is in Hell. Covens are doing their evil work among us. They are at work in our churches. They are at work in politics. They are at work wherever you find money and power. The following is an outline of their evil work:

Coven Prayer
Praying over the Structure and Assignments of Satanic Covens

1. Coven Leader
2. Coven Members
3. Formations, Operation, Rituals
4. Outcomes
   Breaking the will and Word of God, Old and New Testament.

A	B
Attack, Afflict	Rob
Harass, Terrorize	Steal
Torment, Accuse	Kill
Oppress	Destroy

5. A—Perversion of all human power, authority, wealth, influence, attributes and time.

   B—To give Satan control—To turn all these over to Satan.[4]

Prayer

Dear Lord Jesus, I thank You that You are able to do exceeding abundantly above all that I could ask or even think. As I pray, I ask for Your protection. I put on the Armor of God provided by You as my protection against the forces of darkness. I bring to bear in the Name of the Lord Jesus Christ of Nazareth the blood of the Lord Jesus, the Word of God, and the power of Almighty God a billion times a billion times a billion. Put on the evil ones' heads the same torment and destruction You put upon Satan's head at Calvary. Raise it to the billionth power for every moment the evil ones resist. Put them in the circle of Your blood. Pour Your blood over them and down their throats 800 billion times per second. Make them obey Your Word and bow before You as the master and ruler of all creation. I ask You, Lord Jesus, to pour Your blood over the workers of iniquity and all their evil outcomes. Pour Your blood over the coven leaders and the coven members. Separate by Your blood and by Your power their ability to work together for evil. Pour Your blood over the formations, operations, and rituals made in the unholy covenants with the Enemy. Lord Jesus, I ask that You would stop the ability of those who would attempt through unholy power to break the will and Word of God, the Old and New Testament. I ask You, Lord Jesus, to shut down the power of those who would afflict, harass, terrorize, torment, accuse, oppress and the like, and all those who would rob, steal, kill, and destroy. Pour Your blood over them and their ability to perpetrate the evil purposes of Your Enemy. Pour Your blood over the evil ones who would attempt to pervert all human power, authority, wealth, influence, attributes, and time and turn all these over to Satan. I ask You, Lord Jesus, to shut down the evil ones' ability at any level to function in this place, over my family and in my life. I ask all of this in the mighty, all-powerful Name of my Lord Jesus Christ.

Prayer for Spiritual Cleansing from Deception
(John 14:6, 16:13, 17:17, Ephesians 4:15,
John 8:32-36, 44, 2 Timothy 2:26, Revelation 12:9)

Prayer

Dear Heavenly Father, I know that You want me to face the truth, tell the truth, believe the truth, trust the truth, and live in accordance with the truth. Thank You that it is the truth that will set me free. I now know I have been deceived by Satan, the father of lies. Through believing his lies, I have deceived myself, as well. Father, I pray in the Name of the Lord Jesus Christ, by virtue of His shed blood and resurrection, asking You to rebuke all of Satan's demons that are deceiving me. I have trusted in Jesus alone to save me, and so I am Your forgiven child. Therefore, since You accept me just as I am in Christ, I can be free to face my sin and not try to hide. I ask for the Holy Spirit to guide me into all truth. I ask You to *Search me, O God, and know my heart; try me and know my anxious thoughts; and see if there be any hurtful way in me, and lead me in the everlasting way (Psalm 139:23-24).* In the Name of The Lord Jesus Christ, who is the truth, I pray. Amen.

Prayer for Spiritual Cleansing from the Spirit of Fear
(2 Timothy 1:7)

Fear is extremely powerful. It reveals the very opposite of the faith the Lord has for us. He has not given us a spirit of fear. Fear weakens us, causes us to be self-centered, and clouds our minds so that all we can think about is the thing that frightens us. Fear can only control us if we let it. God, however, does not want us to be mastered by anything, including fear *(I Corinthians 6:12)*. Jesus Christ is to be our only master. He is the only true Lord. All others are impostors *(John 13:13; 2 Timothy 2:21)*.

Fear can manifest itself in many different ways: Thoughts of inadequacy, rejection, paranoia, lack of trust, fear of men (because of abuse), fear of women, and the like. When a person is controlled by the spirit of fear, he may so manipulate his life and those around him to create a false sense of success and security. These fears can often be a cover for the chief cause of our fears. For instance, I have found, in many cases, where fear is in manifestation, that the root spirit, the root cause, is a spirit of abandonment. In order to begin to experience freedom from the bondage of fear and the ability to walk by faith in God, pray the following prayer from your heart:

Prayer

Dear Heavenly Father, I confess to You that I have listened to the Devil's lies and have allowed fear to master me. Please forgive me for not living by faith in You. Thank You for forgiving me each time I refused to believe Your Word. Right now, I renounce the spirit of fear and all other spirits that have their assignment with fear. I ask You to bind them with the three-fold cord that cannot be broken, in the Name of the Father, Son, and the Holy Spirit. All evil spirits must come to attention and receive the judgment of God. You will go where Jesus tells you to go, when Jesus tells you to go. There will be no manifestations except the manifestation of the Holy Spirit. All voices must be silent in the presence of Holy God. I believe Christ has not given the spirit of fear but of power, love, and a sound mind. Lord, please reveal to my mind now all the fears that have been controlling me so I can renounce them and be free to walk by faith in You. I renounce the (name the fear) because God has not given me a spirit of fear. I choose to live by faith in the God who has promised to protect me and meet all my needs as I walk by faith in Him. I thank You for the freedom You give me to walk by faith and not by fear. You have never left me, nor forsaken me. Please forgive me for believing the lie that You left me. Thank You for

Your never-ending faithfulness to me according to Your Word *(Heb. 13:5)*. In Jesus' powerful Name, I pray. Amen *(2 Cor. 4:16-18; 5:7; Psalm 27:1; Matthew 6:33-34; 2 Timothy 1:7)*. After you have finished renouncing all the specific fears you have allowed to illicitly control you, pray the following prayer:

Prayer

Dear Heavenly Father, I thank You that I can trust Your Word. I choose to believe Your truth, even when my feelings and circumstances tell me to fear. You have not given me a spirit of fear. You have told me not to fear, for You are with me. I am not to anxiously look about me, for You are my God. You will strengthen me, help me, and surely uphold me with Your righteous hand. You are my strength. I pray that when I am faced with the choice to embrace fear or to trust You, You will strengthen me to trust in You. I pray this with faith in the Name of the Lord Jesus Christ, my Master. Amen *(Isaiah 41:10)*.   •

Prayer for Spiritual Cleansing from Bitterness
(Eph. 4:31-32, Heb. 12:5)

Bitterness only destroys the one who allows its spiritual cancer to remain in his/her heart. We need to forgive others so Satan cannot take advantage of us. The Bible teaches that we must forgive others with the same love that our Heavenly Father has forgiven us. If you have not allowed the Lord to forgive any sin in your life, do so right now. Once you are right before God, ask God to bring to your mind the people you need to forgive by praying the following prayer aloud *(2 Cor. 2:10-11)*:

Prayer

Dear Heavenly Father, I thank You for the riches of Your kindness, forbearance, and patience toward me, knowing that Your kindness has led me to repentance. Please forgive me for my unwillingness to trust You to take care of my hurts. Thank You that you bore my pain and carried my sorrows. You were wounded for my iniquities, and by Your stripes I am healed. You alone are Lord. You can and will handle all wickedness and unrighteousness. You alone are the judge and will reconcile all things to Yourself. You have said in Your Word that vengeance is Yours, and that You will repay. Through my disobedience in not trusting You, I have not allowed the Holy Spirit to manifest His love in me and through me to others. I confess I have not shown Your love, kindness, and patience toward those who have hurt me. Instead, I've held on to my anger, bitterness, and resentment toward them. Because You have forgiven me, I now can forgive those who have hurt me. Please bring to my mind all the people I need to forgive in order that I may forgive them now. In Jesus' mighty Name I pray, Amen *(Romans 2:4)*.

Speak aloud: Lord, I choose to forgive (name the person) for (name what they did or failed to do) because it made me feel (share the painful feeling). After you have forgiven each person for all the offenses that came to your mind, and after you have honestly expressed how you felt, conclude your forgiveness of that person by praying aloud: Lord, I choose not to hold on to my resentment. I thank You for setting me free from the bondage of my bitterness. I relinquish my right to seek revenge and ask You to heal my damaged emotions. I now ask You to bless those who have hurt me. Please, Lord, do a great work of Your love and mercy in their life. May they come to serve You with all their hearts. For the sake of the glory of Your Name, I pray. Amen.

Getting Rid of Bitterness

We are most like Satan when we are bitter and angry. We are most like Christ when we unconditionally love and forgive those who have hurt us. Bitterness is a powerful chief demonic system that allows the Enemy ground to destroy ultimately everyone and everything it touches. I have learned that bitterness is much more than just a powerful emotion, even though emotions are involved. Bitterness is like an octopus. It has many tentacles that hang on for ultimate control and power. Each arm or tentacle must be removed individually before bitterness will leave. If one of its underlings is allowed to hang on, bitterness will hang on. Get alone with our Heavenly Father. Ask Him to silence all other voices but His. Humble yourself and ask Him to tell you where any of the underlings of bitterness listed below are still at work in your heart. When He tells you, agree with Him. Confess each one aloud. Ask Him to forgive you for cooperating with the Evil One through His demonic system of bitterness. When all areas of cooperation with the underlings are confessed before God, ask the Lord by His power, by His blood, and by His Word to remove bitterness from you. Once it's done, ask the Lord to give you the same love for the one who has hurt you that our Lord has so freely expressed toward you in the sacrifice of His Son, Christ Jesus. It's all a gift. Receive it!

Bitterness is a Principality—the Chief Demon in this system

The Underlings in the Demonic System:

- Unforgiveness—to enhance the normal feeling of unforgiveness

- Resentment—Plays the record of the wrong

- Retaliation—Plotting to get even for wrong done

- Anger/Wrath/Rage—Physical manifestation of defilement

- Hatred—Stage of elimination

- Violence—Bitterness in motion- The full blown manifestation

- Murder—The full completed work of Satan. (We can murder someone with our tongues and in our heart. Mitigated murder is still murder.)[5]

Prayer for Spiritual Cleansing from Rebellion
(I Samuel 15:23)

Rebellion is as the sin of witchcraft. Whether rebellion against civil government *(Romans 13:1-7, I Timothy 2:1-4, I Peter 2:13-17)*, parents or legal guardians *(Eph. 6:1-3)*, teachers or school officials *(Romans 13:1-4)*, employers *(I Peter 2:18-23)*, husbands *(I Peter 3:1-4)*, church leaders *(Hebrews 13:7)*, or God *(Daniel 9:5, 9)*, it is still rebellion and

God's Word forbids it. Ask the Lord to bring to your mind all the ways you have been rebellious; use the following prayer to specifically confess the sin of rebellion:

Prayer

Lord, I confess that I have been rebellious toward (name) by (say what you did specifically). Thank You for forgiving my rebellion. I choose now to be submissive and obedient to Your Word in the Name of my Lord Jesus Christ. Dear Heavenly Father, You have said that rebellion is as the sin of witchcraft and insubordination is as iniquity and idolatry (I Samuel 15:23). I choose to turn from rebellion and turn to You. Cleanse my heart of all rebellion by the New Covenant in Your blood. In my rebellion, I now know I have sinned against You. I ask Your forgiveness for my rebellion and pray that by the shed blood of the Lord Jesus Christ all ground gained by evil spirits because of my rebellion would be canceled. All spirits assigned to rebellion must come to attention. You may not separate, you may not divide, and you may not call on reinforcements. You must face the judgment of God. I ask the Lord to bind all evil spirits under the assignment of rebellion in the Name of the Father, Son, and the Holy Spirit. You will go where Jesus tells you to go, when Jesus tells you to go. I pray that Christ will shed His light in my life that I may know the full extent of my rebellion. Cleanse me with your blood, which was shed for my sin on Calvary. Heal the wounds left by the work of the Enemy. I ask You to fill me with Your Holy Spirit. May Your presence fill all the areas that the Enemy has now left. In the Name of Christ Jesus my Lord. Amen.

Prayer for Spiritual Cleansing from Pride
(Prov. 16:18-19, James 4:6-10, Phil. 2: 3-8)

Pride separates us from God. That separation always leads to death for only in God is there life. "God resists the proud, but gives grace to the humble." God is not in charge of your heart. You are! Humility is your choice. Without genuine humility, true spiritual cleansing and victory over the powers of darkness is impossible. Ultimately, all sin comes down to pride. The Devil knows that our pride can be the most effective area to attack to keep us from believing and trusting God. In the believer's life, there is a constant battle between the flesh and the spirit *(Romans 6-8)*. Pride allows the flesh to rule. Remember, a man cannot serve two masters. *Proverbs 3:5-7* says:

> *Trust in the Lord with all your heart, and do not lean on your own understanding. In all your ways acknowledge him, and he will make your paths straight. Do not be wise in your own eyes; fear the Lord and turn away from evil.*

I Peter 5:1-10 warns us that serious spiritual problems will result when we are proud. Pray the following prayer to express your commitment to living humbly before God:

Prayer

Dear Heavenly Father, You have said that pride goes before destruction and an arrogant spirit before stumbling *(Prov. 16:18)*. I confess that I have been thinking mainly of myself and not of others. I have not denied myself, picked up my cross daily, and followed You. I have not lived my life as a living and holy sacrifice unto You. I have not allowed the Holy Spirit to fill my life with the humility of Christ. As a result, I have given ground to the Devil in my life. I have sinned by believing I could be happy and successful on my own. I confess that I have placed my will before Yours. I have centered my life around myself instead of You. I have ruled on the throne of my life instead of allowing Jesus to be the Lord of my life. I have been selfish in my relationship with You and with others. I repent of my pride and selfishness and pray that all ground gained in my members by the enemies of the Lord Jesus Christ would be canceled. I choose to rely on the Holy Spirit's power and guidance so I will do nothing from selfishness or empty conceit. With humility of mind, I will regard others as more important than myself. I choose to make You, Lord, the most important of all in my life. Please show me now all the specific ways in which I have lived my life in pride. Enable me through love to serve others and in honor to prefer others. I ask all of this in the mighty and able Name of Jesus, my Lord. Amen (See *Matthew 6:33, 16:24, Romans 12:10*). Now that you have made a commitment to God in prayer, ask Him to show you any specific ways you have allowed pride to rule in your life. As He shows you these pride areas in your life, pray this prayer out loud:

Prayer

Lord, I agree I have been proud in (name the area). Thank You for answering my prayer. Thank You for showing me every area of pride that needs Your cleansing. Thank You for forgiving me for my pride. I choose to humble myself before You and others. I choose to place all my confidence in You and none in my flesh. I choose to follow and serve only You all the days of my life. You alone are worthy of all praise. Please forgive me for allowing any self-praise to find a place in my heart. In the Name of the Lord Jesus Christ, I pray. Amen.

Prayer for Spiritual Cleansing from Sexual Bondage

Prayer

Dear Heavenly Father, You have told us to put on the Lord Jesus Christ and make no provision for the flesh in regard to its lust *(Romans 13:14)*. I acknowledge that I have given in to fleshly lusts which wage war against my soul *(I Peter 2:11)*. I thank You that in Christ my sins are forgiven, but I have transgressed Your holy law and given the Enemy an opportunity to wage war in my members *(Romans 6:12-13; James 4:1; I Peter 5:8)*. I come before You to acknowledge all sins of the flesh and to seek Your cleansing *(I John 1:9)*. Please forgive me for not agreeing with You when You told me these evil thoughts and actions were wrong. I now believe You. Lord Jesus, You alone can cleanse me of my sin. I put my faith in Your Word and ask that You will come and do in my life what You alone can do. Please reveal to my mind the ways that I have transgressed Your moral law and grieved

the Holy Spirit. In Jesus' precious Name, I pray. Amen. The deeds of
the flesh are numerous. You may want to open your Bible to *Galatians
5:19-21* and pray through the verses, asking the Lord to reveal the ways
you have specifically sinned. It is our responsibility not to allow sin to
reign in our mortal bodies by not using our bodies as instruments of
unrighteousness *(Romans 6:12-13)*. If habitual sexual sins, such as pornography, masturbation, sexual promiscuity, are controlling your life,
come humbly before the Lord Jesus and ask Him to break these areas
of bondage in your life.

Prayer

In the Name of the Lord Jesus Christ, I call upon You, Lord, to silence all other voices but the voice of the Lord Jesus. Lord, I ask You
to reveal to my mind every sexual use of my body as an instrument of
unrighteousness. I pray this knowing that You are able to do exceeding
abundantly above all that we ask or think according to the power that
works within me. Amen. As the Lord brings to your mind every sexual
use of your body, whether you were willing or unwilling, (rape, incest,
or any sexual molestation), renounce every sexual involvement.

Prayer

Lord, I renounce (name the specific use of your body) with (name
the person) and ask You to break that (soul-tie) bond. Lord Jesus, I call
on You to break all soul-ties that have remained as the result of any of
my sexual involvement that was not of You. Please separate me to serve
only You. I give You my body for the glory of Christ. I rededicate my
body as the dwelling place (the Temple) of the Holy Spirit. Now commit your body to the Lord by praying:

Prayer

Lord, I renounce all these uses of my body as an instrument of unrighteousness and in so doing ask You to break all bondages that Satan
has brought into my life through that involvement. I confess my participation. Through the New Covenant in Your blood, I now present my

body to You as a living sacrifice, holy and acceptable to You. I reserve that sexual use of my body only for the marriage partner that You have chosen for me. I renounce the lie of Satan that my body is not clean, that it is dirty or in any way unacceptable as a result of my past sexual experiences. Lord, I thank You that I am totally cleansed and forgiven through the shedding of Your blood for my sin. Thank You for loving and accepting me unconditionally. Because You have accepted and forgiven me, I forgive and accept myself. In the Name of the Lord Jesus Christ, I Pray. Amen.

Homosexuality/Lesbianism
(Lev. 18:22, 20:13, Romans 1, 1 Tim. 1:9-10, 1 Cor. 6:9)

Prayer

Dear Heavenly Father, You have created me. I am not a mistake. I am not a piece of junk. Lord, I renounce the lie that You have created me or anyone else to be homosexual, and I affirm that Your Word clearly forbids homosexual behavior. I accept myself as a child of God and declare that You created me a man (or woman). I renounce any bondages of Satan and their effects that have perverted my relationships with others. I ask You to bring to attention all evil spirits that have gained any ground in my life. I ask You to bind them with a three-fold cord that cannot be broken in the Name of the Father, Son, and the Holy Spirit. All spirits working under the assignment of homosexuality must go where Jesus tells you to go when Jesus tells you to go. I announce that I am free to relate to the opposite sex in the way that You intended. Please release my body from all bondage of the Enemy to serve the one and true living God *(Romans 12:1-2)*. I pray in the Name of The Lord Jesus Christ, my Creator and my Lord, Amen.

Abortion
(Psalm 139:13-16)

Prayer

Dear Heavenly Father, I confess that I have believed Satan's lies. I am so sorry that I joined the Devil's rebellion against You by allowing the child that You gave me to be killed. I am so sorry that I was more concerned about what people would think of me than what they would think of You. Lord, I confess that I did not assume stewardship of the life You entrusted to me, and I ask Your forgiveness. You have promised that, if we confess our sin, You are faithful and just to forgive us our sin and to cleanse us from ALL unrighteousness *(I John 1:9)*. I choose to accept Your forgiveness. Because You who are just have forgiven me, I choose by faith to forgive myself. I do love the child You gave to me. Please let my baby know I am so sorry. Please let my baby know that I do love him/her. I now commit that child to You for Your care in eternity. I look forward to seeing my child one day when we shall gather in Heaven around Your Throne. In the Name of the Lord Jesus Christ, I pray. Amen.

Suicidal Thoughts
(Deut. 5:17, 1 Cor. 6:19-20)

Prayer
Dear Heavenly Father, Please forgive me for not believing Your Word. I renounce the lie that I can find peace and freedom by taking my own life. Please forgive me for being so selfish and thinking only of myself. I give my grief, pain and sorrows, and my wounds to You—for You have carried them in Your body *(Isaiah 53:4-5)*. Satan is a thief, and he comes to steal, kill, and destroy. Please forgive me for not believing Your truth and believing Satan's lie. I now know that if You wanted me dead, I would be, for You are the giver of life. You have the keys to Hell and death *(Rev. 1:18)*. I choose life in Christ, who said He came to give me life and to give it abundantly. In the Name of my Lord Jesus Christ, I pray. Amen.

Eating Disorders, Self-Mutilation
(Psalm 139:14, 1 Cor. 10:20-21)

Eating disorders such as anorexia nervosa, bulimia, and self-abusing conduct such as cutting oneself, self-mutilation, becomes a blasphemous ritual of counterfeit spiritual cleansing without the blood of Christ. Even though we may not realize as blasphemous the activity in which we have been involved, by not believing God's Word, Satan joins us to his rebellion through our unbelief. Humble yourself as you go before God to ask His forgiveness:

Prayer
Dear Heavenly Father, I renounce the lie that my worth is dependent upon my appearance or performance. I renounce cutting myself. I renounce purging, or defecating as a means of cleansing myself of evil; and I announce that only the blood of the Lord Jesus Christ can cleanse me from my sin. I ask You to cleanse all the ground that the Enemy has taken in my life because of my sin and disobedience. I ask You to bind all evil spirits involved in this unholy ritual of trying to cleanse my sin without You. It is You, Lord, and You alone who is able to cleanse my sin. I ask the Lord to bind all evil spirits with the three-fold cord that cannot be broken in the Name of the Father, Son, and the Holy Spirit. All spirits that have found refuge in my life must go where Jesus tells you to go, when Jesus tells you to go. I renounce the lie that I am evil, or that any part of my body is evil. I announce the truth that I am totally accepted by Christ just as I am *(Eph. 1:6)*. Dear Lord, release my body as a living sacrifice unto the glory and praise of the Lord Jesus Christ. Amen *(Romans 12:1-2)*.

Substance Abuse, Drug Addiction
(Rev. 21:8)

The word for sorcery in the Scriptures is pharmachia from which we get the words pharmacist and pharmacy. It implies the physical, behavioral, and spiritual manipulation by the use of drugs. Using drugs for manipulating one's behavior is in fact witchcraft, sorcery. Drugs are not evil in and of themselves; however, the placing of our trust in a drug over faith in Christ is spiritually dangerous and can have devastating effects. Addiction, by definition, assumes someone is "out of control." When someone is out of control, someone else is in control. Remember spiritual warfare is about dominion. Who is in control? Whenever you find addiction, you will find a wound. Most of the time addiction is the symptom, not the cause. Even though addictions are extremely dangerous spiritually, physically, mentally, and emotionally, for the spiritual cleansing to be possible the hurt behind the addictions must be healed:

Prayer

Dear Heavenly Father, I confess that I have misused substances (alcohol, tobacco, food, prescription or street drugs) I chose them for the purpose of pleasure or to escape reality, I chose them to cope with difficult situations resulting in the abuse of my body, the harmful programming of my mind, and the quenching of the Holy Spirit. In doing so I have profaned my body, which is the temple of the Holy Spirit. I have been involved in witchcraft through allowing the Enemy to control my body through the use of (name it). Please forgive me for believing the lies of Satan. I ask Your forgiveness, and I renounce any satanic connection or influence in my life through the misuse of chemicals or food. Thank You for carrying my grief, my pain and my sorrow, and all my wounds in Your body on Calvary. I cast my anxiety onto Christ who loves me, and I commit myself to no longer yield to substance abuse, but to the Holy Spirit. I ask You, Heavenly Father, to fill me with Your Holy Spirit. In the Name of my Lord Jesus Christ, I pray. Amen. After you have confessed all known sin, pray:

Prayer

I now confess these sins to You and claim through the blood of the Lord Jesus Christ my forgiveness and cleansing. I cancel all ground that evil spirits have gained through my willful involvement in sin. I ask

You to gather all wicked spirits that have found a place to work their evil in my life. I pray that You will bind them with the three-fold cord that cannot be broken, in the Name of the Father, Son, and Holy Spirit. All wicked spirits must go where Jesus tells you to go, when Jesus tells you to go. I thank You, Lord, that You are able to do exceeding, abundantly above all that I ask or think according to the power that You have invested in me through Your Holy Spirit. I ask this in the wonderful Name of my Lord and Savior, Jesus Christ. Amen.

Divorce
(Malachi 2:16)

Prayer

Dear Heavenly Father, please forgive me for my disobedience in my marriage that ended in divorce. I believe Your Word when it says that You hate divorce. Please show me the ways I have been deceived by the Enemy to believe his lies instead of Your truth. Please forgive me for not believing that You are able to do exceeding abundantly above all that I ask or think according to the power that works within me. (As the Lord shows you every area of disobedience on your part of the marriage, confess it to Him.) Lord, I agree with You that I have been wrong and selfish. I am so sorry I have not believed You. Please forgive me for trying to fix my life my way. Please forgive me for not keeping my vows I made to You. I am so sorry that I have dealt treacherously with You and the mate You gave me. I ask You to cleanse my life of every vestige of hurt and bitterness. Please forgive me for being so selfish and hurting my children. I ask You to come and heal all the hurts caused by my divorce. I pray that You will take charge of my life. If it pleases You, put my marriage back together for Your glory. Please cleanse me from any working of Satan in my life as the result of my divorce. In the Name of the Lord Jesus Christ I pray, Amen.

Prayer for Spiritual Cleansing from Ancestral Curses
(Exodus 20:5, Numbers 14:18, Jeremiah 32:18)

None of us knows what works of Satan may have been passed on to us from our ancestry. Therefore, it is well for every child of God to make the following "Renunciation and Affirmation." It is advisable to speak it aloud:

Renunciation and Affirmation
(Eph. 1:7, Col. 1:13, Gal. 2:20, Romans 6:4, Gal. 3:13, Eph. 2:5-6)

Prayer
As a child of God purchased by the blood of the Lord Jesus Christ, I here and now renounce and repudiate all the sins of my ancestors. As one who has been delivered from the power of darkness and translated into the Kingdom of God's dear Son, I cancel all demonic working that has been passed on to me from my ancestors. As one who has been crucified with Jesus Christ and raised to walk in newness of life, I cancel every curse that may have been put upon me. I announce to Satan and all his forces that Christ became a curse for me when He hung upon the Cross. As one who has been crucified and raised with Christ and now sits with Him in heavenly places, I renounce any and every way Satan may claim ownership of me. I declare myself to be eternally and completely signed over and committed to the Lord Jesus Christ. All this I do in the Name and authority of the Lord Jesus Christ.[6]

Prayer for Spiritual Cleansing for your Home or Room
(Deuteronomy 7:26, Isaiah 1:16, 2 Cor. 7:1, Psalm 51:1-2, Proverbs 3:33)

This prayer of spiritual cleansing of a home or a room is far more than a superstitious little ritual. This is a powerful claiming of your home, your child, and all aspects of his life for God. It's standing up and proclaiming, *As for me and my house, we will serve the Lord (Joshua 24:15).* It is saying, "My home is sanctified and set apart for God's glory." One does not know what horrible sins may have been committed in your home or on the ground where your home sits. The Enemy may have gained ground (dominion) given over to him through sin and great sorrow. Taking this ground back and giving it to its rightful ruler, the Lord Jesus Christ, is being obedient to our Lord and sharing in His authority to accomplish His will *(I John 3:8, Eph. 2:4-6):*

Prayer

Heavenly Father, I acknowledge that You are the Lord of Heaven and earth. In Your sovereign power and love, You have given me all that I have. Every good and perfect gift comes from You. Thank You for this place to live. Thank You for this place of refuge for me and for my family. I ask for Your protection from all the attacks of the Enemy. As a child of God, raised up and seated with Christ in the heavenly places, I command every evil spirit claiming ground in this place, based on the activities of past or present occupants, including me, to leave and never return. I renounce all curses and spells directed against this place. I ask You, Heavenly Father, to post Your holy, warring angels around this place to guard it from every attempt of the Enemy to enter and disturb Your purposes for my family and me. I thank You, Lord, for doing this in the Name of the Lord Jesus Christ, Amen.

Prayer for Spiritual Cleansing of a Child's Room

Remove and destroy all objects of false worship, and pray this prayer aloud in every room, if necessary:

Prayer

Lord Jesus, I invite Your Holy Spirit to dwell in this room which belongs to (name of child). You are Lord over heaven and earth, and I proclaim that You are Lord over this room as well. Flood it with Your light and life. Crowd out any darkness which seeks to impose itself here, and let no spirit of fear, depression, anger, doubt, anxiety, rebelliousness, or hatred (name anything you've seen manifested in your child's behavior) find any place here. I pray that nothing will come into this room that is not brought by You, Lord. If there is anything here that should not be, show me so it can be taken out. I ask that You will post Your holy guardian angels in this place.

From the North and the South, from the East and the West, from above and below, I call on You to bring your protection in this place through the New Covenant in Your blood. Fill this room with Your love, peace, and joy. I pray that my child will say, as David did:

"I will walk within my house with a perfect heart. I will set nothing wicked before my eyes (Psalm 101:2-3)."

I pray that You, Lord, will make this room a holy place, sanctified for Your glory.

(For more information concerning the spiritual cleansing of your house and property, study the material in the book, *Spiritual House Cleaning*, by Eddie and Alice Smith, Regal Books, 2003.)

Prayer for our Children

Satan is a legalist. He brings to the battle for the control and ultimate destruction of our lives his legal right or ground to continue his evil. These rights have been given to him by the Word of God. Satan can only do what the Scriptures allow Him to do. The Scripture says:

Be angry, and yet do not sin; do not let the sun go down on your anger, and do not give the Devil an opportunity (Eph. 4:26-27).

To disobey this or any scriptural admonition is to say to Satan, "I'm giving you the legal right—the Scriptural right—to destroy me." Any area of unbelief or disobedience in our lives gives Satan and his minions the legal right to proceed to steal, kill, and destroy. The Word of God speaks of a certificate of decrees that are against us:

Having canceled out the certificate of debt consisting of decrees against us and which was hostile to us; and He has taken it out of the way, having nailed it to the cross (Col. 2:14).

Hallelujah, what a wonderful Savior! Oh, what He has done for you and me. As I have stated, the victory is already won for us in Christ; though the battle continues to rage. You will find, as you pray for your children, that you will have great authority as long as they are in your home and under the age of maturity; however, once they are gone to college or out of your home, the battle in the prayer closet can become more intense. Below is a contract, a legal document that I have found to be extremely effective especially as we battle for our children. Let me encourage you to get each of your children to sign this document and give it to you. When you are in the heat of the battle, pull it out. Remind Satan that you too have a legal right given to you by God and by your children to war on their behalf. The following Prayer Covenant signed by your children is extremely powerful against the powers of darkness:

My Prayer Covenant with my Parents
My Commitment to Christ

I, _____ do hereby declare my holy commitment to Jesus Christ as my Lord and my Savior. As a child of God purchased by the blood of the Lord Jesus Christ, I here and now announce to Satan and all his forces that Christ became a curse for me when He hung on the cross for my sin. All my sin, past, present and future was placed upon Christ when He died on Calvary. It was on an old Roman cross where Christ paid the penalty for all my sin. When Jesus said, "It is finished," He meant that the price of my sin that God demanded was paid in full.

I do hereby give my full consent to my Guardians, Father, _____, and my Mother, _____, to battle on my behalf against the forces of darkness according to the leading of the Holy Spirit in their lives. I request for them to pray in my behalf and plead my case before the Righteous Judge of all Creation, Yahweh, God. Through the power given to them through their union with Christ

Jesus, I do hereby allow them to stand in my behalf, as the need would arise under the leadership of the Holy Spirit. Because the Word of God says, *"That if two of you agree on earth about anything that they may ask, it shall be done for them by My Father who is in heaven. For where two or three have gathered together in My name, there I am in their midst (Matt. 18:19)."*

I do hereby declare my faith in the Word of God by requesting them to pray on my behalf expecting our mighty Lord and Savior, Jesus Christ, to hear their prayer and answer their prayer according to His sovereign will. Signed, sealed, and committed this day all under the authority of the Lord Jesus Christ.

Signed _____

Date _____

RENUNCIATION of MAMMON
And any Involvement in the
False Religious System of Christian Materialism

A Declaration of my commitment to Christ as my Provider
(Phil. 4:19, Rom. 8:17, Matt. 6:19-21, 25-34, 7:9-11, 13:22,
James 5:1, Prov.30:8)

The following prayer is a prayer of confession and repentance concerning any unbiblical relationship to Mammon and the practice of Christian Materialism that has or is being used of the Enemy in your life.

Prayer

As a child of God purchased by the blood of the Lord Jesus Christ, **I hereby renounce** any ground where Satan and all His forces may claim ownership of me with regard to my finances. I come before my Heavenly Father through the shed blood of Calvary to ask forgiveness and repent of my disobedience and unbelief.

I repent that I have exchanged the value of the Kingdom of Heaven for the desires of my heart. I repent for laying up treasures on earth *(Matt. 6:19-21).*

I repent for loving money, for serving riches, for my greed and covetousness *(1 Tim. 6:10).*

I repent for making money my defender, security and protection *(Matt. 13:22).*

I repent for believing that chants, spells, fate, superstition and luck will provide the money I need *(Deut. 18:10-12).*

I repent for the dishonest ways I have gained wealth. *(Gal. 5:19-21, Eph. 2:2-3).*

I repent for seeking, accepting, treasuring or profiting from money received from the sorrow and pain of others *(2 Tim. 3:6-9).*

I repent for my robbing God by the withholding of His tithes and my offerings *(Malachi 3:8- 11).*

I repent for not feeding the poor nor taking care of the widows and orphans *(James 1:27).*

I repent for my critical spirit concerning the supporting of missionary and evangelistic ministries *(3 John).*

I repent for any and all the ways I have allowed myself to worship at the false altar of Mammon. I ask the Lord Jesus to break all ties to Mammon either as a result of my disobedience or that which has been assigned to me as the result of my ancestors disobedience *(Matt. 6:24).*

I hereby affirm that My Creator and Heavenly Father is my provider. I receive all that God has for me through my inheritance as a joint-heir with His Son, Christ Jesus. I ask the Holy Spirit to help me see money from God's eyes. Help me worship our Heavenly Father for every financial need He meets according to His riches in glory by Christ Jesus. Only give me that which brings glory and honor to You, Lord Jesus.

Name_____   Date_____

For more information concerning prayers for spiritual cleansing, study Neil Anderson's "Seven Steps to Freedom." These steps and prayers are found in his work entitled, The Bondage Breaker, Harvest House, Eugene, OR, 1993. Also Mark I. Bubeck's work on spiritual cleansing entitled, The Adversary, Moody Press, Chicago, Ill, 1975, is a wonderful resource in understanding how to pray for those in spiritual bondage. Jim Logan's book entitled Reclaiming Surrendered Ground, Moody Press, Chicago, Ill. 1995, is a must in any study of spiritual cleansing. For many years Dr. Logan has taught these spiritual truths and helped many hundreds and thousands of God's people find freedom in Christ through the International Center for Biblical Counseling and now Biblical Restoration Ministries in Sioux City, Iowa. Dr. Logan's work was used of God in my life at the precise moment I needed God's truth the most. I will forever be grateful to our Lord for these wonderful dedicated men of God who have allowed the Lord to use them to set the captives free.

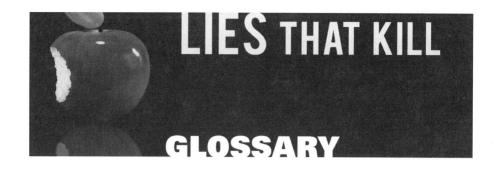

GLOSSARY

In any study of the supernatural, it is necessary that the terms used be clearly defined. There are words such as demon, blasphemy, cult, etc. that carry different meanings to different people. When you encounter such terms in this book, the following list will give you how it is being used by the author.

Abyss
Pit, Tartarus, The place of confinement for demons. The place of demons. Demons do not want to be sent to the abyss for they will then be rendered inactive except for some that will evidently be let out at a future date (*Rev. 9:1*).

Alters
Alter personality, Dissociation DID – Dissociative Identity Disorder, Fractures, Fragments, Personality Splitting, Segmented Personalities, MPD- Multiple Personality Disorder. God created each human being with one unique personality. However, that personality can be shattered, segmented, broken and smashed into pieces or separate parts, through trauma.

Anathemas
To declare that its demise is to the glory of God.

Ancestral spirits
The spirits of dead people in Hell.

269

Assignments
A duty or spiteful piece of work allotted to a spirit being who is obligated to complete the allotted task or experience of pain.

Authority
The level of power given for the purpose of ruling.

Batteries
The most wounded and sensitive part of our personalities that can easily move us into self-defeating thoughts and behaviors that will destroy us.

Bindings
To refuse permission to continue.

Blasphemy
To willfully lie about God in opposition to Him.

Covin, covine, coven
Demonized individuals who come together to carry out demonic activities, usually in secret.

Cult
A system of false religious beliefs or rituals. A false religion.

Curses
The natural results of breaking God's laws, a prayer or calling down harm or injury upon someone or something.

Dead Works
Anything man does that the Holy Spirit cannot use for God's glory.

Deceptions
To mislead, delude, cheat; to lead astray or frustrate by confusing the distinction between true and false, fantasy and reality, leading to confusion.

Denounce

To openly declare one's disbelief.

Demon creature

A fabricated being, not a true spirit; acts for the demon when he is not present. These just disappear when covered with the blood of the Lord Jesus.

Demonization, Demonize, Demonized

Being under the control of one or more demons. One who has or had a demon.

Demons

Fallen angels who work under Satan's authority to bring Satan's will on earth as it is in Hell.

Destructions

To bring to nothing by putting out of existence, to kill, to demolish.

Discernment

The practice of listening to the Holy Spirit as He reveals the thoughts and intentions of the heart and the workings of Satan.

Disposing

To cast out. To remove an evil spirit and the evil work of Satan.

Dominion

Authority, Rule.

Fasting

The spiritual act of denying the flesh. Preparation for spiritual battle.

Formation
How and what a particular stronghold of demonic activity is constructed and used to produce a particular outcome, i.e. alcohol plus addiction produces irresponsible behavior, abuse, and death.

Function
What a particular demonic activity is designed to do; and how the stronghold/structure works.

Ground
A place given to the Devil to control through sin, blasphemy, and disobedience to God's Word.

Inerrancy
The belief that God's Word is truth without error.

Infidel
One who opposes the teaching of the Word of God.

Judgments
A calamity regarded as sent by Satan by way of punishment; a calamity permitted by God to bring about discipline for godly purposes.

Legalism
The false belief that keeping man's rules brings righteousness.

Levels
These structures all have essential levels. See stronghold—environment, place to the devil, walls, foundations, cornerstone. For example: A subhead plus alters that are given certain responsibilities within a dissociative personality.

Light
That which is in the light. That which is known.

Loosing
To allow permission to continue.

Manifestation
A public demonstration of the supernatural presence and power of demons or the Holy Spirit.

Materials
The behavioral, psychological and spiritual realities from which abnormal personality traits are constructed.

Motors
The psychological/spiritual power source that drives personality defects and sinful, self-defeating, self-destructive behaviors.

Mourning
The expression of Godly sorrow and repentance.

New Covenant
The work of Christ on Calvary. The shedding of the blood of Jesus Christ for all sin.

Never
Things that Satan never wants revealed.

No Gods
Demons, Devils, Spirits who manipulate the pagan god systems and actually receive homage and worship.

Occult
A belief in or study of supernatural powers and the possibility of subjecting them to human control.

Pharmachia
The New Testament word for sorcery, witchcraft.

Pit
The place of confinement for demons. Abyss.

Principalities
Demons of greater power and authority assigned to spiritually significant areas. Territorial spirits.

Programming
Developing in a person certain specific responses based on particular stimuli, i.e. as in a computer program; produces activity that is involuntary and /or compulsive.

Reclaim
To restore the creation to its Creator.

Reconciliation
To bring together two opposing positions or beings.

Relativism
The prevailing philosophy of the postmodern western education system that rejects absolute truth.

Religious Flesh
The works of the flesh that are cloaked in a counterfeit religious cover.

Renounce
To declare one's opposition.

Repentance
To turn. To change one's thinking which changes the direction of his/ her life. To turn from sin and disobedience and to turn to Christ.

Rhema

A personal word from God's heart to your heart from His Word.

Sanctification

The process of being made holy like Jesus.

Shadow

Things which remain hidden by Satan through a persons denial.

Soul-ties

Supernatural bondings as a result of sexual intercourse.

Spirits

Human spirits, alive or dead, god demons, angels, supernatural beings that are real but not material in nature.

Spirit of living flesh

A portion of human spirit projected out of a person: 1) to carry out an assignment; 2) to be projected into another human being as a human tie from one to another.

Spiritual Cleansing

To remove all hindrances in the supernatural process of sanctification— becoming like Christ.

Spiritual Flesh

The works of the flesh empowered by the spirit world that cannot be used by the Holy Spirit for the glory of God.

Stronghold

The inability to believe the truth because of the ground given to the Devil. The places of hiding for the demonic in a life.

Structures
All demonic activities within individuals and societies; spiritual/psychological structures to rob, destroy, and kill, i.e. rage, alcoholism, sexual addictions, lying, etc..

Supernatural
The existence beyond the visible observable realities.

Sword of the Spirit
The Bible, The Word of God.

Testing of Spirits
The confrontation of a spirit to determine the source of a spiritual manifestation.

Theological Liberal
Anyone who holds anything other than the Bible as his final and ultimate authority.

Ties
To join one being to another by means of transfer of demonic spirits thus gaining a certain amount of control over that person.

Times
At whatever point in time that a generational curse, assignment, judgment, etc. was loosed—permitted to take effect..

Topos
A place given to the Devil to control through sin, blasphemy, and disobedience to God's Word.

Triggers
A psychological mechanism that releases a preprogrammed response, i.e. acting out, lying, stealing, inappropriate or antisocial behaviors.

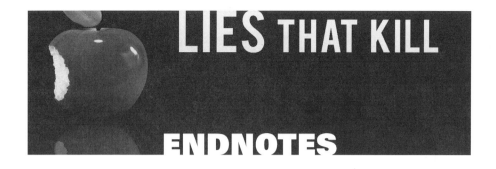

LIES THAT KILL

ENDNOTES

Chapter One

1. Lindsell, Harold, The Battle for the Bible, Zondervan Publishing House, Grand Rapids MI, 1976, pg. 45.

2. Pinnock, Clark, A New Reformation" A Challenge to Southern Baptists, Tigerville, SC., Jewel Books, 1968, pg. 2.

3. Newport, John, Why Christian's Fight over the Bible, Thomas Nelson Publishers, Nashville/NY, 1974, pg. 61.

4. Criswell, W.A., Look Up, Brother!, Broadman Press, Nashville, TN., 1970, pg. 96.

5. Geisler, Norman L., Nix, William E., A General Introduction to the Bible, Moody Press, Chicago, IL, 1968, pg. 26-29.

6. Criswell, W. A., Why I Preach the Bible is Literally True, Broadman Press, Nashville, TN, 1969, pg.71.

7. Geisler, Norman L., Nix, William E., A General Introduction to the Bible, Moody Press, Chicago, IL, 1968, pg. 248.

8. Geisler, Nix, pg. 271, 273.

9. Geisler, Nix, pg. 261.

10. Torrey, R.A., Editor, The Fundamentals, Baker Book House, Grand Rapids, MI, 1917, pg. 109.

11. Criswell, W. A., Why I Preach the Bible is Literally True, Broadman Press, Nashville, TN, 1969, pg.19.

12. Criswell, pg. 20-21.

13. Riley, W.B., My Bible an Apologetic, Eerdmans Publishing Co., Grand Rapids, MI, 1937, pg. 131.

14. Couch, Mal, God has Spoken: Inspiration and Inerrancy, AMG Publishers, Chattanooga, TN, 2003, pg. 2.

15. Knox, John, The World's Great Sermons, Funk and Wagnalls Co. New York, NY, 1908, pg. 197.

Chapter Two

1. Van Der Toorn, Karel, Becking, Bob, Van Der Horst, Pieter W., Editors, Dictionary of Deities and Demons in the Bible, Brill Academic Publishers, Grand Rapids, MI, 1999, pg. 943-960.

2. Spurgeon, Charles, World Digital Library Edition of The Treasury of David and The Collected Works of Charles H. Spurgeon, The Electric Bible Society, Dallas, TX, 1999, pg. 993.

3. Federer, William J., America's God and Country, Encyclopedia of Quotations, Fame Publishing Co., Coppell, TX, 1994, pg. 153.

4. Gingrich, Bob, Founding Fathers vs. History Revisionists, Author House, Blooming, IN, 2008, pg. 5-6.

5. Hudson, Winthrop S., Religion in America, An Historical Account of Religion in American Life, Charles Scribner's Sons, NY, 1981, pg.155.

6. Matthews, Harlan J., Chairman of Editorial Committee, Centennial Story of Texas Baptists, Hammond Press, Chicago, IL, 1936, pg. 131.

7. Cannadine, David, The Speeches of Winston Churchill, Houghton Mifflin Co. Boston, MA, 1989, pg. 154.

8. Cannadine, pg. 177.

9. Kavanaugh, Patrick, The Spiritual Lives of Great Composers, Sparrow Press, Nashville, TN, 1992, pg. 13.

Chapter Three

1. McBeth, J.P., *Exegetical and Practical Commentary on Romans*, Crescendo Book Publications, Dallas, TX, 1937, pg. 115.

2. McBeth. pg. 119.

3. Luther, Martin, *A Mighty Fortress Is Our God, The Baptist Hymnal*, Convention Press, Nashville, TN, 1991, Hymn #8.

4. Sanford, Jenny, *Jenny Sanford, Wife of Cheating Governor tells all*, *People Magazine*, February 15, 2010, Vol. 73, No. 6, pg. 91.

5. Woods, Tiger, *Tiger's Apology, CNN Transcript*, February 19, 2010.

6. Gaebelein, A.C., *The Annotated Bible, Volume 3, Philippians to Hebrews*, Our Hope Publishers, NY, 1913, pg. 283.

7. Hochastetler, Dean, *Ancestral Sin and Resultant Bondage, Studies and Lectures in Spiritual Warfare*, Sioux City, IA, International Center for Biblical Counseling, December 1989.

8. Warner, Timothy, *Spiritual Warfare*, Good News Publishers, Wheaton, IL, 1991, pg. 107.

9. William Cowper, *There is a Fountain, The Baptist Hymnal*, Convention Press, Nashville, TN, 1991, Hymn #8.

10. Marshall, I Howard, F.F. Bruce, Editor, *The New International Commentary on the New Testament, The Epistles of John*, William B. Eerdmans Publishing Company, Grand Rapids, MI, 1978, pg. 113.

Chapter Four

1. Moore, Beth, *Breaking Free*, Broadman and Holman Publishers, Nashville, TN, 2000, pg. 214.

2. Johnson, Norman, Peterson, John W. Compilers *Praise, Our Songs and Hymns*, Kaiser, Kurt, *O How He Loves You and Me*, Singspiration Music, Zondervan Corporation, Grand Rapids MI, 1979, pg. 214.

3. Klein, Laurie, *I Love You, Lord, Songs For Praise and Worship*, Word Music, Waco, TX, 1992, pg. 72.

4. Kanaly, Pam, *Will the Real Me Please Stand Up*, Tate Publishing and Enterprises, Mustang, OK, 2007, pg. 15.

5. Anderson, Neil T., Miller, Rich, Travis, Paul, *Breaking the Bondage of Legalism*, Harvest House Publishers, Eugene, OR, 2003, pg. 266-267.

6. *Father's Love Letter*, used by permission, Father Heart Communications, Copyright 1999-2010, www.FathersLoveLetter.com.

Chapter Five

1. Nee, Watchman, *The Normal Christian Life*, Tyndale House Publishers, Carol Stream, IL, 1957, pg. 70-71.

2. Billheimer, Paul E., *Destined for the Throne*, Christian Literature Crusade, Fort Washington, PA, 1975, pg. 71.

3. Hession, Roy, *The Calvary Road*, Christian Literature Crusade, Fort Washington, PA, 1950, pg. 28-29.

4. Orr, J. Edwin, *My All His All*, International Awakening Press, Wheaton, IL, 1989, pg. 14.

5. Logan, Jim, *Reclaiming Surrendered Ground*, Moody Press, Chicago, IL, 1995, pg. 85.

6. Taylor, Jack R., *The Key to Triumphant Living*, Broadman Press, Nashville, TN, 1971, pg. 37.

7. Thomas, Major W. Ian, *The Mystery of Godliness*, Zondervan Publishing House, Grand Rapids, MI, 1964, pg. 162.

8. Thomas, Major W. Ian, *The Saving Life of Christ*, Zondervan Publishing House, Grand Rapids, MI, 1961, pg. 85.

9. Thomas, pg. 22.

10. Nee, Watchman, *The Normal Christian Life*, Tyndale House Publishers, Carol Stream, IL, 1957, pg.179.

11. Stott, John R.W., *Baptism and Fullness*, InterVarsity Press, Downers Grove, IL, 1976, pg.48.

12. Orr, J. Edwin, *My All His All*, International Awakening Press, Wheaton, IL, 1989, pg. 127,131.

13. Stewart, James A., *Heaven's Throne Gift*, Caring is Doing Press, Ft. Worth, TX, 1956, pg.157.

14. Nee, Watchman, *The Normal Christian Life*, Tyndale House Publishers, CarolStream, IL, 1957, pg. 163.

15. Stewart, James A., *Heaven's Throne Gift*, Caring is Doing Press, Ft. Worth, TX, 1956, pg. 186-192.

16. Stewart. pg. 85.

Chapter Six

1. Patterson, Paige, *Beyond Worship Wars, Southwestern News*, SWBTS, Fort Worth, TX, Volume 68, No. 1, pg. 9.

2. Hollandsworth, Skip, *The Private Hell of Joel Gregory, Texas Monthly*, October 1994, pg. 142.

3. Anderson, Neil; Miller, Rich; Travis, Paul; *Breaking the Bondage of Legalism*, Harvest House Publishers, Eugene, OR, 2003, pg. 31.

4. Kerns, Phil; Wead, Doug; *People's Temple People's Tomb*, Logos International, Plainfield, NJ, 1979, pg. 55.

5. Anderson, Neil; Miller, Rich; Travis, Paul; *Breaking the Bondage of Legalism*, Harvest House Publishers, Eugene, OR, 2003, pg. 31.

6. Anderson, Neil; Miller, Rich; Travis, Paul; pg. 158.

7. Prince, Derek, *Blessing or Curse*, Chosen Books, Grand Rapids, MI, 1990, pg. 88-89.

8. Moore, Beth, *Breaking Free*, Broadman and Holman Publishers, Nashville, TN, 2000, pg. 211.

Chapter Seven

1. Basham, Don, *Can a Christian Have a Demon*, Whitaker Books, Monroeville, PA, 1971, pg. 29.

2. Moreau, Scott, *The World of Spirits*, Evangel Publishers, Nairobi, Kenya 1990, pg. 90.

3. Arnold, Clinton, *The Powers of Darkness*, Inter Varsity, Downers Grove, IL, 1992, pg. 128.

4. Anderson, Neil, *The Bondage Breaker*, Harvest House, Eugene, OR, 1993, pg. 187-188.

5. Dickason, C. Fred, *Demon Possession and the Christian*, Crossway Books, Wheaton, IL, 1987, pg. 81-127.

6. Rockstad, Ernest. B., *Demon Activity and the Christian*, Faith and Life Publications, Andover, KS, pg. 7.

7. Anderson, Neil, *The Bondage Breaker*, Harvest House, Eugene, OR, 1993, pg. 186.

8. Warner, Timothy, *Spiritual Warfare*, Crossway Books, Wheaton, IL, 1991, pg. 79-80.

9. Warner. pg. 80.

10. Anderson, Neil, *Released from Bondage*, Here's Life Publications, San Bernardino, CA, 1991, pg. 16.

11. Murphy, Ed. *The Handbook for Spiritual Warfare*, Thomas Nelson Publishers, Nashville, TN, 1996, pg. 432-433.

12. Murphy. pg. 433.

13. Swindoll, Charles R., *Victory Over Darkness*: Winning the Spiritual Battle, Insight for Living, Anaheim, CA, 1981, pg. 23.

14. Bubeck, Mark, *The Adversary*, Moody Press, Chicago, IL, 1975, pg. 87.

15. Larson, Bob, *Larson's Book of Spiritual Warfare*, Nelson Publications, Nashville, TN, 1999, pg. 384.

Chapter Eight

1. *Webster's Seventh New Collegiate Dictionary*, G.& C. Merriam Company, Springfield, MA, 1966, pg. 177.

2. Fagan, Patrick F., Rector, Robert, *The Effects of Divorce on America*, The Heritage Foundation Backgrounder Executive Summary Newsletter, June 5, 2000.

3. Stanton, Glen, *Divorce: Bible Belt Style*, Citizen (June 2000), http://www.family.org/cforum/citizenmag/ controversy/a0011624.cfm.

4. Henderson, Daniel, *Think Before You Look*, Living Ink Books, Chattanooga, TN, 2005, pg. 136.

5. Stanton, Glen, *Divorce: Bible Belt Style*, Citizen (June 2000), http://www.family.org/cforum/citizenmag/ controversy/a0011624.cfm.

6. Stanton, Glen.

7. Ensign, Grayson H., Howe, Edward, *Counseling and Demonization*, Recovery Publications, Amarillo, TX, 1989, 4b.

8. Gil, Eliana, *Training Seminar for Survivors and Service Providers on Ritual Abuse*, University of California-Berkeley, June 9,1988.

9. Van Der Toorn, Karel, Becking, Bob, W., Van Der Horst, Pieter, Editors, *Dictionary of Deities and Demons in the Bible*, Brill Academic Publishers, Grand Rapids, MI, 1999, pg. 95.

10. Logan, Jim, *Reclaiming Surrendered Ground*, Moody Press, Chicago, IL, 1995, pg. 102.

11. Reardon, David C., *The Abortion Suicide Connection*, Springfield, IL, Elliot Institute, 1993.

12. *The Internet Filter Review,* 2006.

13. ABC News, SEC, *Pornography: Employees Spent Hours Surfing Porn Sites*, 4/23/2010.

14. Tech Mission, Safe Families, *Keeping Children Safe Online, Statistics on Pornography, Sexual Addiction, and Online Perpetrators*, safefamilies.org.

15. Henderson, Daniel, *Think Before You Look*, Living Ink Books, Chattanooga, TN, 2005, pg. 91.

16. Van Der Toorn, Karel, Becking, Bob, W., Van Der Horst, Pieter, pg. 768-770.

Chapter Nine

1. Anderson, Neil, *The Bondage Breaker*, Harvest House Publishers, Eugene, OR, 1993, pg. 195.

2. Kendall, R.T., *Total Forgiveness*, Charisma House Publishers, Lake Mary FL, 2007, pg. 101.

3. Logan, Jim, *Reclaiming Surrendered Ground*, Moody Press, Chicago, IL, 1995, pg. 65.

4. Prince, Derek, *Blessing or Curse*, Baker House Company, Grand Rapids, MI, 1990, pg. 152.

5. Bounds, E.M., *Winning the Invisible War*, Whitaker House Publishers, Springdale, PA, 1984, pg. 109.

6. Lahaye, Tim, *Spirit Controlled Temperament*, Tyndale House Publishers, Wheaton, IL, 1966, pg. 69-70.

7. Kendall, R.T., *Total Forgiveness*, Charisma House Publishers, Lake Mary FL, 2007, pg. 41-42.

8. Logan, Jim, *Reclaiming Surrendered Ground*, Moody Press, Chicago, IL, 1995, pg. 61.

9. Wright, Henry W., *A More Excellent Way, Be in Health*, Pleasant Valley Publications, Thomaston, GA, 2003, pg. 163.

10. Wright. pg. 184.

11. Wright. pg. 92-95.

Chapter Ten

1   Coad, Norman, Coad Word Christian Counseling Services, 1161 S.W. Wilshire Blvd. Suite 118, Burleson, TX, 2002.

2   Dickerman, Don, Don Dickerman Ministries, Box 575, Hurst, TX, 2008.

3   Anderson, Neil, *The Bondage Breaker*, Harvest House, Eugene, OR, 2000, pg. 208.

4   Coad, Norman, Coad Word Christian Counseling Services, 1161 S.W. Wilshire Blvd. Suite 118, Burleson, TX, 2002.

5   Wright, Henry W, *A More Excellent Way*, Be in Health, Pleasant Valley Publications, Thomaston, GA, 2003, pg. 92-95.

6   Rockstad, Ernest B, *Setting the Captives Free*, Tape Lectures and Materials, Faith and Life Publications, Andover, KS, 1970.

LIES THAT KILL

BIBLIOGRAPHY

Alsobrook, David. *Understanding the Accuser*. Ventura: Renew, 1999.

Anderson, Neil. T., Miller, Rich., Travis, Paul. *Breaking the Bonds of Legalism,* Eugene: Harvest House, 2003.

Anderson, Neil. T. *Release from Bondage*. Eugene, San Bernardino: Here's Life Publications, 1991.

_____. *The Bondage Breaker*. Eugene: Harvest House, 2000.

_____. *Winning Spiritual Warfare*. Eugene: Harvest House, 1990.

Arnold, Clinton E. *Powers of Darkness: Principalities and Powers in Paul's Letters.* Downers Grove: InterVarsity, 1992.

_____. *3 Crucial Questions About Spiritual Warfare*. Grand Rapids: Baker, 1997.

Basham, Don. *Can a Christian Have a Demon,* Monroeville: Whitaker Books, 1971.

Barnhouse, Donald Grey. *The Invisible War: The Panorama of the Continuing Conflict Between Good and Evil,* Grand Rapids: Zondervan, 1965

Beeson, Ray and Patricia Hulsey. *Strategic Spiritual Warfare*. Nashville: Thomas Nelson, 1995.

Billheimer, Paul E. *Destined for the Throne,* Fort Washington: Christian Literature Crusade, 1975.

Birch, George A. *The Deliverance Ministry*. Camp Hill: Horizon, 1988.

Bounds, E.M. *Guide to Spiritual Warfare*. New Kensington: Whitaker House, 1984

Bounds, E.M. *Satan.* Grand Rapids: Baker, 1972.

_____. *Winning the Invisible War.* Springdale: Whitaker House, 1864.

Boyd, Gregory A. *God at War: The Bible and Spiritual Warfare.* Downers Grove: InterVarsity, 1997.

Bubeck, Mark I. *Overcoming the Adversary.* Chicago: Moody, 1984.

_____. *The Adversary.* Chicago: Moody, 1975.

Buntain, Mark. *Waging Spiritual Warfare.* Springfield: Gospel, 1993.

Cannadine, David. *The Speeches of Winston Churchill,* Boston: Houghton Mifflin, 1989.

Cathey, Sam. *Spiritual Warfare.* Orlando, Golden rule Book Press, 1987.

Chafer, Lewis S. *Satan: His Motives and Methods.* Rev. ed. Grand Rapids: Kregal, 1990.

Cornwall, Judson. *It's God's War: A Biblical View of Spiritual Warfare.* Hagerstown: McDougal, 1998.

Couch, Mal. *God has Spoken: Inspiration and Inerrancy,* Chattanooga: AMG Publishers, 2003.

Criswell, W.A. *Look Up, Brother!,* Nashville: Broadman, 1970.

Criswell, W.A. *Why I Preach the Bible is Literally True,* Nashville: Broadman, 1968.

Day, Peggy L. *An Adversary in Heaven: Satan in the Hebrew Bible.* Atlanta: Scholars Press, 1988.

Dickason, C. Fred. *Demon Possession & the Christian.* Wheaton: Crossway books, 1987.

_____. *Angels, Elect and Evil.* Chicago: Moody Press, 1975

Downame, John. *The Christian Warfare.* 2nd Ed. London: Printed by Felix Kyngston for Elizabeth Burby, 1608.

Eastman, Dick. *The School of Victorious Warfare.* Colorado Springs: Every Home for Christ, 1995.

Eckhardt, John. *Deliverance and Spiritual Warfare Manual.* Chicago: Crusaders Ministries, 1993.

Ensign, Grayson H., Howe, Edward. *Counseling and Demonization,* Amarillo: Recovery Publications, 1989.

Ernest, Victor H. *I Talked with Spirits.* Wheaton: Tyndale, 1970.

Evans, Eifion. *The Welsh Revival of 1904.* Bryntirion: Evangelical Press of Wales, 1969.

Evans, Tony. *The Battle is the Lord's: Waging Victorious Warfare.* Chicago: Moody, 1998.

Federer, Williams J. *America's God and Country, Encyclopedia of Quotations*, Coppell: Fame, 1994.

Foster, K. Neill. *Warfare Weapons.* Camp Hill: Christian Publications, 1995.

Frangipane, Francis. *The Three Battlegrounds.* Cedar Rapids: Arrow, 1989.

Garrett, Susan R. *The Demise of the Devil.* Minneapolis: Fortress, 1989.

Gay, Robert. *Silencing the Enemy.* Orlando: Creation House, 1993.

Geisler, Norman L., Nix, Williams E. *A General Introduction to the Bible,* Chicago: Moody, 1968.

Gingrich, Bob. *Founding Fathers vs. History Revisionists,* Blooming: Author House, 2008.

Graham, Billy. *Angels: God's Secret Agents.* Garden City: Doubleday and Co., 1975.

Graves, Kersey. *The Biography of Satan: Or a Historical Exposition of the Devil and His Fiery Dominions.* Kila: Kessinger Publishing, 1993.

Gross, Edward N. *Miracles, Demons, and Spiritual Warfare: An Urgent Call for Discernment.* Grand Rapids: Baker, 1990.

Gurnall, William. *The Christian in Complete Armour [sic]:A Treatise of the Saint's War Against lthe Devil.* Reprint. Carlisle: Banner of Truth, 1995.

Hall, Charles A. *With The Spirit's Sword: The Drama of Spiritual Warfare in the Theology of John Calvin.* Richmond: John Knox Press, 1970.

Hanegraaff, Hank. *Counterfeit Revival.* Dallas: Word Publishing, 1997.

Henderson, Daniel. *Think Before You Look,* Chattanooga: Living Ink Books, 1966.

Henton, Richard D. *Christian Warfare.* Tulsa: Vincom, 1992.

Hession, Roy. *The Calvary Road,* Fort Washington: Christian Literature Crusade, 1950.

Hix, Randy. *Blood War: The Blood Covenant and Spiritual Warfare.* Costa Mesa: Embassy, 1994.

Horn, Thomas H. *Spiritual Warfare: The Invisible Invasion.* Lafayette: Huntington House, 1998.

Horsford, Elizabeth-Ann. *Created to Conquer.* London: Hodr and Stoughton, 1996.

Hudson, Winthrop S. *Religion in America, An Historical Account of Religion in American Life,* NY: Scribner's, 1981.

Ing, Richard. *Spiritual Warfare.* Springdale: Whitaker House, 1990.

Kallas, James. *The Real Satan From Biblical Times to the Present.* Minneapolis: Augsburg, 1975.

Kanaly, Pam. *Will the Real Me Please Stand Up,* Mustang: Tate, 2007.

Kavanaugh, Patrick. *The Spiritual Lives of Great Composers,* Nashville: Sparrow Press, 1992.

Kendall, R.T. *Total Forgiveness,* Lake Mary: Charisma House, 2007.

Kerns, Phil., Wead, Doug. *People's Temple People's Tomb,* Plainfield: Logos International,1979.

Kirkwood, David. *Modern Myths About Satan and Spiritual Warfare.* Pittsburgh: Ethnos, 1994.

Knox, John. *The World's Great Sermons,* New York: Funk and Wagnalls, 1908.

Koch, Kurt. *Demonology Past and Present.* Grand Rapids: Kregel, 1973.

_____. *The Devil's Alphabet.* Grand Rapids: Kregel, 1969.

Kuhatschek, Jack. *Spiritual Warfare.* Downers Grove: InterVarsity, 1999.

Lahaye, Tim. *Spirit Controlled Temperament,* Wheaton: Tyndale, 1966.

Lane, Anthony N.S., ed. *The Unseen World: Christian Reflections on Angels, Demons, and the Heavenly Realm.* Grand Rapids: Baker, 1996.

Larson, Bob. *Larson's Book of Spiritual Warfare.* Nashville: Thomas Nelson, 1999.

Lewis, C.S. *The Screwtape Letters*. San Francisco: Harper, 1942.

Lindsell, Harold. *The New Paganism.* San Francisco: Harper and Row, 1987.

Lindsell, Harold, *The Battle for the Bible,* Grand Rapids: Zondervan, 1976.

Logan, Jim *Reclaiming Surrendered Ground.* Chicago: Moody, 1995.

Lovett, C.S. *Dealing with the Devil.* Baldwin Park: Personal Christianity Chapel, 1981.

Lowe, Chuck. *Territorial Spirits and World Evangelism.* London: Mentor, 1998.

Lutzer, Erwin W. *Satan's "Evangelistic" Strategy for this New Age.* Wheaton: Victor, 1989.

MacMillan, John A. *The Authority of the Believer.* Camp Hill: Christian Publications, 1980.

Malone, Henry *Shadow Boxing.* Irving: Trophy, 1999.

Matthews, Harlan J. *Centennial Story of Texas Baptists,* Chicago: Hammond, 131

McBeth, J.P. *Exegetical and Practical Commentary on Romans,* Dallas: Crescendo, 1937.

McCall, Thomas S., Levitt, Zola. *Satan in the Sancturary.* Chicago: Moody, 1973.

Meyers, Jeff. *God vs. god: Spiritual Warfare in Heavenly Places.* Springfield: 21st Century Press, 2000.

Miller, Calvin. *Disarming the Darkness.* Grand Rapids: Zondervan, 1998.

Moore, Beth. *Breaking Free,* Nashville: Broadman and Holman, 2000.

Moore, Steve. *Insights on Spiritual Warfare.* Self Published: Kingdom Building Ministries, 1989.

Moreau, A. Scott. *Spiritual Warfare.* Wheaton: Harold Shaw, 1995.

_____. *The World of Spirits*, Nairobi: Evangel, 1990.

Murphy, Ed. *The Handbook for Spiritual Warfare.* Rev. and Updated. Nashville: Thomas Nelson, 1996.

Nee, Watchman, *The Normal Christian Life,* Carol Stream: Tyndale, 1957.

Newport, John P. *Demons, Demons, Demons.* Nashville: Broadman 1972.

Newport, John P. *Why Christians Fight over the Bible,* Nashville/NY: Thomas Nelson, 1974

Nugent, Christopher. *Masks of Satan: The Demonic in History.* London: Sheed and Ward, 1983.

O'Grady, Joan. *The Prince of Darkness: The Devil in History, Religion, and the Human Psyche.* Shaftsbury: Element, 1989.

Orr, J. Edwin. *My All His All,* Wheaton: International Awakening Press, 1989. Penn-Lewis, Jesse. *Spiritual Warfare.* Fort Washington: Christian Literature Crusade, 1998.

Penn-Lewis, Jesse. with Roberts, Evan *War on the Saints.* Unabridged Addition. New York: Thomas E. Lowe, 1998

Pentecost, Dwight J. *Your Adversary the Devil.* Grand Rapids: Kregel, 1997.

Petzoldt, Ruth, and Paul Neubauer, eds. *Demons: Mediators Between this World and the Other: Essays on Demonic Beings from the Middle Ages to the Present.* New York: Peter Lang, 1998.

Pinnock, Clark. *A New Reformation – A Challenge to Southern Baptists,* Tigerville: Jewell Books, 1968.

Prince, Derek. *Blessing or Curse,* Grand Rapids: Chosen Books, 1990.

_____. *Spiritual Warfare.* Springdale: Whitaker House, 1987.

Randall, Rob. *The Invisible War – Living in Victory Over the Enemy.* Springfield: 21st Century Press, 2003

Randles, Bill. *Making War in the Heavenlies: A Different Look on Spiritual Warfare.* Published by the author: N.D.

Reapsome, James, and Martha Raepsome. *Spiritual Warfare.* Grand Rapids: Zondervan, 1992.

Riley, W. B. *My Bible an Apologetic,* Grand Rapids: Eerdmans, 1937.

Rockstad, Ernest. B. *Demon Activity and the Christian,* Andover: Faith and Life Publications, 1984.

Royster, Roger. *The Word on Spiritual Warfare.* Ventura: Gospel Light, 1996.

Rumph, Jane L. *Stories from the Front Lines: Power Evangelism in Today's World.* Grand Rapids: Chosen Books, 1996.

Scanlon, Michael and Randall J. Cirner. *Deliverance from Evil Spirits: A Weapon for Spiritual Warfare.* Ann Arbor: Vine, 1980.

Schlier, Heinrich. *Principalities and Powers in the New Testament.* Freiburg, West Germany: Herder, 1966.

Showers, Ronald E. *What on Earth is God Doing?: Satan's Conflict with God.* Neptune: Loizeaux Brothers, 1973.

Shuster, Marguerite. *Power, Pathology, Paradox: The Dynamics of Good and Evil.* Grand Rapids: Academie, 1987.

Spurgeon, Charles. *The Power in Praising God.* New Kensington: Whitaker House, 1998.

_____. *Power Over Satan.* New Kensington: Whitaker House, 1997.

_____. *World Digital Library Editions of the Treasury of David and The Collected Works of Charles H. Spurgeon,* Dallas: The Electronic Bible Society, 1999.

Stott, John R.W. *Baptism and Fullness,* Downer Grove: InterVarsity Press, 1976.
Stedman, Ray C. *Spiritual Warfare.* Waco: Word, 1975.

Stewart, James A. *Heaven's Throne Gift,* Fort Worth: Caring is Doing Press, 1956.

Swindoll, Charles R. *Victory Over Darkness: Winning the Spiritual Battle,* Anaheim: Insight for Living Publications, 1981.

Taylor, Jack. *The Key to Triumphant Living,* Nashville: Broadman Press, 1971,

_____. *Victory Over the Devil.* Nashville: Broadman Press, 1973.

Thomas, Major W. Ian. *The Mystery of Godliness,* Grand Rapids: Zondervan, 1964.
_____. *The Saving Life of Christ,* Grand Rapids: Zondervan, 1961.

Torrey, R.A. *The Fundamentals,* Grand Rapids: Baker Book House, 1917.

Tozar, A. W. *The Warfare of the Spirit.* Camp Hill: Christian Publications, 1993.

Unger, Merrill F. *Biblical Demonology: A Study of the Forces Behind the Present Unrest.* Wheaton: Van Kampen, 1952.

_____. *Biblical Demonology: A Study of Spiritual Forces at Work Today*. Grand Rapids: Kregel, 1994.

Unger, Merrill F. *Demons in the World Today*. Wheaton: Tyndale House Publishers, 1971.

Upchurch, T. Howell. *Strategy for Spiritual Warfare*. Columbus: Brentwood Christian Press, 1987.

Van Der Toorn, Karel, Becking, boc, Van Der Horst, Pieter W., eds. *Dictionary of Deities and Demons in the Bible,* Grand Rapids: Brill Academic Publishers, 1999.

Wagner, C. Peter, Ed. *Engaging the Enemy: How to Fight and Defeat Territorial Spirits*. Ventura: Regal, 1991.

Warner, Timothy M. *Spiritual Warfare*. Wheaton: Crossway Books, 1991

White, Thomas B. *The Believer's Guide to Spiritual Warfare*. Ann Arbor: Servant, 1990.

Wiersby, Warren. *The Strategy of Satan: How to Detect and Defeat Him,* Wheaton: Tyndale, 1985.

Wimber, John, and Kevin Springer. *Power Evangelism*. London: Hodder and Stoughton, 1992.

Wink, Walter. *Engaging the Powers: Discernment and Resistance in a World of Dominion*. Minneapolis: Fortress, 1992.

Wise, Terry S. *Fundamentals of Spiritual Warfare*. Needham Heights: Simon and Schuster, 1996.

Wright, Henry W. *A More Excellent Way, Be in Health,* Thomaston: Pleasant Valley, 2003.
Youssef, Michael. *Know Your Real Enemy*. Nashville: Thomas Nelson, 1997.

LIES THAT KILL

SCRIPTURE INDEX

LIES THAT KILL

TOPICAL INDEX

Dr. Rob Randall is a third generation evangelist. For the past quarter of a century, he has been at the forefront of the spiritual battle within the church. Through area-wide crusades, conferences and local church revivals Dr. Randall has held over 700 gospel meetings, presenting the claims of Christ upon the lives of men, women, boys, girls, and young people. He holds the B.A., M.Div., and Ph.D. Degrees from Baylor University, Southwestern Baptist Theological Seminary, and Louisiana Baptist University. Dr. Randall's book, *The Invisible War*, is being widely used within the church to help bring spiritual healing and cleansing to many. Rob and his wife Pattie have been married for thirty-six years and have their home in the Dallas Fort Worth Metro Area.

For more information concerning
The Revival and Conference Ministry
Of Evangelist Rob Randall
Contact:

Rob Randall Evangelistic Ministries, Inc.
P.O. Box 5
McKinney, Texas 75070

www.theinvisiblewar.org